PROGRAMMING
IN occam® 2

occam is a registered trademark of the INMOS Group of Companies

Prentice Hall International
Series in Computer Science

C. A. R. Hoare, Series Editor

BACKHOUSE, R. C., *Program Construction and Verification*
BACKHOUSE, R. C., *Syntax of Programming Languages: Theory and practice*
DE BAKKER, J. W., *Mathematical Theory of Program Correctness*
BIRD, R., and WADLER, P., *Introduction to Functional Programming*
BJÖRNER, D., and JONES, C. B., *Formal Specification and Software Development*
BORNAT, R., *Programming from First Principles*
BUSTARD, D., ELDER, J., and WELSH, J., *Concurrent Program Structures*
CLARK, K. L., and MCCABE, F. G., *micro-Prolog: Programming in logic*
DROMEY, R. G., *How to Solve it by Computer*
DUNCAN, F., *Microprocessor Programming and Software Development*
ELDER, J., *Construction of Data Processing Software*
GOLDSCHLAGER, L., and LISTER, A., *Computer Science: A modern introduction (2nd edn)*
GORDON, M. J. C., *Programming Language Theory and its Implementation*
HAYES, I. (ed.), *Specification Case Studies*
HEHNER, E. C. R., *The Logic of Programming*
HENDERSON, P., *Functional Programming: Application and implementation*
HOARE, C. A. R., *Communicating Sequential Processes*
HOARE, C. A. R., and SHEPHERDSON, J. C. (eds), *Mathematical Logic and Programming Languages*
HUGHES, J. G., *Database Technology: A software engineering approach*
INMOS LTD, *occam Programming Manual*
INMOS LTD, *occam 2 Reference Manual*
JACKSON, M. A., *System Development*
JOHNSTON, H., *Learning to Program*
JONES, C. B., *Systematic Software Development using VDM*
JONES, G., *Programming in occam*
JONES, G., and GOLDSMITH, M., *Programming in occam 2*
JOSEPH, M., PRASAD, V. R., and NATARAJAN, N., *A Multiprocessor Operating System*
LEW, A., *Computer Science: A mathematical introduction*
MACCALLUM, I., *Pascal for the Apple*
MACCALLUM, I., *UCSD Pascal for IBM PC*
MEYER, B., *Object-oriented Software Construction*
PEYTON JONES, S. L., *The Implementation of Functional Programming Languages*
POMBERGER, G., *Software Engineering and Modula-2*
REYNOLDS, J. C., *The Craft of Programming*
RYDEHEARD, D. E., and BURSTALL, R. M., *Computational Category Theory*
SLOMAN, M., and KRAMER, J., *Distributed Systems and Computer Networks*
TENNENT, R. D., *Principles of Programming Languages*
WATT, D. A., WICHMANN, B. A., and FINDLAY, W., *ADA: Language and methodology*
WELSH, J., and ELDER, J., *Introduction to Modula-2*
WELSH, J., and ELDER, J., *Introduction to Pascal (3rd edn)*
WELSH, J., ELDER, J., and BUSTARD, D., *Sequential Program Structures*
WELSH, J., and HAY, A., *A Model Implementation of Standard Pascal*
WELSH, J., and MCKEAG, M., *Structured System Programming*
WIKSTRÖM, Å., *Functional Programming using Standard ML*

PROGRAMMING IN occam® 2

Geraint Jones
Michael Goldsmith

Oxford University Computing Laboratory,
Programming Research Group

PRENTICE HALL

NEW YORK   LONDON   TORONTO   SYDNEY   TOKYO

First published 1988 by
Prentice Hall International (UK) Ltd,
66 Wood Lane End, Hemel Hempstead,
Hertfordshire, HP2 4RG
A division of
Simon & Schuster International Group

Printed and bound in Great Britain by
A. Wheaton & Co. Ltd, Exeter.

Library of Congress and British Library Cataloguing in
Publication Data are available from the publisher.

1 2 3 4 5   92 91 90 89 88

ISBN 0-13-730334-3

Contents

Preface

This is a book about designing and writing certain sorts of parallel program. As parallel computers become more common, and as common computers become more parallel, it is important that the programmer cast off the shackles of sequential thought. Although the principal virtue of parallel computers would appear to be their speed, this book is not greatly concerned with writing programs in parallel to make them go faster. Rather, in this book what is important about parallel programs is that they can be simpler to write and understand than sequential programs which achieve the same effect.

It used to be that writing a program meant finding some strict sequence of steps to achieve the desired end. This odd constraint is a legacy of the time when programs were written only to be executed by computers, and computers were machines that did one thing at a time. Programmers knew that any attempt to get such a machine to take on two tasks at once was to give themselves the additional burden of making sure that these tasks did not interfere with each other.

The occam language, intended by its designers as the assembly language of the INMOS transputer[12], takes the revolutionary step of enforcing the independence of parts of the program. An occam programmer can start from the assumption that the parts of a program cannot interfere with each other. Unless the programmer makes explicit provision to the contrary, parallel processes in an occam program are guaranteed to be entirely unaware of each other.

Theoretical models like CSP[8] and CCS[9] describe parallel computation using only *synchronization*: no process engaged in a synchronizing communication may proceed until its partners are simultaneously doing so. The handling of parallelism in occam is based on these models: the job of programming is making the otherwise independent processes in a program co-operate by explicit communication. As it happens, programs written in this way are quite likely to be suitable for execution on computers made of several processors, but that is incidental to our purpose in this book.

The occam programmer is encouraged to think of process creation, and of synchronization and scheduling operations, as being as cheap as any other 'primitive' actions. Indeed, even on a conventional processor, neither process creation nor scheduling need be any more expensive than, say, procedure invocation. This startling scale of costs gives the programmer much greater freedom of expression, and leads to an unaccustomed programming style. If you think the book is about anything, we would prefer you to think it is about this style.

The language used in this book, occam 2, supplements the program structures of the earlier prototype occam languages with some concrete data structuring. To the sequential sub-language of occam is added a conventional system of data types, which makes it easier to read and write programs and easier for a compiler to check that the programmer's intentions are properly implemented. The system of protocols on communications between parallel processes is the natural extension of this type scheme to the parallel sub-language.

This book begins with an introduction to occam 2, intended to make the rest of the work intelligible to anyone who is already able to write and understand sequential programs. Several short examples exercise some occam 2 idioms illustrating the way the language can be used. The bulk of the text is devoted to developing a number of sizeable examples. Most of these programs solve the same problems as those in the earlier *Programming in occam*[5], although the differences between the two languages alter the emphasis; some of the examples have been substantially reworked and expanded.

At the back of the book there is a concise summary of the occam 2 language, drawn from material in INMOS's *occam 2 Reference Manual*[1], which is also published in this series. The complete source code of the larger examples is reproduced; we do not expect that anyone might want to read hundreds of lines of code, but their presence may make it easier to settle ambiguities earlier in the presentation. A short bibliography contains some suggestions for related reading.

*   *   *

Many will find that their conversations have contributed to this book, among them Steven Ericsson Zenith and David May of INMOS, Geoff Barrett, Jim Davies and Andrew Kay of the Programming Research Group. To these and others whom we have negligently omitted, we are grateful for their time, patience, and insights. Such inaccuracies and obfuscations as you will find herein we were, as our colleagues could testify, able to concoct entirely unaided.

Oxford
March, 1988

G.J.
M.H.G.
occam-book@uk.ac.oxford.prg

1

An introduction to occam

The occam notation was designed to simplify the programming of parallel computers. Arranging that several things happen 'at the same time' in a program is as simple in occam as is arranging that they happen in any particular order. The language was designed to be used as a low-level programming language and as a compiler target for machines built of INMOS transputers.

The language, occam 2, described and used in this book is a development of an earlier occam language, variously called 'proto-occam' or just 'occam'. It provides facilities for describing and checking the types of data items used and communicated by a program, and for structuring the communications between processes. It has also a richer set of program structures.

There is an unfortunate confusion of different languages all called occam. Where it is necessary to distinguish, this book will refer to the earlier language, that of the *Programming Manual*[4], as proto-occam. At the time of writing, the occam compilers available for transputer-based machines accept a language which is neither proto-occam, nor occam 2 as described by the *Reference Manual*[1]. The language used in this book is, as far as possible, occam 2 as described in the *Reference Manual*.

An occam 2 program is a process, that is, it is a description of some actions possibly with a description of the data on which those actions are performed. Indeed, the principal difference between proto-occam and occam 2 is that there is in the newer language a richer sub-language for describing the types and structures of the data on which a program operates. Where there are new program structures in occam 2, these reflect the new data types and structures.

Accordingly, this discussion of occam 2 takes the following sequence: the data and the types of data acted on by an occam program; the channels and the protocols on channels by which programs communicate; the processes and structures of processes from which programs are built. Because it might be a bit confusing (and rather tedious) to come at things in this order, the rest of this chapter is an outline of the key peculiarities of occam. All this will come around again in its proper order, but is here so that the next chapters will make sense in the order in which they appear.

First of all, just as in other procedural languages, there are assignments in occam; the assignment

```
x := y
```

changes the value of *x* to be the same as that of *y*. Conventional, sequential programs can be written, although the syntax is a bit unusual: what might, in another language like PASCAL or ALGOL, have been written

```
BEGIN x := y; y := 3 * x + 2; z := x + y + 1 END
```

is written in occam as

```
SEQ
  x := y
  y := (3 * x) + 2
  z := (x + y) + 1
```

This means that the value of *y* should be stored in *x*; that the new value of *x* is used to calculate $3x + 2$, and the value of that expression stored in *y*; and only the new values of *x* and *y* be used to store a new value in *z*.

The format is rigidly fixed: each process (in this case, each assignment) starts on a line to itself, and in a column indented a little (two columns) from the start of the keyword SEQ (for *seq*uential).

As a concession, if a line gets too long for comfort, it can be broken in most of the places where the first part cannot be confused with a complete line, provided that the continuation is indented at least as far as the first part of the line. Comments are introduced by a pair of dashes, --, and extend to the end of the line. So as to avoid making the layout obscure, a comment must not start to the left of the next line of program.

```
SEQ             -- this is a keyword
  x := y
  -- notice that there is no precedence
  -- between the operators in expressions

  y := (3 * x) +
       2        -- this is a continuation

  -- notice that + is not associative
  z := (x + y) + 1
```

Expressions have to be written with enough parentheses to make the evaluation order explicit. There is no precedence between, say, multiplication and addition; addition is not associative, because there might be an arithmetic overflow in one order of evaluation, but not in another.

The reason for the fuss about SEQ introducing a sequentially executed list of processes is that there are also concurrent, or *par*allel, lists of processes. The notation is similar

```
PAR
  x := y + 1
  z := y + 2
```

This process executes by executing both of its components, but it is not defined which of them happens first. Indeed they are allowed to happen 'at the same time'. A process like this is only legal if the components are *disjoint*: none of them changes a variable which appears in one of the others.

Branches of a parallel process can communicate by input (written with a ? mark) and output (written with an ! mark) over a common channel

```
PAR
  c ! x + y
  c ? z
```

which executes so as to have the same effect as z:=x+y.

Parallel and sequential constructions can be nested without any limitation,

```
SEQ
  PAR
    p1
    SEQ
      p2.1
      SEQ
        p2.2.1
        p2.2.2
      p2.3
    p3
  q
  SEQ
    r1
    PAR
    r3
```

Notice that the last of those PAR keywords, with nothing indented after it, is like a pair of brackets with nothing between them: it has an empty list of processes. To execute such an empty parallel is to do no-things, all at once. In the same way, a sequential list of no processes does nothing, and is immediately completed. The same effect can be achieved more clearly by writing SKIP. This is a process which does nothing, and then terminates.

Conditional processes make decisions about which of a collection of processes will be executed. What might, in other notations, have been written

```
IF odd(x) THEN x := 3 * x + 1 ELSE x := x / 2
```

is written in occam as

```
IF
  odd(x)
    x := (3 * x) + 1
  NOT odd(x)
    x := x / 2
```

A conditional process contains a list of pairs of expressions and processes, each of the expressions being either true or false. It executes by executing the first of the processes paired with a true expression.

It would be wrong for there not to be a true expression, and in that case none of the components can be executed, but neither can the conditional terminate. An invalid conditional like this, and in particular an IF with no components, does nothing but it is not like SKIP because it does not terminate successfully. This turns out also to be such a useful process that it has a name: STOP.

The other thing that a programmer must be able to specify is that some piece of program be executed repeatedly. The notation in occam for what is written

```
WHILE even(x) DO x := x / 2
```

in other languages is

```
WHILE even(x)
  x := x / 2
```

and it means the same as

```
IF
  even(x)
    SEQ
      x := x / 2
      WHILE even(x)
        x := x / 2
  NOT even(x)
    SKIP
```

Something to notice about loops that do not terminate, like for example

```
WHILE TRUE
  SKIP
```

is that although this is a process which does nothing, it is not the same as SKIP because it never terminates; on the other hand, it is not the same as STOP, because you can expect an implementation of occam to do something intelligent with STOP.

Do not confuse STOP with a non-terminating loop: STOP is used to explain what is meant to happen in an occam program that goes wrong; it is a potentially detectable failure. For example, a process that divides by zero, or which accesses an array outside its bounds, is meant to 'behave like STOP'. A non-terminating loop, on the other hand, can carry on not terminating for a long time without an implementation of the language having (or indeed being able) to notice.

2
Data

Expressions in occam have values which represent, in the usual way for programming languages, integers, floating-point numbers, Boolean (truth) values, characters, and arrays (sequences) of these values.

Every expression in occam has a mechanically determinable type. There are no automatic translations of values from one type to another, as there are in some other programming notations. Whenever a value of one type is turned – coerced – into a corresponding value of another type, the coercion has to be made explicit.

Integers

The usual type used for discrete arithmetic is INT, which is a set of integers represented in twos-complement. Numerals like 42, or 0, represent the corresponding values of type INT. (When it comes to putting parentheses into expressions, it will transpire that for pragmatic reasons, negative numerals like -137 are not literal numerals, but are expressions.) For definiteness, the type of an INT literal may also be noted along with the numeral, 27(INT), and so on.

It is not defined which twos-complement range of integers have to be representable as INTs, but in any particular implementation arithmetic with INTs is meant to be the most efficient. To be sure of representing a particular large value, or to be definite about a value communicated with another program, there are fixed length integer types which include INT16, INT32 and INT64. Values of these types are integers with twos-complement representations in sixteen, thirty-two and sixty-four bits respectively. The type of a literal of fixed length always has to be given explicitly, for example 9223372036854775807(INT64).

It is sometimes handy to construct integer constants, especially very large or very small ones, which happen to be represented by a convenient bit pattern. In this case you can use hexadecimal numerals preceded by a hash sign, #, or a dollar sign, $. Thus, #010A is the same as 266(INT), and the constant just a little under nine and a quarter trillion at the end of the previous paragraph is #7FFFFFFFFFFFFFFF(INT64).

In fact, the sensible way of describing that particular constant is as MOSTPOS INT64, since it is the most positive (largest) possible value of an INT64. The same holds for the most positive value of each of the integer types, and MOSTNEG for the smallest values, like MOSTNEG INT64 which is #8000000000000000(INT64).

Characters

There is a type BYTE of small non-negative integers, usually used for characters and similar data. The values of type BYTE are the non-negative integers less than 256. Although BYTE literals can be written as numerals, like 0(BYTE), 255(BYTE), there are also character denotations, like 'a', 'b', whose values are the ASCII codes of the corresponding characters represented as BYTEs.

In fact, the BYTE type is usually used for characters, and the denotation you would normally use for the code of most printable characters – 33(BYTE) to 126(BYTE) – is that character between single quotes. To avoid confusion, you cannot put the single- or double-quote characters between quotes; for these characters there is an escape notation, which uses up the asterisk character as well: '*'' is 39(BYTE), a single-quote character; '*"' is 34(BYTE), a double-quote character; '**' is 42(BYTE), an asterisk character.

There are escape denotations for some layout characters: '*s' and '*S' are clearer alternatives for ' ', a space character; similarly '*c' and '*C' for carriage-return, '*n' and '*N' for the newline character, '*t' and '*T' for the tab character. You can also denote any BYTE by a two-character hex numeral in a character escape, so that for example '*#0A' is the same as #0A(BYTE).

Notice that the character type is different from integer types; that whilst #FF(BYTE) is positive, #FFFF(INT16) is negative.

Floating-point numbers

Approximate reals can be represented as values of type REAL32 or REAL64. These types are defined by ANSI/IEEE Standard 754-1985[13], and are sometimes called *single-* and *double-length real numbers*. They are, of course, not *really* real numbers in the sense that mathematicians use the words, and arithmetic with REAL32s and REAL64s is only approximate.

A literal of one these types is written as a mantissa, optionally followed by an exponent, and necessarily qualified by its type. The mantissa is a sequence of digits with a decimal point; the exponent, if there is one, is written with an E, a sign, and a sequence of digits. Thus, 2.71828(REAL32) and 0.000314159265359E+4(REAL64) are each floating-point literals. The value of the second is 3.14159265359 (which is $0.000314159265359 \times 10^4$) rounded to a value representable as a double-length number according to the Standard.

Notice that the approximation inherent in floating-point numbers means that there really is not a representation as a (say) REAL64 for some numbers that you can represent with a few decimal digits. There are some literals, such as 0.5(REAL64), which have the values you would expect: one-half is exactly representable as a binary fraction. Others, such as 0.2(REAL64), have values which are only approximations to what you might expect. Since one-fifth – 0.2_{10} – when represented as a binary fraction is necessarily a recurring sequence – $0.0011\dot{0}01\dot{1}_2$ – the value of 0.2(REAL64) is $0.2_{10} \times (1 + 2^{-54})$ which is the rounded approximation with a fractional part of fifty-two bits.

Booleans

The literals TRUE and FALSE have type BOOL, a type which has only those two different values. Expressions with Boolean values are usually used in decisions that control the sequencing of programs.

Arrays

A finite sequence of values all of the same type can be organized as an array. The type of an array of n values of type T is written [n]T. A constant value of such a type, a *table*, can be denoted by a sequence of constant expressions between brackets, separated by commas. So

    [3, 2, 1]

is an [3]INT (read as 'an array of three INTs', or 'a row of three INTs') and the unlikely

    [[[MOSTNEG INT64]]]

is an [1][1][1]INT64. For no particular reason, when you write down the type of an array, the expressions that determine the number of components must be of type INT, and of no other integer type.

Perhaps it is worth emphasizing that arrays have to be sequences of components all of the same type: [1(INT32),1.0(REAL32)] is not an array, nor is [1,[2,3]]. Since the type of an array includes the number of components in the sequence, an array of arrays has to have components of uniform length, so

    ["That man,", "I wish him well.", "I wish him grass."]

is not a valid [] []BYTE. On the other hand, while arrays of arrays do have to be 'rectangular', they need not be 'square'. An array of one length can have components of another length:

    [[[TRUE, TRUE, FALSE], [FALSE, FALSE, TRUE]]]

is an [1] [2] [3] BOOL; both of the components of the array with two components are of length three.

Arrays of characters can be denoted by *strings* of characters between double quotes, like

    "Jetzt geht*'s um die Wurst."

which is a much clearer way of denoting the array of twenty-six BYTEs

    ['J', 'e', 't', 'z', 't', '*s',
     'g', 'e', 'h', 't', 39(BYTE), 's', '*s',
     'u', 'm', '*s',
     'd', 'i', 'e', '*s',
     'W', 'u', 'r', 's', 't', '.']

Any of the character escape sequences can also be used in a string.

Expressions

All of the expressions described so far denote constants; there are also various ways of giving names to values, some of which are fixed, some of which change. Every named value also has a determinable type.

A name can be given to the value of an expression by *abbreviating* the expression. An abbreviation like

    VAL REAL64 fine.structure IS 1.0(REAL64)/137.0388(REAL64) :

identifies the name *fine.structure* with the value of the expression

    1.0(REAL64) / 137.0388(REAL64)

in the *scope* of the abbreviation. (Roughly speaking, this is the subsequent process.)

Not only can you use the name, rather than having to write out the value of the expression, but you can expect that an implementation might evaluate the expression only once, irrespective of how often you use the name to stand for its value. This means, of course, that it would be wrong for an abbreviated expression to be invalid, even if the subsequent process happens not to use the name. On the other hand, an implementation is not *obliged* to evaluate and store the values of abbreviated expressions. There are restrictions on the use of abbreviations which mean that whenever an abbreviation is valid, the meaning of the program in which it appears is unaffected by whether the expression is evaluated once and a stored value used, or the expression is evaluated every time its name is used.

Because the type of an expression can be determined, it is allowed to omit the sizes of arrays from an abbreviation, or even to leave out the type altogether. Each of

```
VAL [30]BYTE detail IS "Who is? Sylvia! What? Is she!*#00" :
VAL []BYTE less.detail IS detail :
VAL do.it.yourself IS "Who is? Sylvia! What? Is she!*#00" :
```

identifies each of the three names as an abbreviation for the same [30]BYTE value.

It is normally good practice to quote the type of an abbreviation, if only to remind the reader; it would also help a mechanical checker to produce sensible error messages in case of type errors. On the other hand if the length of an array is relatively unimportant, as in the case of a string that will just be typed out as a message, it would be tedious to require the type to be quoted in full.

Integer arithmetic

The usual arithmetic operators: + for addition, - for subtraction, * for multiplication, / for division apply to any pair of integers of the same type, returning a value of the same type, provided that the result is representable as a value of that type. A process which causes the evaluation of an expression that overflows the range of representable values, or which does something invalid such as dividing by zero, behaves like STOP.

Provided that they are in the representable range, the results of addition, subtraction and multiplication are what you would expect for arithmetic on the signed integers. Integer division returns a result which is rounded towards zero, so that for example the value of 9/4 is 2, and that of (-9)/4 is −2. The corresponding remainder is given by \, which can also be written REM; again it is applicable to any pair of integers of the same type and returns an integer of the same type. So, the value of (-9)\4 is −1, and in general the sign of a non-zero remainder is the same as the left operand, and $((x\,/\,y)*y)+(x\setminus y)$ has the same value as x provided no sub-expression leads to an overflow.

The operators PLUS, MINUS, TIMES represent cyclic addition, subtraction, and multiplication of integers. Cyclic, or modulo, arithmetic cannot lead to overflows; the result of an operation is that value in the representable range which differs from the result that you might expect by a multiple of the range of representable values. For example, the value of

(MOSTNEG INT32) MINUS 1(INT32)

is the same as MOSTPOS INT32; the value of

(MOSTPOS INT64) TIMES (MOSTPOS INT64)

is 1(INT64), which is the INT64 which differs from $(2^{63} - 1)^2$ by a multiple of 2^{64}. Although all of the other operators treat integer representations as signed twos-complement numbers, you will get the same result for the three cyclic operations if you think of them as unsigned modulo arithmetic. (Of course, there is no such thing as cyclic division or cyclic remainder!)

Both the normal and cyclic subtraction operators can be used as a unary prefix, so that -x is the same as 0 - x, and MINUS x as 0 MINUS x. (There is exactly one value x of each integer type for which -x does not mean the same as MINUS x.)

Bit-pattern arithmetic

It is sometimes handy for a programmer to treat a word of storage as if it were just a sequence of bits. In occam this is done with the bit-pattern operators which operate on the representations of integers. The bit-by-bit *and, or*, and *exclusive-or* operations produce results which are integers of the same type as both of their operands, each bit of the representation of the result depending on the corresponding bits in the representations of the operands.

The bit-by-bit *and*, written either as /\ or as BITAND, has a one bit in its result precisely where both of its operands have one bits, so

#00FF(INT16) /\ #1234(INT16)

is #0034(INT16). Notice that this really is an operation on perfectly ordinary integers, and you can write expressions like x/\(x MINUS 1). (If you are unfamiliar with bit-manipulation operations, check that you understand why, for any integer x that has a non-zero value, there is one less bit set to one in x/\(x MINUS 1) than in x.)

The bit-by-bit *or*, written as \/ or as BITOR, has a one bit in its result precisely where either or both of its operands has a one bit, so

#00FF(INT16) \/ #1234(INT16)

is #12FF(INT16). The bit-by-bit exclusive-or, written ><, has a one bit in its result precisely where exactly one of its operands has a one bit, so

#00FF(INT16) >< #1234(INT16)

is #12CB(INT16).

The bit-by-bit negation or *inversion* operation, written as ~ (a tilde sign) or as BITNOT, is a monadic operation, applicable to integers and returning an integer of the same type. The result has a representation with one bits exactly where the representation of the operand has zero bits. For example ~#1234(INT16) is #EDCB(INT16), and in general if x is an INT, ~x is the same as (-1) >< x, and similarly for other integer types.

The shifting operations, << and >>, operate on a bit pattern by shifting it left or right, respectively, by a specified number of bits. Bits that are shifted out of the pattern are lost, and the vacated bit positions are filled by zeros, so both 1(INT16)<<15 and #FFFF(INT16)<<15 have the same value as MOSTNEG INT16; and #87654321(INT32)>>16 is #00008765(INT32).

The result of a shift is of the same integer type as the left argument, but notice that the number of bits over which to shift is of type INT in each case. The operation is valid only when this number of bits over which to shift is between zero and the length of the representation being shifted; other values can be treated as overflows.

A particularly common use of << is in raising two to an integer power, because the value of 1 << n is 2^n provided this value is in the representable range. Similarly, for small enough n, $(1 << n)$ MINUS 1 is the integer $2^n - 1$, having a representation in which the n least significant bits are set; although ~$((~0) << n)$ is perhaps a neater way of saying the same thing.

Floating-point arithmetic

Floating-point arithmetic is quite similar to integer arithmetic: +, -, *, and / can be used between any two floating-point numbers of the same length and return a result of the same type. Of course, it is quite likely that the result of a floating-point operation cannot be represented exactly by a value of its type, and it is defined that the result is *rounded* to the nearest representable value. Rounding returns a value which is wrong by at most a half of the value of the least significant bit in the representation, choosing a zero in the least significant bit if the required value is out by exactly half a bit value.

The remainder operator \ or REM can also be used between pairs of floating-point expressions. Its result is not related to division in the same way as for integers; in effect, the result of a division is rounded to an infinite precision integer, and the result of a remainder operation is the difference between the numerator and that integer number of times the denominator. Only then is the result rounded to the length of the result, so it is more accurate than a result which could be calculated from the quotient.

Consider 6.0(REAL64) REM 4.0(REAL64); in this case both the numbers have exact representations, and the result of the corresponding division is exactly 1.5. Rounding this to the nearest integer yields 2, which is the nearest integer with zero as its least significant bit. It follows that the result of 6.0(REAL64) REM 4.0(REAL64) is 6 − (2 × 4) as a REAL64, that is it is the same as -2.0(REAL64).

In some programming notations, all floating-point arithmetic is carried out to double-length or longer and the result of the calculation reduced to the required precision. To do this might mean rounding the result of an operation to double-length, and then rounding that value to a single-length value. Notice that it is defined that expressions in occam are evaluated in the arithmetic of the type of the arguments. This means that fewer rounding operations are needed, giving results that may be more accurate. In particular, since storing an intermediate value cannot cause rounding, it is safe for a compiler to rearrange evaluation of floating-point expressions to optimize performance.

It is, of course, possible that an expression of a REAL type does not have a numeric value representable in that type: the value may be too large or small, or too near zero without being exactly zero. Although the Standard defines bit patterns to represent these overflows and underflows, a process which evaluates floating-point expressions that overflow or underflow is normally invalid, and stops. Implementations of occam may provide a library of predefined routines which implement the extensions of floating-point operations to these non-numbers.

Relational expressions

Pairs of expressions of the same integer, byte, floating-point, or Boolean type can be compared for equality, or inequality: $x = y$ is TRUE if x is exactly equal to y, and FALSE otherwise; $x <> y$ is TRUE exactly when x is not equal to y. Notice that, whilst you can test whether or not two floating-point numbers are equal it is unlikely to be exactly what you intend. For example,

(1.0E+16(REAL64) + 1.0(REAL64)) = 1.0E+16(REAL64)

and although

68.0(REAL32) * (1.0(REAL32) / 127.0(REAL32)) =
                    (68.0(REAL32) / 127.0(REAL32))

is TRUE, the corresponding equality does not hold in double-length arithmetic, because

68.0(REAL64) * (1.0(REAL64) / 127.0(REAL64)) <
                    (68.0(REAL64) / 127.0(REAL64))

The difference is caused by the rounding errors happening to be equal in single-length arithmetic but differing by 2^{-53} in the two double-length expressions.

Pairs of expressions of the same integer, byte, or floating-point type can be compared by <, >, <=, >=. The result is TRUE when the left operand is less than, greater than, no greater than, or no less than, respectively, the right operand. Again, relying on the distinction between < and <= on floating-point values is unwise.

There is also a cyclic comparison, AFTER, defined on pairs of integers of the same type so that

    (a AFTER b) = ((a MINUS b) > 0)

It is intended for comparing the readings on a clock or timer: a clock counts cyclically, like the turning hands of a physical clock, and almost half of all integers are AFTER a given integer of the same type.

Boolean expressions

The operations AND, and OR operate on a pair of truth values and return a truth value. The result of an expression in AND is FALSE if its left operand is FALSE, and is the same as the right operand otherwise. Similarly, the result of an expression in OR is TRUE if its left operand is TRUE, and is the same as the right operand otherwise.

Notice that these operations are distinguished from others in that because of the left-to-right asymmetry it is safe to use them with invalid sub-expressions, such as divisions by zero or representation overflow. It is not possible for the expression

    (x = 0) OR ((y / x) > 1) OR ((y / x) < (-1))

to be invalid because of a division by zero. Notice as well that you are allowed to leave brackets out of expressions in AND and OR because of their associativity.

Monadic negation, NOT, returns TRUE if its operand is FALSE and vice versa, so for example NOT$(x = y)$ is the same as x <> y.

Type coercion

Because the types of the arguments to an operator must exactly match the requirements of the operator, it is often necessary to replace an expression of one type by another of a different type but a corresponding value. Generally, writing the name of a type in front of an expression returns a result of the specified type and the 'corresponding' value.

In the case of integer types and characters, the corresponding value is the same integer, and the coercion is valid only if the integer is within the range representable by the result type. For the purpose of coercion, Booleans are also treated as integers with INT FALSE being 0, and BOOL 1 being TRUE.

Similarly, a REAL32 can be recast as the REAL64 which represents the same number. Thus REAL64 0.5(REAL32) is the same double-length number as 0.5(REAL64). As ever, beware rounding errors: REAL64 0.2(REAL32) is not quite the same as 0.2(REAL64), the latter being a fifty-three bit approximation to one fifth, the former only a twenty-seven bit approximation.

In the case of other conversions, between integers and floating-point values, between floating-point values and integers, or from double-length to single-length floating-point values, you have to specify whether to round or truncate the value on conversion. It should be obvious that turning a REAL64 into an integer might require rounding because there might be a fractional part to its value. Notice, additionally, that since there are more bits in an INT64 than in the mantissa of a REAL64, you sometimes have to round or truncate integers to get representable floating-point values. In occam, you always have to specify the rounding when converting an integer to a floating-point value, even between INT16 and REAL64.

Rounding has already been described: the result value differs from the desired value by at most a half of the value of the least significant bit; the representation with a zero in the least significant bit is chosen where there are two alternatives. You can also specify *truncation* of the result: any bits in excess of the size of the representation are simply lost. For example, the value of INT ROUND 1.5(REAL32) is 2, but the value of INT TRUNC 1.5(REAL32) is 1. Again, since there are only twenty-three bits in the mantissa of a REAL32,

```
REAL32 TRUNC ((1(INT32) << 31) \/ #FF(INT32))
```

is 2^{31} as a REAL32, whereas

```
REAL32 ROUND ((1(INT32) << 31) \/ #FF(INT32))
```

is $2^{31} + 2^8$ as a REAL32.

Components of arrays

If the value of *exp* is of an array type, then SIZE *exp* is the number of components in the array, so if

```
VAL [39]BYTE circumflex IS
          "Qu*'est-ce qu*'il y a sur l*'eau du Rhone?" :
```

then SIZE *circumflex* is 39. Do not confuse the SIZE of an array with the amount of space it occupies. The SIZE of a [39]INT is also 39, as is the SIZE of a [39][39][39]REAL64, but the SIZE of a [1][39]BYTE is only 1. Like other expressions to do with the indexing of arrays, SIZE *e* is always of type INT.

The components of a value which is an array can be selected individually, by *subscripting* or indexing them. They are indexed by consecutive non-negative integers (of type INT), counting from zero; for example the value of *circumflex*[0] is 'Q', and that of *circumflex*[38] is '?'. Of course, the components of an array of arrays are themselves arrays, so if *a* is an [3][2][1]BYTE, *a*[2] is an [2][1]BYTE, *a*[2][1] is an [1]BYTE, and *a*[2][1][0] is a BYTE. For an indexed expression to be valid, the index must be non-negative and smaller than the size of the array.

Whole sub-arrays of contiguous components from an array can be selected together; for example

```
["Lost lanes of Queen Anne*'s lace" FROM 14 FOR 10]
```

is the [10]BYTE value "Queen Anne" which is the same as the character of the string indexed by fourteen, the character indexed by fifteen, and so on for ten characters. A *segment* expression like this is valid only if it lies entirely within the array of which it is a segment: any valid subscription of a segment has to correspond to a valid subscription of the array of which it is a segment.

Notice that a segment is indexed from zero, just like any other array value, so

```
["Lost lanes of Queen Anne*'s lace" FROM 14 FOR 10][6]
```

is "Queen Anne"[6], which is 'A'.

Constant expressions

You should expect an implementation of **occam** to require that certain expressions in a valid program have to be 'constants' that could reasonably be evaluated by a compiler, without having to execute the program. In particular, the sizes of various arrays will usually have to be constant. Roughly speaking, an expression made only of sub-expressions described in this chapter is a constant expression.

3

Assignment and communication

There are two essentially different ways of communicating information from one part of a program to another. Just as in conventional programming languages, a process may modify the values of variables which are subsequently read by another process executed in sequence with the first. A process may also send values over channels to other processes executing in parallel with it.

Variables and assignment

A variable is a name with a specific type, associated with a value that can be changed by the program. At any time, the value of a variable is the last value assigned to it by the program, so communication through variables is essentially sequential.

A variable is introduced by a declaration consisting of its type, and its name, for example

    INT Exe, Wye :

which could also be written as two separate declarations

    INT Exe :
    INT Wye :

declares two INT variables called *Exe*, and *Wye*.

    [3][3][3]REAL64 tensor :

declares an [3][3][3]REAL64 variable called *tensor*, or you could think of it as declaring twenty-seven component variables called *tensor*[0][0][0], *tensor*[0][0][1], *tensor*[0][0][2], *tensor*[0][1][0], and so on. Segments of an array of variables can also be used as arrays of variables. If *row* is an [100]INT

17

variable, then [row FROM 50 FOR 10] is a [10]INT variable which consists of the ten variables $row[50]$, $row[51]$, to $row[59]$.

Variables can be renamed by abbreviations, for example, if *Windscale* is an INT variable

```
INT Sellafield IS Windscale :
```

makes *Sellafield* a name for the same variable. Assignment to *Sellafield* changes the value of *Windscale*, but it is not permitted to use the name of *Windscale* in the scope of the declaration of *Sellafield*. It is a good idea to quote the type of a variable abbreviation, but it can be omitted in the same way as for value abbreviations.

Abbreviation of variables is most commonly used to give a short or efficient name for a component or segment of an array, for example

```
REAL64 middle IS tensor[1][1][1] :
```

Having made such an abbreviation, an implementation can be expected to be able to refer more efficiently to *middle* than to $tensor[1][1][1]$, but the abbreviation is valid only if the selection is valid. Abbreviating a component of an array like this makes the name of the whole array inaccessible, except that the name can be used in other abbreviations which refer to other parts of the array. This concession means that it is possible to make disjoint abbreviations, for example in the scope of

```
left  IS [row FROM 0 FOR n] :
right IS [row FROM n FOR (SIZE row) - n] :
```

it is possible to refer to *left* and *right*, but not to *row*.

In the scope of its declaration, the name of a variable can be used in expressions, and its value is the last value that was assigned to it. That means, amongst other things, that a variable has no defined value until the first time that a value is assigned. The rules governing the use of variables in valid parallel programs mean that an expression cannot need to use the value of a variable while another process is able to change that value.

Just as in conventional languages, the values of variables can be changed by *assignment*. After the execution of

```
variable := expression
```

the value of the variable is the value which the expression had before its execution. For an assignment to be valid, the variable has to have the same type as the expression, and the expression has to be valid, as does any expression (for example, an array index) which occurs in the variable.

More generally, a multiple assignment

```
v1, v2, v3, ..., vn := e1, e2, e3, ..., en
```

is valid only if there are as many variables as expressions, and corresponding pairs have the same types. The effect is to assign to each variable in the list the value before all of the assignments of the corresponding expression. This means that, for example, you can write

```
yin, yang := yang, yin
```

to exchange the values of two variables *yin* and *yang*.

You may be wondering about assignments like

```
i, a[i] := p, q
```

where it is not plain whether the value of *i* is changed before or after it is used to decide which component of *a* is selected. In fact, in occam, such an assignment would be invalid. There is no implication that any part of the assignment executes from left to right: the expressions on the right may be evaluated in any order; the values of the variable on the left may be changed in any order. A multiple assignment behaves as though it were

```
SEQ
  PAR
    t1 := e1
    ...
    tn := en
  PAR
    v1 := t1
    ...
    vn := tn
```

where *t*1 up to *tn* are new variables of the right types.

It is invalid for any variable assigned to by an assignment to appear in an expression selecting any of the variables; it is also invalid for the same variable to be assigned to twice by an assignment,

```
x, x, x := hay, bee, sea
```

or as would be the case in

```
a[i], a[j] := a[j], a[i]
```

were *i* to be equal to *j*.

Communication by channels

In parallel programs, the analogue of the variable is the *channel*. You can think of a channel as being something like a wire between the processes; indeed, if two processes running on different processors in a multiprocessor computer communicate over a channel, then there will be a real physical wire implementing the channel. On the other hand, you should not think of occam communication as necessarily involving signals moving into or out of a computer. In occam, input and output are component processes just like assignment. An output process

```
channel ! expression
```

which sends the value of the expression over the channel, executed in parallel with a corresponding input process

```
channel ? variable
```

which reads a value from the channel and assigns it to the variable, is exactly the same as the assignment

```
variable := expression
```

In suitable circumstances – when both parties to a communication are implemented on a single processor – an input and an output reduce to just the corresponding assignment, and some synchronization to ensure that both parts of the communication happen at the same time.

A channel is used for communication in only one direction: if two concurrent processes (branches of a PAR) use a single channel, one of them must use it exclusively for input, the other exclusively for output. The synchronization of input and output is an important part of the communication. An input is not complete until the corresponding output is complete, and vice versa, so each partner in a communication has to wait for the other to be ready before the communication is complete.

Protocols and channel declarations

The equivalent, for channels, of the type of a variable is the *protocol* operated on that channel. Channels are declared, just like variables, by quoting a description when introducing the name. A protocol describes the values that are to be communicated, in the same way that the type of a variable constrains the values that can be stored.

The simplest protocols are just types; any type can be used as a simple protocol, and to declare a channel with such a protocol, say

```
CHAN OF REAL64 control :
```

is to say that it will only be used for outputs of a single value of that type,

```
control ! 1.0(REAL64) / (REAL64 ROUND 15)
```

and inputs to a single variable of that type,

```
[3] [3] [3] REAL64 tensor :
...
control ? tensor [0] [0] [0]
```

Of course, a single value of an array type is a whole array, so

```
CHAN OF [34] BYTE stream :
```

would be used for outputs of rows of thirty-four bytes, like

```
stream ! "pleated bagpipes without the pipes"
```

and inputs of rows of thirty-four bytes, like

```
[34] BYTE accordion :
stream ? accordion
```

This example illustrates another case where the precise sizing of arrays can be annoying, and there is a protocol for counted arrays which is like not quoting the length of an array when specifying an abbreviation.

Because it is important to be able to determine the sizes of arrays, in order to confirm that accesses to them are valid, a counted array consists of an integer describing the size of the array accompanied by that number of components of the array. Channels of counted array protocols are declared by quoting the type of the integer, and specifying the array type without giving an exact length

```
CHAN OF INT:: [] [3] INT vectors :
```

Outputs on such a channel have to specify the number of components being sent, so

```
vectors ! 2:: [[1,1,1], [1,2,3], [1,4,9], [1,8,27]]
```

will send $[[1,1,1],[1,2,3]]$. Inputs receive the length and a number of components, so

```
INT d :
[100] [3] INT buff :
...
vectors ? d::buff
```

together with the above output would have the effect of setting d to 2, and setting

```
[buff FROM 0 FOR d] :=
        [[[1,1,1], [1,2,3], [1,4,9], [1,8,27]] FROM 0 FOR 2]
```

Of course, neither the input nor the output is valid if the count which is sent or received is greater than the number of components in the array of which a segment is sent, or the array to a segment of which an assignment is made.

Counted array protocols are often used with strings of characters, and it is quite usual to use

```
c ! SIZE v :: v
```

for moving strings around.

Protocols can be given names, for example

```
PROTOCOL BIT IS BOOL :
PROTOCOL STRING IS INT::[]BYTE :
```

and in the scope of such a declaration the name can be used in a channel declaration

```
CHAN OF STRING file :
```

to have exactly the same meaning as declaring the channel with the corresponding protocol

```
CHAN OF INT::[]BYTE file :
```

In fact, for more complicated protocols you have to give a name to the protocol and use that name in declaring channels.

Sequential protocols

A sequential protocol is a sequence of (possibly different) simple protocols – types and counted arrays – and a channel declared to have a sequential protocol can be used for communicating sequences of values, each value conforming to the corresponding component of the protocol. In the scope of

```
PROTOCOL COMPLEX IS REAL64; REAL64 :
```

a channel declared by

```
CHAN OF COMPLEX complex :
```

can only be used for outputs of pairs of REAL64s

```
complex ! r * sin.th; r * cos.th
```

and inputs to pairs of REAL64 variables

```
complex ? x; y
```

In this case there is a defined left-to-right sequence, so it is perfectly in order to use a channel with a sequential protocol

```
PROTOCOL RECORD IS INT; INT::[]BYTE :
CHAN OF RECORD update :
```

for inputs like

```
update ? i; length[i]::data[i]
```

The input to i happens first; then, using the new value of i variables are selected for the input of the counted array.

There is no significance to our use of an upper-case name for the protocol, except that this is a convention which we will adopt to make protocol names look like type names.

Discriminated protocols

In general, the communications between a pair of processes will at different times conform to different protocols. In the same way that in some programming languages you can store values of different types in a variable, and keep track of which type of value is stored, so in occam 2 values of different types can be sent over a channel by indicating with *tags* which type of value is to come. The declaration

```
PROTOCOL NUMBER IS
  CASE
    whole; INT64
    floating; REAL64
    complex; REAL64; REAL64
  :
```

introduces a protocol called NUMBER, but it also declares tags called *whole*, *floating*, and *complex* with the same scope. The protocols which appear in the component lists of a discriminated protocol have to be simple protocols – types, and counted arrays.

If a channel is declared to use such a protocol,

```
CHAN OF NUMBER c :
```

the only outputs which are legal have the forms

```
c ! whole; n
```

where n is an INT64,

```
c ! floating; r
```

where *r* is a REAL64, or

```
c ! complex; r; theta
```

where *r* and *theta* are both REAL64s.

The corresponding discriminated input has the form of a case discrimination on the tag of the communicated value,

```
c ? CASE
  whole; n
    wurble.int64(n)
  floating; r
    wurble.real64(r)
  complex; r; theta
    wurble.complex64(r, theta)
```

This process accepts a tag, and depending on which of the tags is received completes the corresponding input. It then proceeds to execute the process that appears in that branch of the case discrimination.

Notice that the first thing to appear in the semicolon-separated list in each branch of a discriminated input is the tag. It is a constant, not a variable into which the tag is read! There is no way of accepting a tag into a variable and then testing the value of the tag: for what type would the variable have; what would be the number and types of the other variables in the input process?

In fact, the discriminated input is very much more like an alternative process

```
CHAN OF INT64 c.whole :
CHAN OF REAL64 c.floating :
CHAN OF COMPLEX c.complex :
...
ALT
  c.whole ? n
    wurble.int64(n)
  c.floating ? r
    wurble.real64(r)
  c.complex ? r; theta
    wurble.complex64(r, theta)
```

over a number of new channels with different protocols.

If some of the tags are not listed in a discriminated input, it is an error for that input to match with an output of one of the missing tags, and the whole input stops. A discriminated input with only one branch can be abbreviated to one line, for example

```
c ? CASE complex; r; theta
```

which is the same as

```
c ? CASE
  complex; r; theta
    SKIP
```

and it is of course wrong for the received tag to be different from the one tag in such an input. In that case, the input fails to terminate, like STOP.

Arrays of channels

Just as arrays of variables of the same type can be declared, so can arrays of channels with the same protocol, and arrays of arrays of channels, and so on. The need for arrays of channels arises naturally when one process needs to communicate with an array of processes.

Individual components and complete segments can be selected from arrays of channels in exactly the same way as from arrays of variables, and channels and arrays of channels can be abbreviated.

```
[100]CHAN OF NUMBER c :
[]CHAN OF NUMBER left   IS [c FROM 0 FOR n] :
CHAN OF NUMBER middle  IS c[n] :
[]CHAN OF NUMBER right IS [c FROM n+1 FOR (SIZE c) - (n+1)] :
```

The same rules as for arrays of variables apply to the use of names of arrays of channels that have been abbreviated.

4

Processes

Each process may be a primitive process indicating a single action; or it may be a composite process consisting of a number of definitions and simpler component processes bound together by process constructors, indicating a combination of the actions of its component processes. The structure of constructed processes is indicated by a prescribed layout of the source text, with each component appearing on a new line, slightly indented from the keyword that introduced the whole construction.

Processes that do nothing

The simplest of the primitive processes is SKIP, which is the process that does nothing at all. In many programming languages, you are obliged to write nothing (that is, not to write anything at all) if you want 'nothing' done; you will see later that SKIP serves as useful a purpose in occam as that of zero in the decimal notation for numbers.

The process STOP also does 'nothing', but unlike SKIP it never terminates. You can think of it as being what happens when something goes wrong, like the program becoming deadlocked, or some illegal operation. Nothing can happen in a sequential process after it has stopped, but things can happen in parallel with a stopped process. You might not expect to write the STOP process very often in your programs, but it is the rational thing to do when something unexpected happens, because it ensures that the part of a network of processes that has failed is brought to a standstill without affecting other processes, at least until they come to depend on the broken part.

It is also useful to have STOP around so as to be able to describe the effect of compound processes that 'go wrong', for example by becoming deadlocked. A process is said to be deadlocked if there is nothing which it is able to do next, but it has not finished properly. A parallel program which

26

becomes deadlocked typically does so because each of its processes is waiting for one of the others to do something. For example, each component process may be prepared to communicate but only to do so with some of the other processes, and not with any process which is ready to communicate with it.

Sequential processes

In programs which execute sequentially, each process communicates with its successors by passing on a record of its state in variables. The work is done by assigning values to variables, and subsequently basing decisions on the values of those variables. The occam assignment has the form

```
variable := expression
```

Each expression has a value, and a type; each variable has a type. The type of the variable in an assignment must be the same as the type of the expression whose value is assigned to it.

A sequence of operations is described by writing them one under the other, under and slightly indented from the keyword SEQ. The sequence is executed by executing each of the components in the sequence in which they are written. Of course, if there are no components at all, then the sequence does nothing, and is just like SKIP. Thus,

```
SEQ
  x := 3
  y := x + 7
  x := x + 6
  z := x + 1
  x := (y + z) / 2
```

has the overall effect of setting each of the variables x, y, z to 10, albeit in a roundabout way, changing x three times.

Conditional processes

Decisions based on the values of variables are made by conditional processes. A conditional process consists of the keyword IF written above a list of components, each slightly indented. Each component is either another conditional nested within the first, or consists of a Boolean expression – the *condition* – and, below the condition and a little further indented, a process.

The whole conditional executes by looking down the list of components, and the components of the nested conditionals, until a condition is found whose value is TRUE. The process part of the first component with a

TRUE condition, and only that process, is then executed before the whole conditional terminates. It is wrong for there to be no TRUE condition, and in that case the conditional stops; of course, a conditional with no branches has no true conditions, and so is like STOP.

```
IF
  n < 0
    sign := -1
  n = 0
    sign := 0
  n > 0
    sign := 1
```

sets the value of the variable *sign* to one of minus one, zero, or plus one, according as the variable *n* has a negative, zero, or positive value.

Since it is defined that the selected process is the first in the order written of those corresponding to a TRUE condition, the process

```
VAL BOOL otherwise IS TRUE :
IF
  n = 0
    sign := 0
  n <= 0
    sign := -1
  otherwise
    sign := 1
```

describes exactly the same effect as the former example, but is much less clear. In general, it is good style to use constraints that describe as precisely as is convenient the conditions under which a process is to be executed. A good conditional has an exhaustive set of conditions, that is one of them is guaranteed to be TRUE; and the truth of a condition is a guarantee that executing the corresponding process would produce the right result.

There is a particularly common form of conditional which can be written more compactly to make a program easier to understand (and, incidentally, to give a hint to a compiler about how to translate it into efficient code). A conditional process selects a branch according to which of a range of constant values is taken by a single expression, for example

```
IF
  (a + b) = (-1)
    x := - a
  (a + b) = 0
    x := 0
  (a + b) = 1
    x := b
```

can be written more clearly as a case discrimination,

```
CASE a + b
  -1
    x := - a
  0
    x := 0
  1
    x := b
```

A case discrimination consists of an expression, the *selector*, written after the keyword CASE, followed by a slightly indented list of selections. Most selections consist of a comma-separated list of constant expressions of the same type as the selector, followed by an indented process. At most one of the selections can be a default selection, consisting of the keyword ELSE followed by an indented process.

The expressions in selections must all have distinct values, and a case discrimination executes by executing the process in the selection with an expression whose value is the same as that of the selector, if there is one. If there is no matching selection, a case discrimination executes by executing the process in its default selection if there is one; otherwise it stops. Notice that this makes an ELSE option different from a constant TRUE condition in a conditional:

```
CASE x
  ELSE
    p
  y, z
    q
```

would be the same if the branches were in a different order, and is the same as

```
IF
  (x = y) OR (x = z)
    q
  TRUE
    p
```

but if the first condition of a conditional were TRUE, then that branch would be guaranteed to be executed.

Parallel processes

Just as a list of actions can be described as happening in a strict sequence, so it is possible to specify that each of a list of actions is to happen, without specifying an order in which they must happen. Such a parallel composition is indicated by writing the actions one under the other, under and slightly indented from the keyword PAR. The parallel composition executes by executing each of its components until each has terminated. Of course, if there are no components, the effect is the same as SKIP; and if any of the components fails to terminate, for example by stopping, then the composition cannot terminate.

```
PAR
  x := y - 1
  z := y + 1
```

sets the values of x and z to be one less than, and one more than, respectively, the value of y. There is, however, no guarantee that the assignments will not happen in the other order, or indeed at precisely the same moment. Because of this, for a parallel composition to be legal, none of its components may change any variable which is used in any of the other branches: it would be an error, for example, to try to write

```
PAR
  x := y - 1
  z := x + 2
```

because x is used in the second component, but changed in the first component.

Since such mutual interference cannot happen, concurrent processes can only communicate by input and output over channels. In combination, an input and an output behave just like an assignment, except that the expression and variable are in different, concurrently executing processes. In particular, the assignment

```
variable := expression
```

is exactly the same as

```
PAR
  channel ! expression
  channel ? variable
```

provided that it is legal to write the latter in the particular context. Just as there are rules about the use of variables in concurrently executing processes, so also each end – the input end, or the output end – of a channel may be used in only one of the components of a PAR construction.

The rules about the use of channels and variables in parallel processes mean that the branches of a PAR are *disjoint*. In order to make the disjointness of processes mechanically checkable, there have to be quite severe restrictions on the use of arrays. If an array of channels or variables is shared by two or more branches of a PAR, and the indices used are not constants, the process is not valid unless the array is divided into non-overlapping segments by abbreviation, and only the abbreviations are used in the different branches.

Arbitrating processes

Decisions may also be distributed across several processes, using an *alternative*, which is like a conditional except in that the choice can depend on whether another process is executing an output. The simplest form of alternative is written with an ALT above an indented list of guarded processes; each guarded process is an input – a *guard* – followed by an accompanying indented process.

```
ALT
  up ? increment
    x := x + increment
  down ? decrement
    x := x - decrement
  read ? request
    reply ! x
```

executes by waiting until another process is ready to perform an output on one of the channels, *up*, *down*, *read*. The first of these offers to be made is taken up, and the corresponding input happens, followed by the accompanying process. If the inputs never become ready, the alternative is never completed. If several of the inputs are ready before the alternative is executed or if several become ready simultaneously, for example if several of them use the same channel, then any one – but only one – of the ready inputs is chosen.

In this example, the alternative acts as a guardian for the variable x which is effectively shared by the three (presumably) distinct processes which communicate on *up*, *down*, and *read*. The alternative arbitrates between them, making sure that their accesses to x happen in some sequence, so that only one of them is using the variable at any time.

It turns out that it is often handy to be able to shut out some of the branches of an alternative. A guard that starts with a Boolean condition and an ampersand sign is ready only if the Boolean is true and the input is ready.

```
ALT
  read ? request
    reply ! x
  NOT fixed & write ? change
    x := x + change
```

is a convenient abbreviation for a family of alternatives, in this case

```
IF
  fixed
    ALT
      read ? request
        reply ! x
  NOT fixed
    ALT
      read ? request
        reply ! x
      write ? change
        x := x + change
```

Of course, because the conditions in guards use only variables accessed by the alternative, their values cannot change while the alternative waits for one of the guards to become ready.

A guard in an alternative may also be SKIP, which is a guard that is always immediately ready. An alternative with a SKIP guard can always choose that guard without considering any of the others. For that reason, SKIP guards are almost always accompanied by a condition; indeed a helpful compiler may insist on a condition! SKIP guards are used to give an explicit default action in case all of the other branches are closed by false conditions,

```
ALT
  readable & read ? request
    reply ! x
  writable & write ? change
    x := x + change
  NOT (readable OR writable) & SKIP
    x := default.value
```

because if all of the guards in an alternative are closed by false conditions they will remain closed forever, and the alternative behaves like an alternative with no branches – that is, it behaves like STOP.

If a guard is an input on a channel with a discriminated protocol, you can use the short form of single-case discriminated input as a guard.

```
ALT
  condition & channel ? CASE tag; variable
    process
```

Notice that a guard which is a discriminated input is ready whenever another process is prepared to output, irrespective of what tag is going to be communicated. If the tag which is sent is not expected then the input stops, but only after the alternative has been committed to that branch.

The full form of a discriminated input takes the place of both the guard and the accompanying process. Both forms of discriminated input appear in

```
ALT
  readable & read ? CASE signal
    reply ! x
  writable & write ? CASE
    increment; i
      x := x + i
    decrement; d
      x := x - d
```

If *write* were a channel with a protocol that had a third tag distinct from both *increment* and *decrement*, and another process were to output that tag to *write*, then this example could opt for the second branch to the exclusion of the first. It would then, of course, stop because the received tag was not one of those present in the discriminated input.

Distinguish carefully between

```
ALT
  write ? CASE increment; i
    x := x + i
  write ? CASE decrement; d
    x := x - d
```

which can arbitrarily decide whether it will stop if sent an *increment* or if sent a *decrement*, and

```
ALT
  write ? CASE
    increment; i
      x := x + i
    decrement; d
      x := x - d
```

which guarantees to accept either tag. The former process is hardly ever what you would want.

Just like conditionals, the other thing that can appear as a branch of an alternative is a nested alternative. An alternative with nested alternatives behaves as though all of the branches of the nested alternatives were written as branches of the outer alternative. That is to say, ALT is associative.

Loops

There are two kinds of loop in occam: unbounded WHILE loops, and indexed, bounded FOR loops. Unbounded loops are necessarily sequential, whereas bounded loops need not be.

An unbounded loop is written with the keyword WHILE, followed by an expression (the condition), with a process (the body) below and slightly indented from it. It executes by testing the value of the condition and then, provided that its value is TRUE, executing the body. When the body has terminated, the condition is re-tested, so that the body is executed a number of times, in sequence, for as long as the condition remains TRUE. The whole WHILE loop terminates when the condition is tested and found to be FALSE.

```
SEQ
    x, v[n] := 0, key
    WHILE v[x] <> key
        x := x + 1
```

sets x to be the index of the first variable in the array v which contains the value *key*, by first posting a sentinel at $v[n]$.

Arrays of processes

A bounded loop may be thought of as being an array of processes, and can be made with any of the SEQ, IF, PAR, and ALT constructors, by putting a replicator of the form

```
name = base FOR count
```

after the keyword, and then writing just a single component (of the kind appropriate to the construction) below and slightly indented from the keyword. The *base* and *count* are expressions of type INT, and the meaning of such a FOR loop is the same as that of a construction formed from the same keyword followed by *count* copies of the component with the *name* taking on the values *base*, *base* + 1, ..., *base* + *count* − 1 in successive copies. In effect, the replicator declares *name* to be an INT constant with the body of the loop as its scope.

A FOR loop stands for a repetition of the constructor with which it is made. In the same way that

$$\prod_{year=1280}^{1341} entity_{year}$$

stands for the multiplication of sixty-two values,

$$entity_{1280} \times entity_{1281} \times \ldots \times entity_{1341}$$

so too the SEQ–FOR loop

```
SEQ year = 1280 FOR 62
    celebrate.easter(year)
```

stands for the sequential composition of sixty-two processes

```
SEQ
  celebrate.easter(1280)
  celebrate.easter(1281)
  ...
  celebrate.easter(1341)
```

or, more precisely,

```
SEQ
  VAL INT year IS 1280 :
  celebrate.easter(year)
  VAL INT year IS 1281 :
  celebrate.easter(year)
  ...
  VAL INT year IS 1341 :
  celebrate.easter(year)
```

So SEQ–FOR loops are quite like FOR loops in languages like ALGOL or PASCAL; but notice that you may not assign to the loop index, and it is not declared outside the body of the loop.

The bodies of parallel PAR–FOR loops are executed concurrently, so such loops are arrays of parallel processes. A conditional loop, written with IF and FOR, performs a bounded search, so

```
SEQ
  v[n] := key
  IF i = 0 FOR n+1
    v[i] = key
      x := i
```

has precisely the same effect as that of the WHILE loop on page 34. The same search can be performed rather more elegantly, without the use of a sentinel, by writing

```
VAL BOOL otherwise IS TRUE :
VAL INT not.found IS n :
IF
  IF i = 0 FOR n
    v[i] = key
      x := i
  otherwise
    x := not.found
```

Here, x is set to *not.found* precisely when there is no occurrence of the value *key* in the array.

In practice, a more useful result from the search would be a Boolean indicating whether or not the *key* was found.

```
VAL BOOL otherwise IS TRUE :
IF
  IF i = 0 FOR n
    v[i] = key
      found, x := TRUE, i
  otherwise
    found := FALSE
```

You should now see the reason for allowing conditionals as components of conditionals! Although you can (and should, where it helps) use redundant nesting to guide a reader through the structure of a large construct, it is necessary in cases like the last example, where one of the branches is a loop. The same applies to alternatives as components of alternatives.

Alternative loops, written ALT–FOR, give a process an opportunity to listen to an array of channels, for example

```
WHILE TRUE
  ALT i = 0 FOR SIZE c
    INT n :
    c[i] ? n
      shared ! i; n
```

gathers integers from the channels of *c* and passes them on, with an identifying index, to the *shared* channel.

5

Abbreviation and abstraction

This chapter is largely about the business of taking parts of a program and giving names to them. We have got so far without saying what a name is, largely because the rules for which are allowable names are much what they are in most programming languages. To be precise, a name is a sequence of letters, digits and full-stop symbols; the first must be a letter. Two names are distinct unless they are exactly the same sequence of characters – the case of letters is significant – so each of the following twenty-four names

```
x           y           z           X           Y           Z
left        right       up          down        seq         par
x0          x1          x2          x.          x..         x...
Imre.Nagy               G.G.Arnold              d2V.by.dr2
Beatrice7               dff.39c                 OX1.3DW
```

can validly be used as a name in an **occam** program. The only exception to this description is that those sequences of upper case letters which are keywords – like SEQ, PAR – are reserved for this purpose and cannot be used as names. There is a list of reserved words on page 206 in the language summary at the back of this book.

Formally, all the names used in a program have to be in the scope of a declaration of the right kind. In practice, an implementation will have libraries of pre-declared names which behave as though they had already been defined. For the present, these can be treated as though they were declared immediately before the text of every program.

Declarations of variables, protocols and channels, and abbreviations of values, variables and channels can appear in front of any process, any branch of a conditional, branch of an alternative, branch of a case discrimination, branch of a discriminated input, or anonymous function. The scope of the name introduced by the declaration or abbreviation is the process or branch, and any declarations or abbreviations appearing between them.

Very roughly, what this means is that everywhere after the declaration or abbreviation and before the end of the subsequent process or branch the new name refers to the declared or abbreviated object. There are two kinds of exception: either another declaration of the same name can knock a hole in the scope of the declaration, or there may be constraints which mean that although a name is in scope it is not valid to use it.

The first kind of exception follows a conventional scoping rule in all ALGOL-like languages. An example of this kind is that in

```
VAL INT x IS 27 :
SEQ
  c ! 1; x
  VAL BYTE x IS '$' :
  d ! 2; x
  c ! 3; x
```

because the x in d!2;x is in the scope of the inner abbreviation, it is taken out of the scope of the outer one; the whole process is equivalent to

```
SEQ
  c ! 1; 27
  d ! 2; '$'
  c ! 3; 27
```

Notice that only the one branch of the sequence is in the scope of the inner abbreviation. Deliberate and unnecessary re-use of names like this is to be discouraged, since it is likely to confuse a human reader – and often the writer – of the program. It is valid to write

```
VAL x IS 63 :
VAL x IS 2 * x :
VAL x IS x + 1 :
c[x] ! x
```

but it would be altogether clearer to write

```
VAL x IS 63 :
VAL y IS 2 * x :
VAL z IS y + 1 :
c[z] ! z
```

which is what it means. On the other hand, it is as well that this scoping rule makes it safe to use a name locally irrespective of an unrelated use that happens to have an enclosing scope.

The second kind of exception is less familiar; in most programming languages, it is simply considered good practice never to have two names for the same variable. For example, it is possible but frowned upon to have a variable passed as an argument to a PASCAL procedure, and to use it as a free variable of that procedure. If there are two different names for a single piece of storage, it becomes difficult to predict the effect of assigning to one of them. An experienced programmer will know at a glance that

```
SEQ
  Casnewydd := Casnewydd >< Newport
  Newport   := Casnewydd >< Newport
  Casnewydd := Casnewydd >< Newport
```

has the effect of interchanging the values of the integer variables *Casnewydd* and *Newport*, admittedly rather less efficiently than

```
Casnewydd, Newport := Newport, Casnewydd
```

(It is an old trick for exchanging the contents of two processor registers without recourse to the use of a third, or of main store, as a temporary storage location.) Yet, there is an unstated assumption that they are different variables: were it allowable to write

```
Newport IS Casnewydd :
SEQ
  Casnewydd := Casnewydd >< Newport
  Newport   := Casnewydd >< Newport
  Casnewydd := Casnewydd >< Newport
```

then presumably this would be equivalent to

```
SEQ
  Casnewydd := Casnewydd >< Casnewydd
  Casnewydd := Casnewydd >< Casnewydd
  Casnewydd := Casnewydd >< Casnewydd
```

which sets *Casnewydd* to zero, three times. Since there might be any amount of text between the abbreviation and its use, it might be difficult for a reader to spot that *Casnewydd* and *Newport* shared the same location.

In occam such dangerous bad style is outlawed by the language definition; such programs are not valid occam, and an implementation of occam must check for violation of these rules. This compulsion is partly because the potential for confusion is enhanced by the possibility of concurrent accesses to shared variables. In part it reflects a growing acceptance that it is a good thing to restrict the programmer's freedom to make a fool of himself, so as to make it easier to check that a program means what it seems to mean.

The rule for channel and variable abbreviations is essentially that when a new name has been given to a variable or channel, use of the old name is no longer valid. In order to be realistically checkable without having to execute the program, the rule for abbreviating components and segments of arrays is that any use of the name of the array is invalid, except for further abbreviations; and that abbreviated parts of an array must be non-overlapping.

The rule for value abbreviations is that it is invalid in the scope of a value abbreviation to appear to change the value of a variable which appears in the abbreviated expression. This means that

```
VAL INT forty.two IS (zero * x) + one.three.seven :
IF
  forty.two = 42
    x := 17
  forty.two <> 42
    SKIP
```

would be invalid, even if *forty.two* were not 42. A variable appears to be changed if there is in the text an assignment to it, an input to it, or a variable abbreviation of it, even though that part of the text might happen not to be executed.

The rule for sharing variables between the branches of a parallel process is essentially that either none of them appears to change it, or exactly one of them can change it and none of the others can access it at all. It might help to remember this rule if you think of it as: either each of the branches can safely take a copy of the initial value of the variable, and it does not change; or one of the branches can take sole possession of the storage represented by the variable. The rule for channels is similar: at most one branch of a parallel process can use a channel for input, at most one of them can use it for output.

Again, to make the disjointness of the branches of a parallel process efficiently checkable by a compiler, there is an additional rule for arrays of variables or channels. If a branch of a parallel process indexes an array with subscripting expressions that include variables, that branch is treated as if it used the whole of the array. Of course, it is valid to abbreviate several disjoint segments of an array and to index those with variable subscripts in different branches of a parallel process.

Procedure definition

A *procedure* definition gives a name to a process, so that in the scope of the definition, the name can be written to have the effect of having written out the whole of the process. In the scope of

```
PROC another()
  number := number + 1
:
```

you can use the *call*

```
another()
```

to stand for the process in the body of the procedure

```
number := number + 1
```

As with other definitions, the scope of a procedure definition is the part of the program *after* the definition, so does not include the process in the definition itself. In **occam**, procedures cannot call themselves.

A word of caution about names: in the rather bizarre program

```
INT number :
PROC another()
  number := number + 1
:
SEQ
  number := 0
  INT number :
  SEQ
    another()
    number := 0
  c ! number
```

the *number* assigned to by *another()* is the one in scope where the procedure is defined, not the one where it is used. The example is the same as

```
INT number :
SEQ
  number := 0
  INT new.number :
  SEQ
    number := number + 1
    new.number := 0
  c ! number
```

The reason for the empty parentheses after the name of *another* is that a procedure definition need not give a name to a simple process. The procedure can be made to depend on abbreviations which are different at each call of the procedure.

```
PROC write.string(CHAN OF BYTE c, VAL []BYTE s)
  SEQ i = 0 FOR SIZE s
    c ! s[i]
:
```

is a procedure which sends an as yet unspecified sequence of bytes along an as yet unspecified character channel. An instance like

```
write.string(output, "Bootifrolo")
```

is effectively

```
CHAN OF BYTE c IS output :
[]BYTE s IS "Bootifrolo" :
SEQ i = 0 FOR SIZE s
  c ! s[i]
```

The formal parameter list in a procedure definition consists of the left hand sides of a sequence of abbreviations, and the actual parameter list in an instance consists of the corresponding right hand sides.

There must be the same number of components in each list of actual parameters as in the formal parameter list, and they must be the right sort of expression, variable, or channel, and of the right type for the equivalent abbreviation to be correct. Since the whole point of procedure definition is to take a piece of the program text and make it self-contained, you cannot leave the type specification from the formal parameter list as you can from an actual abbreviation. On the other hand, where there is a sequence of parameters of the same type and kind, you can leave out the second and subsequent specifiers:

```
PROC set.min.max(INT min, max, VAL INT a, b)
  IF
    a <= b
      min, max := a, b
    a >= b
      max, min := a, b
  :
```

is exactly the same definition as if it had been introduced by

```
PROC set.min.max(INT min, INT max, VAL INT a, VAL INT b)
```

Since the meaning of parameters is defined in terms of abbreviation, they are governed by the same rules as abbreviation: a variable may not be passed twice as two variable parameters, nor a channel twice as two channel parameters; neither should a variable which appears in an expression which is passed as a value parameter also be passed as a variable parameter. An instance like

```
set.min.max(a, b, a, b)
```

is not valid, because the argument list abbreviates the variables *a* and *b* before they appear as value arguments. This is a problem which cannot be cured by changing the order of the arguments:

```
PROC set.min.max(VAL INT a, b, INT min, max)
  ...
:
set.min.max(a, b, a, b)
```

would be invalid because *a* and *b* are abbreviated after they appear in value abbreviations.

In addition, of course, the parameter abbreviations must not interfere with free names – those names like *free* in

```
PROC remember(VAL INT arg)
  free := free >< arg
:
```

which appear in a procedure definition and are not defined within it, but refer to definitions in an enclosing scope. An invocation like *remember*(137) is all right, but *remember*(*free*) would have been invalid; to be precise, in

```
INT free :
PROC remember(VAL INT arg)
  free := free >< arg
:
SEQ
  ...
  INT expensive :
  SEQ
    ...
    remember(expensive)   -- valid
    remember(free)        -- invalid
    INT nothing IS free :
    SEQ
      ...
      remember(something) -- invalid
    INT free :
    SEQ
      ...
      remember(free)      -- valid
```

the first instance is all right; the second is invalid because it means

```
INT free :
...
VAL INT arg IS free :
free := free >< arg
```

which assigns to a variable mentioned in an abbreviated expression; the third is invalid because it means

```
INT free :
...
INT nothing IS free :
...
free := free >< something
```

which assigns to an abbreviated variable; and the fourth is valid because it is the same as

```
INT free :
...
INT new.free :
...
VAL INT arg IS new.free :
free := free >< arg
```

because the apparent clash of names is entirely accidental. Notice that – as in all ALGOL-like languages – the assignment is always to the same variable irrespective of what names are in scope at the instance.

Similarly the procedure

```
PROC invalid(CHAN OF INT channel)
  PAR
    channel ! 0
    INT dummy :
    channel ? dummy
:
```

is invalid even though the channel is used for input in the one case and output in the other. This is because of an additional rule that a channel argument or free channel of a procedure may not be used both for input and for output. Of course, this causes no great hardship to the programmer, since such a channel might as well have been declared locally to the body of the procedure.

Anonymous functions

An anonymous function contains a process which calculates a value; for example

```
INT sum :
VALOF
  SEQ
    sum := 0
    SEQ i = 0 FOR SIZE v
      sum := sum + v[i]
  RESULT sum
```

is an INT expression – its value is the value of the variable *sum*, which appears as its RESULT, after the execution of the process which is its body:

```
SEQ
  sum := 0
  SEQ i = 0 FOR SIZE v
    sum := sum + v[i]
```

and so is the sum of all the components of the array *v*. (In INMOS documentation, anonymous functions are called *value processes*, but notice that they are expressions, and not processes.)

In order for an anonymous function to be side-effect free it is forbidden for its body to assign to free variables. This means that in practice, the result will almost always consist of variables declared immediately in front of the VALOF. Additionally, the body may not input or output, and must contain no parallel or alternative processes. This means that the value of the expression is fully determined by the values of its free variables.

When an anonymous function appears in an expression, it must be enclosed in a pair of parentheses one above the other, and the whole of its text must be to the right of these parentheses.

```
sum.of.sums := (INT sum :
                VALOF
                  SEQ
                    sum := 0
                    SEQ i = 0 FOR SIZE v
                      sum := sum + v[i]
                  RESULT sum
                ) + sum.of.sums
```

If the process in the body of an anonymous function fails, for example if it stops, then the expression using the anonymous function is just like any other invalid expression: a process which uses it stops.

As well as returning a single value for use in an expression, an anonymous function may also return a list of values, for example

```
INT min, max :
VALOF
  IF
    a <= b
      min, max := a, b
    a >= b
      max, min := a, b
  RESULT min, max
```

which returns two INTs. These functions can be used on the right hand side of a multiple assignment

```
less, more := (INT min, max :
               VALOF
                 IF
                   a <= b
                     min, max := a, b
                   a >= b
                     max, min := a, b
                 RESULT min, max
               )
```

again, between and to the right of vertically disposed parentheses. In practice, anonymous functions will rarely be written in expressions and assignments: they are usually only used as the bodies of function definitions. You can expect some compilers not to implement anonymous functions in expressions.

Function definitions

Function definition generalizes value abstraction, in a way like procedure definition. For example, in the scope of

```
REAL64 FUNCTION square(VAL REAL64 a) IS a * a :
```

you can write

```
r.square := square(x) + square(y)
```

to mean

```
VAL REAL64 a IS x :
VAL REAL64 b IS y :
r.square := (a * a) + (b * b)
```

or, rather, something more like

```
r.square := (VAL REAL64 a IS x :
             VALOF
               SKIP
               RESULT a * a
             ) + (VAL REAL64 a IS y :
                  VALOF
                    SKIP
                    RESULT a * a
                  )
```

The formal parameters of a function definition must all be value parameters, and the value of an instance of the function is the value of the expression in the body of its definition, in the scope of the value abbreviations corresponding to its parameters.

Notice that there is an important difference between

```
VAL INT initial.x IS x :
```

and the definition of a 'constant' function like

```
INT FUNCTION recent.x() IS x :
```

In the scope of a value abbreviation it is invalid to try to change the value of the abbreviated expression; the value of the abbreviating name is therefore fixed. Each instance of a constant function is evaluated afresh:

```
INT FUNCTION recent.x() IS x :
SEQ
  x := 42
  c ! recent.x()
  x := 137
  c ! recent.x()
```

has the same meaning as

```
SEQ
  x := 42
  c ! 42
  x := 137
  c ! 137
```

As a syntactic concession, if the body of a function definition is an anonymous function, it can be written to look as though it were a procedure definition,

```
INT FUNCTION max(VAL INT a, b)
  INT max :
  VALOF
    IF
      a <= b
        max := b
      a >= b
        max := a
    RESULT max
  :
```

Remember that the process in the body of such a function definition, being the body of an anonymous function, cannot assign to free variables, communicate, or make arbitrary choices. This ensures that the defined function is free from side-effects.

More generally, a function can return a list of values, for example

```
INT64, INT64 FUNCTION divide (VAL INT64 x, y) IS x/y, x\y :
```

and instances of such functions can be used as the right hand side of a multiple assignment or as the RESULT of an anonymous function.

```
x, y := ( INT64 p, q :
          VALOF
            p, q := divide(x, y)
            RESULT divide(p, y)
        )
```

Notice that calling a function which returns multiple results can be more efficient than calling several functions. The assignment

```
INT, INT FUNCTION min.max(VAL INT a, b)
  INT min, max :
  VALOF
    IF
      a <= b
        min, max := a, b
      a >= b
        max, min := a, b
    RESULT min, max
  :

a, b := min.max(a, b)
```

makes only one comparison of *a* against *b*, whereas

```
a, b := min(a, b), max(a, b)
```

necessarily makes two comparisons.

Since a function with multiple results can ultimately only be used on the right hand side of a multiple assignment, it might seem that you would be as well to have written a procedure with variable parameters. For example

```
x, y := min.max(a, b)
```

being the same as

```
set.min.max(x, y, a, b)
```

Notice, however, that

```
a, b := min.max(a, b)
```

is valid, whereas

```
set.min.max(a, b, a, b)
```

is not.

6

Local time

One of the principal applications of **occam** is to be programming what are commonly called *embedded* applications, that is programs to be executed on a computer that is only a part of some machine or system. Programs which interact in this way with parts of the world outside the computer on which they are executed often have a need to measure and record the passage of time. For this reason, facilities for dealing with real-time clocks are incorporated in the language.

This chapter is here to complete the presentation, but timers will hardly be used in the rest of the book so you may want to pass over this chapter on a first reading.

Timers

A *timer* is an object in a program rather like a channel; two timers are declared by

```
TIMER gmt, bst :
```

As with variables, arrays of timers can be declared, timers can be renamed by abbreviation,

```
[24]TIMER time.zone :
TIMER universal IS time.zone[12] :
```

and they can be passed as parameters to procedures, but not to functions.

Each timer is associated with a *clock*, which is rather like another process operating in parallel with the program. This process behaves as though it had a hidden **INT** variable; the value of this variable is called the *reading* of the clock. Each clock has a characteristic period, and increments its reading with the passage of each period. The expected implementation of a timer would be a hardware counter driven by a constant frequency clock signal.

The reading on a timer can be read by a process that looks like an input process

```
universal ? now
```

which immediately stores in an INT variable, *now*, the current reading of the specified timer. It is a trifle misleading for this to look like an input process: there are no restrictions on the use of timers in different branches of a parallel command as there are for channels; many concurrent processes may read the same timer without interference.

Because the reading on a clock passes through the whole range of INTs, with t being followed by t PLUS 1, the reading will be the same again after 2^n periods, where n is the number of bits in an INT. The right way of comparing two times is with AFTER. If two readings are taken from a clock less than MOSTPOS INT periods apart, then the second will be AFTER the first. As a guide to what this means, the clock visible to low priority processes on an IMST800 transputer has a period of 64 μs, and counts around in 2^{32} periods – about seventy-six and a half hours. This means that AFTER gives the expected answer if used to compare two readings taken less than a day and a half apart.

Later in the book, we assume that you can provide a definition

```
VAL INT second IS ... :
```

indicating by how much the reading on a timer changes in a second; this would only be possible for a clock which did not complete its cycle in less than two seconds. It is not unreasonable to assume that you can compare readings taken a minute apart, although the cycle time of a sixteen-bit 1μs clock would only be a sixteenth of a second or so.

Delay

The *delay* process

```
universal ? AFTER midnight
```

is another process, like SKIP, which does nothing in the sense that it eventually terminates, having neither communicated on any channel, nor changed any variable. It may, however, suspend execution, and does not terminate until the reading of *universal* has satisfied *reading* AFTER *midnight*. That is a carefully worded sentence: notice that there is no guarantee about the value of *variable* after the execution of

```
SEQ
  universal ? AFTER midnight
  universal ? variable
```

nor is there any guaranteed upper limit on how long it takes to execute a delay process. As before, a delay is not really an input process, but it can be used either as an ordinary process or as a guard in an alternative. A guard which is a delay is ready as soon as the delay could have terminated.

Notice that there is no way of setting the reading of a timer, nor is there any guaranteed relationship between the reading on two different clocks. That means that the normal way of setting a deadline for a delay is by taking a reading from the same timer, and calculating what the reading will be at the deadline.

Using timers

There are a very few idioms that encompass almost all uses of timers.

To suspend execution for (at least) ten seconds, it suffices to take a reading from any timer, and to wait until that timer has moved on by ten seconds.

```
TIMER t :
INT start :
SEQ
  t ? start
  t ? AFTER start PLUS (10 * second)
```

This might be done as a once-only action in a program while starting or stopping some mechanical peripheral device.

If an action is to be performed at regular intervals, say once every ten seconds, the program must wait for the passage of a succession of deadlines, each ten seconds later than the previous one. The process

```
TIMER t :
INT dead.line :
SEQ
  t ? dead.line
  WHILE ...
    SEQ
      dead.line := dead.line PLUS (10 * second)
      t ? AFTER dead.line
      ... perform the regular action
```

will do this, provided that the regular action can be completed in under ten seconds. Notice that each deadline is set relative to the previous deadline, so as to avoid slippage.

Finally, using delay guards allows a process to limit the time for which it is prepared to wait for input.

```
TIMER t :
INT prompted :
SEQ
  write.string(terminal.screen, "Yer wot, mate? ")
  t ? prompted
  ALT
    BYTE ch :
    terminal.keyboard ? ch
      to.program ! operator.typed.character; ch
    t ? AFTER prompted PLUS (30 * second)
      to.program ! operator.asleep.or.dead
```

Provided that the input from the *terminal.keyboard* arrives within thirty seconds of the clock being read, the alternative will select its first guard. After that time, the other guard is ready and the process is no longer obliged to wait for its input.

7
Configuration

Because it was intended as a medium for programming embedded systems, occam includes facilities for describing the way in which the abstract data objects of the program are related to the concrete hardware. Most of the explanations in this chapter have to be in terms of what an implementation would do, and how it would do it. On the whole, you would not expect to have to use the material here unless and until you needed to make your program fit some particular piece of hardware. You may want to pass by this chapter on a first reading.

Biased alternatives

Recall that alternative processes are symmetric: each of the branches of an alternative is given the same chance of being selected. If a number of guards are ready when the alternative is executed, any one of them may be selected.

There are circumstances in which this is inconvenient; in a process

```
WHILE TRUE
  ALT
    interruption ? CASE signal
      unusual()
    INT message:
    input ? message
      usual(message)
```

the intention is that receipt of a signal from *interruption* should cause the execution of the *unusual* procedure, whereas normally a stream of messages from *input* are dealt with by the *usual* procedure. But consider what would happen were the process writing to *input* producing new messages in less time than it would take to execute *usual*: each time the alternative was executed the *input* guard would be ready. Irrespective of the readiness of the *interruption* guard, it would be open to the alternative to choose the *input*, and a ready *interruption* could be ignored indefinitely. Notice especially that this is nothing to do with the order in which the branches of the alternative were written: an alternative is symmetric, and the same argument would hold were the branches written in the other order.

There is, for precisely this reason, an asymmetric alternative process, written with a PRI qualifier. (Some people read this, it appears, as *prioritized*!) An asymmetric alternative favours its earlier branches – those nearer the top of the paper – over the later ones. Like the symmetrical construct, it waits until some of its guards are ready and then selects one for execution, subject to the additional constraint that no branch can be selected which is later in the text than that which first became ready.

In particular, if some of the guards of an asymmetric alternative are ready when the alternative is executed, no branches later than these ready ones can be selected. In the example above, this is just what is needed:

```
WHILE TRUE
  PRI ALT
    interruption ? CASE signal
      unusual()
    INT message:
    input ? message
      usual(message)
```

is obliged to service a signal from *interruption* after the completion of at most one execution of the body of the loop after the signal is sent.

Check that you understand that an implementation of occam would be allowed to ignore the PRI if it implemented *all* alternatives as if they were asymmetric. An implementation must guarantee the asymmetry of a PRI ALT, and a programmer can rely on that; an implementation is free to implement any selection strategy that meets the specification of a symmetric alternative, and a programmer can only rely on the existence of some strategy. There is no guarantee of the fairness of an alternative which happens to have the freedom to make a choice.

Beware the temptation to over-use PRI!

Priority on a single processor

If several branches of a parallel process are to be executed by a single processor, it may be that one of them has to wait for another not because of any communication between them, but because they each need the processor. This is a hidden shared resource, but it does not usually matter because the guaranteed disjointness of parallel processes in occam gives the programmer the illusion that every process has its own machine with its own store (variables) and processor.

The illusion breaks down when the programmer is allowed to measure the performance of a program. There are times when it really matters how long it takes to execute a piece of code, or how long it takes to get a response to an attempt to communicate with a program. One process being executed by a processor shared with another process can be unexpectedly delayed by the other, in a way that cannot be predicted simply by studying the code of the program.

Usually, where performance matters, there is some small collection of processes in a program that must be given priority. There may, for example, be signals from a piece of hardware external to the program to which a response must be given in a bounded time. In checking that a sequential program could achieve the required response time, the programmer – or better still, the compiler – could count the instructions to be executed. The count of instructions executed by a process in a parallel program, however, is only a lower bound on how long it takes to be executed. To achieve that bound the process has to be guaranteed access to the processor when it is needed.

A parallel process is symmetric; the order of the branches is immaterial. Sequential, single-processor implementations are allowed to make progress in executing it by executing any one of the branches that are not blocked waiting for a communication. On the other hand, an asymmetric parallel process, introduced by PRI PAR, favours the textually earlier branches – those nearer the top of the paper – over the later ones. If there are two branches that are not blocked, the earlier one must be executed; if an earlier branch becomes unblocked while a later one is executing, the implementation must rapidly switch to executing the higher priority branch.

Once again, an implementation of occam would be allowed to ignore the PRI if it implemented *all* parallels as if they were asymmetric. An implementation must guarantee the asymmetry of a PRI PAR, and a programmer can rely on that; an implementation is free to implement any execution strategy that meets the specification of a symmetric parallel, and a programmer can only rely on the existence of some strategy. There is no guarantee of the fairness of a parallel which happens to have the freedom to make a choice.

Notice that the priority is ascribed dynamically to a piece of code. It is possible for the same piece of code, the procedure p in this example

```
PROC p(...)
  ...
:
PRI PAR
  p(...)
  p(...)
```

to be executed with several different urgencies in the same program.

An implementation will normally impose quite a small limit on the number of branches in an asymmetric parallel construction; on present transputer implementations, the limit is two. In a parallel like

```
PRI PAR
  PAR
    incoming.router(...)
    outgoing.router(...)
  PAR
    user.routine(...)
    background.task(...)
```

the high priority branch encompasses both —.*router* processes; the low priority processes are the *user.routine* and the *background.task*. Within each pair, there is no priority given to the one process over the other.

Once again, beware the temptation to over-use PRI! Like an exclamation mark at the end of a sentence, the PRI qualifier should be used only when it is necessary. If one exists, the algorithm that solves a problem without requiring asymmetric constructs is likely to be simpler and easier to understand than one which relies on asymmetry.

Distributing a process over several processors

If an occam program is to be executed by a multi-processor machine, it is the programmer's responsibility to decide which processor executes which processes. This is in keeping with the philosophy that the programmer should be in control, knowing best what performance measure is important. This mapping of text to processors has no effect on the behaviour of the program, apart from deciding where in a machine a particular variable or channel will exist, or altering the time it takes to execute the program.

The outermost parallel constructor of a program can be annotated PLACED, meaning that each branch is to be executed by a different processor. Each processor will be allotted an INT identifier in a very machine-dependent way, and the part of the program text which is to be executed by a particular processor is announced by a PROCESSOR line with that processor's number. Suppose that the program

```
[(2*n)+1]CHAN OF INT16::[]BYTE c :
PAR
  inpull(c[0])
  PAR i = 0 FOR 2*n
    wurdle(c[i], c[i+1])
  outpush(c[2*n])
```

is to be executed on a linearly indexed array of processors that are connected each to its two second nearest neighbours.

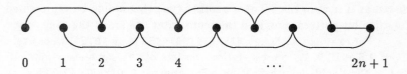

$$0 \quad 1 \quad 2 \quad 3 \quad 4 \quad \cdots \quad 2n+1$$

This could be done by grouping the $2n$ processes that *wurdle* into an odd-numbered n and an even-numbered n.

```
[(2*n)+1]CHAN OF INT16::[]BYTE c :
PLACED PAR
  PROCESSOR 0
    inpull(c[0])
  PLACED PAR i = 0 FOR n
    PROCESSOR (2*i) + 2          -- even numbers ascending
      wurdle(c[i], c[i+1])
  PLACED PAR i = n FOR n
    PROCESSOR ((4*n)+1) - (2*i)  -- odd numbers descending
      wurdle(c[i], c[i+1])
  PROCESSOR 1
    outpush(c[2*n])
```

The behaviour of this program is indistinguishable from the original, except that each instruction of the code has been allocated to a specific processor.

Variables and timers may not be declared 'outside' a PROCESSOR, so only constants, channels, and procedures and functions can be shared by different processors. If executed on a machine constructed from transputers, the channels shared by branches of a placed parallel would be implemented by the physical serial links between the transputers. The mechanism for associating channels with links is described later in this chapter.

In any particular implementation of **occam** it will usually be necessary to include other information about each processor: for example current transputer implementations require an indication of which type of transputer is to execute the code. Since branches of a placed parallel can be executed by different types of processor, it is perfectly possible for the 'natural' integer type INT to have a different range of values in different branches. Not only does this mean that it would be unwise to try to communicate INT values between different branches, but it is also necessary to be careful of algorithms that use expressions like MOSTPOS INT which might have different values in different parts of the same program. Beware, also, the replicator index of a replicated placed parallel; it is of an INT type that may not have the same range of values as the natural INT of any of the branches.

Concrete representation of data

A value of one type which is represented by a certain bit pattern can be viewed as if it were the value of another type that would be represented by the same bit pattern, provided the representations are of the same size.

For example, although #3FF(INT64)<<52 is an INT64, whose value is about 4.6×10^{18}, its representation consists of the same sixty-four bits as that of the double-length floating-point number 1.0(REAL64). This means that the retyping conversion

```
VAL REAL64 one RETYPES #3FF(INT64) << 52 :
```

is the same abbreviation as

```
VAL REAL64 one IS 1.0(REAL64) :
```

There is an important difference between retyping and type coercion: the REAL64 with the same representation as an INT64 is nothing like the REAL64 of about the same value, in this case

```
VAL REAL64 huge IS REAL64 ROUND (#3FF(INT64) << 52) :
```

which would be approximately the same as 4.6E+18(REAL64).

A retyping variable abbreviation is similar; it gives a distorting window through which to view the variable as if it were a variable of a given type, so long as that type has the same sized representation as the type of the variable. For example,

```
INT64 register.dump :
...
[8]BYTE register RETYPES register.dump :
```

allows the program to read and write individual bytes of the INT64 by indexing the array. The same rules apply to the use of names of retyped values and variables as apply to abbreviation: it is invalid to refer to a retyped variable by its original name; it is invalid to change a variable in a retyped expression.

In general, the meaning of a retyping is allowed to depend on the implementation. For example, different implementations of occam could quite reasonably interpret

```
PAR i = 0 FOR 8
  register[i] := BYTE i
```

as setting the integer *register.dump* either to #0001020304050607(INT64) or to #0706050403020100(INT64). Other values are not ruled out either, but an implementation is required to be consistent with itself.

There may be circumstances in which an occam program needs to communicate with a process that is implemented in hardware, and which communicates sequences of bit patterns for which there is no description as a protocol. For example, something like a disk controller may send to the program various sized blocks of data from its disks along a serial link. Such a communication requires that the link be represented by a channel with the anarchic protocol

```
CHAN OF ANY from.disk :
```

Inputs from a channel of this protocol can be made into a variable of any type, not necessarily all of the same type. Each communication is treated as though it were an array of bytes, and is retyped, as if by a RETYPES conversion, to be of the type of the variable. All that is necessary is that each input is into a variable represented by the right number of bytes for the value communicated. Similarly, outputs to a channel with an anarchic protocol transmit the byte array which retypes whichever value, of whatever type, is presented for output.

Notice that the use of anarchic channels effectively suppresses checking; if a process makes an anarchic input into a small variable, and receives a larger array of bytes than will fit, anything might happen. The process must be able to determine in some other way what type or size of variable to use. Anarchic communication should only rarely be used on channels between two occam processes, rather than between one software process and one hardware process. Indeed, the only circumstance in which internal anarchic channels are reasonable is when simulating a piece of hardware for testing the process which will drive it.

Attaching a program to hardware

If a program is to be executed on a particular machine, with no operating system to insulate the programmer from the machine's peculiarities, there has to be some way of referring to the parts of the hardware from within the program. The usual thing is to associate each type of hardware object with a corresponding type of abstract object in the program.

The store of each processor is treated as though it were an []INT, and each addressable object will correspond to an element or elements of this array. For example, the serial links of a transputer are located at specific addresses at the bottom of memory; say that one of them corresponds to the $link^{\text{th}}$ location in the memory, where

```
VAL INT link IS ... :
```

A channel, say a channel of counted arrays of characters,

```
CHAN OF INT::[]BYTE c :
```

that is to be implemented by that particular link from a transputer would
be placed

```
PLACE c AT link :
```

In the same way, timers can be placed at particular addresses that correspond
to hardware real-time clocks.

It is also possible to place variables at specific hardware addresses,
although this should not be done in a way that invalidates the anti-aliasing
rules. Placing of variables and arrays of variables is allowed principally to
let the programmer decide which variables will lie in different types of store.
There is, for example, a large performance benefit obtainable from placing
heavily used variables in the internal store of a transputer, rather than in the
relatively slower external store.

There is an additional abstraction for describing peripherals which
are to be handled by the processor's reading and writing particular locations
in store. Because accessing a store address which is mapped onto a peripheral device, even if the access is only for reading, can change the state of
the peripheral it would be dangerous to treat the peripheral as if it were a
variable. An occam implementation is free to access the variables referred to
in expressions in any order, even several times as often as they occur in the
expression. It would not be possible to explain the behaviour of a program
in which the variables changed their values without their being assigned, at
least not in terms of the abstraction of the variable.

A *port* of a given type, placed at a given location in store, is a mechanism for controlled reading and storing of values of that type at that location.
A port

```
PORT OF [4]BYTE uart :
PLACE uart AT ... :
```

can be used in two sorts of process:

```
uart ? buffer
```

reads four bytes exactly once from the location of the port, and stores them
in the [4]BYTE variable *buffer*;

```
uart ! table
```

writes the [4]BYTE value *table* to the location of the port, writing to it exactly
once.

Ports and arrays of ports and so on can be abbreviated, placed, and
passed as parameters in the same way as channels.

8

Programming structures

The simplest thing that you can usefully want a process to be doing, at the same time as another process is doing something else, is to copy data from one channel to another. This is just a matter of repeatedly taking input from one channel, storing it in a local variable, and then sending the value of the variable along another channel. Think of

```
INT local :
SEQ
  source ? local
  sink ! local
```

Why you might possibly want this done should be apparent: the local variable acts as a buffer in the data stream passing along the two channels. This copying process can be packaged as a named process that can be used to buffer an infinite stream of integers passing between two processes:

```
PROC buffer(CHAN OF INT source, sink)
  WHILE TRUE
    INT local :
    SEQ
      source ? local
      sink ! local
  :
```

Now, whereas the producer and the consumer process are tightly synchronized in a program like

```
CHAN OF INT data.stream :
PAR
  producer(data.stream) -- sends output to data.stream
  consumer(data.stream) -- takes input from data.stream
```

with neither able to get ahead of the other, by adding a buffer

```
CHAN OF INT data.from.producer, data.to.consumer :
PAR
  producer(data.from.producer)
  buffer(data.from.producer, data.to.consumer)
  consumer(data.to.consumer)
```

the two are slightly decoupled. The producer is now able to run up to one item of data ahead of the consumer. (It remains difficult to let the consumer get ahead of the producer!)

More buffering is easily provided by inserting more buffers in the data path. This is like a 'fall-through' first-in–first-out store, where each item of data is passed along a sequence of registers until it reaches the last unoccupied location. Several items can be in independent passage at once – several of the component processes of the buffer can be active – if the buffer is fairly empty.

```
CHAN OF INT data.stream[number.of.buffers + 1] :
PAR
  producer(data.stream[0])
  PAR index = 0 FOR number.of.buffers
    buffer(data.stream[index], data.stream[index + 1])
  consumer(data.stream[number.of.buffers])
```

There is an apparent paradox here: although channels implement only unbuffered communication, it is not possible to write a process that joins two channels together without introducing some buffering. The best that can be done is something like the *buffer* procedure, which ensures that the same data are communicated on two channels, without being able to make the communications happen at the same time. Specifically, a process is a *buffer* if it

o consumes data from one channel and performs outputs, on the other channel, of the same data in the same sequence

o is prepared to perform an output whenever it has consumed more than it has subsequently output

o is prepared to consume more input whenever it has disposed of everything that it has input

So the procedure *buffer* is a buffer for infinitely long streams of INTs, and

```
CHAN OF INT data.stream[number.of.buffers + 1] :
PAR index = 0 FOR number.of.buffers
  buffer(data.stream[index], data.stream[index + 1])
```

is a buffer between *data.stream*[0] and *data.stream*[*number.of.buffers*] for infinitely long streams of INTs.

If there is a bound on how much more data a buffer can consume than reproduce before it is *full* – no longer ready for more – this is called the *length* of the buffer. The length of *buffer* is one, the length of an array of *number.of.buffers* of them is *number.of.buffers*.

Synchronization without data

Even when there is no transfer of data, a communication between an output process and an input process synchronizes the two processes concerned. The protocol

```
PROTOCOL SIGNAL
  CASE
    signal
:
```

allows of only one message, so a channel declared with this protocol

```
CHAN OF SIGNAL handshake :
```

can be used in only one sort of output process

```
handshake ! signal
```

and only one sort of input process

```
handshake ? CASE signal
```

Inputs on channels with this or an equivalent protocol are usually used as guards in alternatives. Since there is no transfer of information between an input and output on a signal channel, the processes are interchangeable except of course that only the input can appear as a guard.

In some notations for parallel programming, the fundamental synchronizing primitive is the *semaphore*, a device for ensuring that only one of a collection of parallel processes has access to a resource at any one time. Process 8.1 is initially prepared to accept a signal on any of the *handshake* channels. After that, the next communication has to be on the same channel. That means that the semaphore can only ever have performed an odd number of communications on at most one of its channels. If each channel is used for output by a 'user' of the semaphore, then each user knows that if it has completed an odd number of outputs, no other user has done so.

In a program like Process 8.2 at most one of the instances of *critical*(i) can be executing at any time. This sort of guarantee is just what you need to ensure that only one process was using a single shared physical resource,

Process 8.1

```
PROC binary.semaphore([]CHAN OF SIGNAL handshake)
  WHILE TRUE
    ALT i = 0 FOR SIZE handshake
      handshake[i] ? CASE signal
        handshake[i] ? CASE signal
:
```

Process 8.2

```
[number.of.users]CHAN OF SIGNAL handshake :
PAR
  PAR i = 0 FOR number.of.users
    CHAN OF SIGNAL resource IS handshake[i] :
    WHILE TRUE
      SEQ
        unimportant(i)
        resource ! signal
        critical(i)
        resource ! signal
  binary.semaphore(handshake)
```

Process 8.3

```
PROC receive(CHAN OF INT another.int, CHAN OF SIGNAL no.more.ints)
  BOOL more :
  SEQ
    more := TRUE
    WHILE more
      ALT
        INT x :
        another.int ? x
          ...
        no.more.ints ? CASE signal
          more := FALSE
:
```

Process 8.4

```
PROC send(CHAN OF INT another.int, CHAN OF SIGNAL no.more.ints)
  SEQ
    WHILE ...
      SEQ
        ...
        another.int ! i
    no.more.ints ! signal
:
```

like a terminal screen: if each process were to guarantee to write characters on the screen only when it was in its critical routine, then no process would be allowed to interrupt a message from another.

A particularly common use of interrupting signals is to mark the end of a sequence of communications. Process 8.3 consumes a sequence of integers from *another.int*, until it receives a signal from *no.more.ints*. This sort of process would probably be used in a program like

```
CHAN OF INT another.int :
CHAN OF SIGNAL no.more.ints :
PAR
  send(another.int, no.more.ints)
  receive(another.int, no.more.ints)
```

to consume the output of a process, Process 8.4, which executes some indefinite number of outputs to *another.int*, and then having sent them all, sends a signal on *no.more.ints*.

In fact, in this case, there is a neater way of coding this example. Because both of the channels pass between the same two processes, and are used in a strict sequence, they can be replaced by a single channel with a discriminated protocol

```
PROTOCOL INT.STREAM
  CASE
    another.int; INT
    no.more.ints
:
```

An output on one channel is replaced by an output of one variant, on the other channel by a signal of the other variant (Process 8.5); and the alternative of

Process 8.5
```
PROC send(CHAN OF INT.STREAM c)
  SEQ
    WHILE ...
      SEQ
        ...
        c ! another.int; i
    c ! no.more.ints
:
```

the two inputs becomes an input discriminating between the two variants of the discriminated protocol (Process 8.6). This code is neater, if a trifle less modular, and an implementation would probably execute it more efficiently than the earlier coding.

Process 8.6

```
PROC receive(CHAN OF INT.STREAM c)
  BOOL more :
  SEQ
    more := TRUE
    WHILE more
      c ? CASE
        INT x :
        another.int; x
          ...
        no.more.ints
          more := FALSE
  :
```

Synchronization by access to shared data

The semaphore is an awkward primitive with which to work; the generality of an occam alternative process can usually express rather better what is intended by keeping the code which handles the shared resource in the same process as the resource. Process 8.7 implements an averaging register; it accepts a sequence of integers from *another.int*. At any time this sequence can be interrupted by a signal on *request.mean* in response to which the averaged sum is sent by an output on *mean.of.stream*. By sequencing all accesses to the variables *sum* and *count*, the alternative process guarantees that an average is not calculated with inconsistent values of the variables. At the same time it encapsulates all accesses to those variables, so that a reader of the program can immediately see that the variables always contain values which guarantee that each output to *mean.of.stream* is the mean of the integers read from *another.int*.

Process 8.7

```
PROC average(CHAN OF INT another.int,
             CHAN OF SIGNAL request.mean,
             CHAN OF INT mean.of.stream )
  INT sum, count :
  SEQ
    sum, count := 0, 0
    WHILE TRUE
      ALT
        INT x :
        another.int ? x
          sum, count := sum + x, count + 1
        count > 0 & request.mean ? CASE signal
          mean.of.stream ! sum / count
  :
```

A perfect example of this sort of arbitration with encapsulation is a buffer process, which effectively shares a local variable between a writer and a reader; the single variable in the earlier example of a buffer of length one required little management, but a longer buffer would be more complex. The usual algorithm for implementing a buffer of length *size* characters uses an array

```
[size]BYTE store :
```

indexed by variables

```
INT reader, writer :
```

which range over zero to *size* − 1 so that the oldest value, about to leave the buffer, will be found at *store*[*reader*], and the next to enter the buffer will be written to *store*[*writer*]. It will be convenient to keep track of the number of unoccupied locations in the buffer by a further variable

```
INT count :
```

whose value ranges from zero, for a full buffer, to *size* for an empty one.

There are two activities in which the buffer must be able to participate: provided that it is not full, that is that *count* > 0, it must be possible to add another value to the buffer

```
SEQ
   source ? store[writer]
   count, writer := count - 1, (writer + 1) \ size
```

and provided that *count* < *size* it must be possible for the oldest value to be read from the buffer

```
SEQ
   sink ! store[reader]
   count, reader := count + 1, (reader + 1) \ size
```

The buffer must allow the producing and consuming processes to control its activity, selecting between writing and reading, provided only that there is room to write, or something to read, respectively.

Arbitration like this requires an `ALT` process, with the reading and writing actions being guarded by the conditions under which they may happen – *count* > 0 and *count* < *size* – and the readiness of the consumer and the producer. Since the consumer is ready when the buffer can output to *sink* and the producer when the buffer can input from *source* it is tempting to write

```
ALT
  count > 0   &   source ? store[writer]
    count, writer := count - 1, (writer + 1) \ size
  count < size   &   sink ! store[reader]
    count, reader := count + 1, (reader + 1) \ size
```

but output processes cannot be used to guard alternatives. The solution is to have a control signal from the consuming process indicating that it is ready to accept an input from *sink*.

```
ALT
  count > 0   &   source ? store[writer]
    count, writer := count - 1, (writer + 1) \ size
  count < size   &   request ? CASE signal
  SEQ
    sink ! store[reader]
    count, reader := count + 1, (reader + 1) \ size
```

There is no need for the corresponding request before a write to the buffer, because the input along *source* serves perfectly well in place of a control signal. It is the responsibility of the consumer, whenever it reads from the circular buffer, Process 8.8, to precede the input from *source* by an output on *request*, performing two communications in sequence

```
SEQ
  request ! signal
  source ? ...
```

The ultimate consumer can be relieved of this burden at the expense of an extra process like *request.buffer*, Process 8.9. This process executing concurrently with the circular buffer has a behaviour, Process 8.10, which is indistinguishable – apart, perhaps from performance – from that of a chain of *size* + 1 single-item *buffer* processes acting in parallel.

Using parallelism for program modularity

Imagine that for some obscure reason you wanted a procedure

```
PROC write.even.parity.string(CHAN OF BYTE c, []BYTE s)
```

that, like *write.string*, sent the characters from its string argument to its output channel, but which only sent the even parity ones and discarded the odd parity ones. (The *parity* of a character is odd or even according as the number of one bits in the representation of the character is odd or even.)

Process 8.8

```
PROC circular.buffer(CHAN OF BYTE source,
                     CHAN OF SIGNAL request,
                     CHAN OF BYTE sink     )
  -- Copy from source to sink buffering up to size items. A signal
  -- is needed on request before each item is read from sink.
  INT reader, writer, count :
  [size]BYTE store :
  SEQ
    count, reader, writer := size, 0, 0
    WHILE TRUE
      ALT
        count > 0   &   source ? store[writer]
          count, writer := count - 1, (writer + 1) \ size
        count < size   &   request ? CASE signal
          SEQ
            sink ! store[reader]
            count, reader := count + 1, (reader + 1) \ size
:
```

Process 8.9

```
PROC request.buffer(CHAN OF SIGNAL request,
                    CHAN OF BYTE source, sink )
  WHILE TRUE
    BYTE datum :
    SEQ
      request ! signal
      source ? datum
      sink ! datum
:
```

Process 8.10

```
PROC multiple.buffer(CHAN OF BYTE source, sink)
  -- Copy from source to sink, buffering up to size+1 items.
  CHAN OF SIGNAL request :
  CHAN OF BYTE data :
  PAR
    circular.buffer(source, request, data)
    request.buffer(request, data, sink)
:
```

Any pair of different values will do for representing *even* and *odd*,

```
VAL even IS 0 :
VAL odd  IS 1 >< even :
```

Each bit in the representation of the character has to be considered, so the simplest thing to do is to consider them one at a time. (An expert bit-twiddler may care to code an algorithm logarithmic in the number of bits in the character.) The expression (pattern >> i) /\ 1 is zero or one according as the ith bit of *pattern* is zero or one, so Process 8.11 returns the parity of its argument.

Process 8.11

```
INT FUNCTION parity(VAL BYTE ch)
  INT p :
  VALOF
    SEQ
      p := even
      VAL INT bits.in.byte IS 8 :
      VAL INT pattern IS INT ch :
      SEQ i = 0 FOR bits.in.byte
        p := p >< ((pattern >> i) /\ 1)
      RESULT p
  :
```

You could certainly code *write.even.parity.string* directly, as shown in Process 8.12, but this is rather a specialized process. It can only be used for selecting even parity characters from arrays of characters, because the code for selecting characters according to their parity is mixed in with the code for turning a string into a sequence of outputs.

A more modular program might re-use *write.string* to convert the string into a sequence of outputs, and a separate process, Process 8.13, to filter the characters on their parities. These components can be plugged together to make a process that almost implements *write.even.parity.string*

```
PAR
  SEQ
    write.string(both, s)
    end.of.both ! signal
  divide.on.parity(both, end.of.both, c, rubbish)
```

One process converts the string *s* into a sequence of communications on the channel *both*; another process divides these characters so that only the even parity characters are communicated on *c*.

The problem is that the odd parity characters are communicated on *rubbish*. Since no process is taking input from *rubbish* the *divide.on.parity* process will be held up indefinitely by the first odd parity character which

Process 8.12

```
PROC write.even.parity.string(CHAN OF BYTE c, []BYTE s)
  SEQ i = 0 FOR SIZE s
    VAL BYTE ch IS s[i] :
    CASE parity(ch)
      even
        c ! ch
      odd
        SKIP
:
```

Process 8.13

```
PROC divide.on.parity(CHAN OF BYTE source,
                      CHAN OF SIGNAL end.of.source,
                      CHAN OF BYTE even.sink, odd.sink )
  -- Copy the even parity chars from source to even.sink,
  -- the odd parity ones to odd.sink, until end.of.source
  BOOL more.expected :
  SEQ
    more.expected := TRUE
    WHILE more.expected
      ALT
        BYTE ch :
        source ? ch
          CASE parity(ch)
            even
              even.sink ! ch
            odd
              odd.sink ! ch
        end.of.source ? CASE signal
          more.expected := FALSE
:
```

Process 8.14

```
PROC discard(CHAN OF BYTE source, CHAN OF SIGNAL end.of.source)
  BOOL more.expected :
  SEQ
    more.expected := TRUE
    WHILE more.expected
      ALT
        BYTE ch :
        source ? ch
          SKIP
        end.of.source ? CASE signal
          more.expected := FALSE
:
```

it encounters. Parallel programs abound with instances where a discarding
process, such as Process 8.14, are useful. There is no real equivalent in sequential programming; this process discards all of its input, never sends any
output, never changes the values of any global variables. Its sole function is
to achieve the necessary synchronizations.

Process 8.15

```
PROC write.even.parity.string(CHAN OF BYTE c, []BYTE s)
  CHAN OF BYTE both, odd.ones :
  CHAN OF SIGNAL end.of.both, end.of.odd :
  PAR
    SEQ
      write.string(both, s)
      end.of.both ! signal
    SEQ
      divide.on.parity(both, end.of.both, c, odd.ones)
      end.of.odd ! signal
    discard(odd.ones, end.of.odd)
:
```

The procedure *write.even.parity.string*, Process 8.15, can be put together from these components so that the effect of

```
write.string(output, "Bootifrolo")
```

for example, can be achieved by

```
write.even.parity.string(output, "Booting from Floppy")
```

In this particular case, the gain in modularity may not seem adequate to
justify the expense, both in programming effort and execution time. The
advantage is clearer in cases where the program must perform a number
of tasks each of which divides its input data into chunks, and where the
boundaries of these components do not coincide.

Using parallelism to resolve structure clash

A structure clash happens whenever a program must perform operations on
data that must be divided into mutually overlapping components. In a text
processing program, for example, it may prove necessary to do something to
every line of a document, and something else to every sentence.

The natural way to code each of these tasks, individually, is to write
programs whose structure reflects the structure of the document. To perform
an action on every line:

```
WHILE ... there are more lines
  SEQ
    ... read a line
    ... process the line
```

and to perform an action on every sentence:

```
WHILE ... there are more sentences
  SEQ
    ... read a sentence
    ... process the sentence
```

Since sentences do not need to contain only complete lines, nor lines complete sentences, it is difficult to combine these two programs in a single sequential program. The somewhat unsatisfactory best that can be done in a sequential program is to treat the document as a sequence of words, these being the largest common sub-components of both lines and sentences.

```
WHILE ... there are more words
  SEQ
    ... read a word
    ... if it completes a line process the line
    ... if it completes a sentence process the sentence
```

In a parallel program, the structure of both component processes can be retained by performing both of the divisions of the document concurrently.

```
CHAN OF LINES lines :
CHAN OF SENTENCES sentences :

PAR
  ... copy the document to lines and sentences

  WHILE ... there are more lines
    SEQ
      ... read a line from lines
      ... process the line

  WHILE ... there are more sentences
    SEQ
      ... read a sentence from sentences
      ... process the sentence
```

The simplest case of a structure clash arises from attempting to pack data into fixed-sized blocks that will not accommodate an exact whole number of items. It might be necessary, for example, to pack a stream of characters into half-kilobyte blocks for transmission or storage on a medium which accepts only such blocks. Consider first a case in which there is no structure clash: the medium is represented as a channel that accepts only outputs of arrays of half a kilobyte, and characters are represented by codes in the range from 0 to 255, so that a whole number of characters exactly fill a block.

The way to perform actions sequentially on the components of an array of bytes declared by

```
VAL INT bytes.in.a.block IS 512 :
[bytes.in.a.block]BYTE buffer :
```

is to use a sequential 'array' of processes created by the constructor

```
SEQ byte.number = 0 FOR bytes.in.a.block
```

so this packing might be done by a process like Process 8.16.

Process 8.16

```
PROTOCOL BLOCK IS [bytes.in.a.block]BYTE :

PROC pack.bytes.into.blocks(CHAN OF BYTE byte.source,
                           CHAN OF SIGNAL end.of.source,
                           CHAN OF BLOCK block.sink    )
  BOOL more.bytes.expected :
  SEQ
    more.bytes.expected := TRUE
    WHILE more.bytes.expected
      [bytes.in.a.block]BYTE buffer :
      SEQ
        SEQ byte.number = 0 FOR bytes.in.a.block
          ALT
            BYTE byte IS buffer[byte.number] :
            more.bytes.expected & byte.source ? byte
              SKIP
            more.bytes.expected & end.of.source ? CASE signal
              more.bytes.expected := FALSE
            NOT more.bytes.expected & SKIP
              SKIP
        block.sink ! buffer
  :
```

The branch of the alternative that does all the work is the first, that guarded by an input from *byte.source* which inputs the next byte into the particular component of the buffer which is being considered. Since the guard does all the work, there is nothing left to be done in the guarded process, so this is SKIP. The condition before the SKIP guard ensures that it is ready when and only when there are no more bytes to be packed into the last block.

That process always sends a partly or completely empty block as its last output. The sending of a completely empty block could be prevented by

Process 8.17

```
VAL INT bytes.in.a.block IS 512 :

PROC pack.bytes.into.blocks(CHAN OF BYTE byte.source,
                            CHAN OF SIGNAL end.of.source,
                            CHAN OF BLOCK block.sink    )
  BOOL more.bytes.expected :
  SEQ
    more.bytes.expected := TRUE
    WHILE more.bytes.expected
      [bytes.in.a.block]BYTE buffer :
      ALT
        byte.source ? buffer[0]
          SEQ
            SEQ byte.number = 1 FOR bytes.in.a.block - 1
              ALT
                BYTE byte IS buffer[byte.number] :
                more.bytes.expected & byte.source ? byte
                  SKIP
                more.bytes.expected & end.of.source ? CASE signal
                  more.bytes.expected := FALSE
                NOT more.bytes.expected & SKIP
                  SKIP
            block.sink ! buffer
        end.of.source ? CASE signal
          more.bytes.expected := FALSE
  :
```

looking ahead for the next byte (Process 8.17). Even so, in case the entire message does not exactly fill a whole number of blocks, it has to be possible for a process that unpacks the characters from the blocks to deduce from those characters that it has reached the actual end of the character stream before the end of the last block.

Full blocks can be unpacked by Process 8.18 so a stream of a number bytes that happened to fit exactly into a number of blocks could be passed by

```
CHAN OF BLOCKS medium :
CHAN OF SIGNAL end.medium :
PAR
  SEQ
    pack.bytes.into.blocks(bytes.in, end.of.in, medium)
    end.medium ! signal
  unpack.bytes.from.blocks(medium, end.medium, bytes.out)
```

This is almost a buffer, but not quite, because it might not be prepared to output its first byte until it has received a full block's worth of bytes of input.

Process 8.18

```
PROC unpack.bytes.from.blocks(CHAN OF BLOCK block.source,
                             CHAN OF SIGNAL end.of.source,
                             CHAN OF BYTE byte.sink        )
  BOOL more.blocks.expected :
  SEQ
    more.blocks.expected := TRUE
    WHILE more.blocks.expected
      ALT
        [bytes.in.a.block]BYTE buffer :
        block.source ? buffer
          SEQ byte.number = 0 FOR bytes.in.a.block
            byte.sink ! buffer[byte.number]
        end.of.source ? CASE signal
          more.blocks.expected := FALSE
:
```

Process 8.19

```
PROC set.bit(BYTE byte, VAL INT bit.number, VAL BOOL bit)
  IF
    NOT bit
      byte := BYTE ((INT byte) /\ (~(1 << bit.number)))
    bit
      byte := BYTE ((INT byte) \/ (1 << bit.number))
:
```

Now consider the problem of trying to achieve a higher packing density, given that it happens that only character codes less than 128 are going to be sent, so that seven bits will suffice rather than eight. Seven bit values will not fit neatly into bytes, nor indeed into half-kilobyte blocks. The problem can, however, be decomposed into two simpler separate problems in which there is no structure clash: turning seven bit character values into a sequence of bits, and packing a sequence of bits into blocks.

The packing of bits into blocks can be done in almost exactly the same way as that suggested for packing bytes into blocks. A byte can be considered to be an array of bits, indexed by using the bit-pattern manipulating operations. The assignment

```
byte := BYTE ((INT byte) /\ (~(1 << bit.number)))
```

sets the *bit.number*[th] bit of *byte* to zero, whilst

```
byte := BYTE ((INT byte) \/ (1 << bit.number))
```

sets that same bit to one, so the conditional in Process 8.19 stores one or zero in the *bit.number*[th] bit of the *byte* according as the given *bit* is true or not. The buffer could be treated as a two-dimensional array, so it would be possible to write a two-dimensional SEQ–FOR array of processes, Process 8.20, over the bit-number and byte-number to pack the buffer.

Process 8.20

```
VAL INT bits.in.a.byte IS 8 :
VAL INT bytes.in.a.block IS  512 :
PROTOCOL BIT IS BOOL :

PROC pack.bits.into.blocks(CHAN OF BIT bit.source,
                           CHAN OF SIGNAL end.of.source,
                           CHAN OF BLOCK block.sink       )
  -- Copy data from bit.source in complete blocks onto
  -- block.sink, until a signal arrives on end.of.source
  BOOL next.bit :
  ALT
    bit.source ? next.bit    -- Read ahead the first bit
      BOOL more.bits.to.pack :
      SEQ
        more.bits.to.pack := TRUE
        WHILE more.bits.to.pack
          VAL INT block.size IS bytes.in.a.block :
          [block.size]BYTE buffer :
          SEQ
            SEQ byte.number = 0 FOR bits.in.a.block
              IF
                more.bits.to.pack
                  SEQ bit.number = 0 FOR bits.in.a.byte
                    IF
                      more.bits.to.pack
                        SEQ
                          set.bit(buffer[byte.number],
                                      bit.number, next.bit )
                          ALT
                            bit.source ? next.bit
                              SKIP
                            end.of.source ? CASE signal
                              more.bits.to.pack := FALSE
                      NOT more.bits.to.pack
                        SKIP
                NOT more.bits.to.pack
                  SKIP
            block.sink ! buffer
    end.of.source ? CASE signal -- No bits at all
      SKIP
:
```

A more modular solution, Process 8.21, would separate the two loops into two processes: one to turn the sequence of bits into a sequence of bytes; the other to turn the sequence of bytes into a sequence of blocks.

Process 8.21

```
PROC pack.bits.into.blocks(CHAN OF BIT bit.source,
                           CHAN OF SIGNAL end.of.source,
                           CHAN OF BLOCK block.sink    )

  PROC pack.bits.into.bytes(CHAN OF BIT bit.source,
                            CHAN OF SIGNAL end.of.source,
                            CHAN OF BYTE byte.sink     )
    BOOL more.bits.expected :
    SEQ
      more.bits.expected := TRUE
      WHILE more.bits.expected
        BYTE byte :
        ALT
          BOOL bit :
          bit.source ? bit
            SEQ
              set.bit(byte, 0, bit)
              SEQ bit.number = 1 FOR bits.in.a.byte - 1
                ALT
                  more.bits.expected & bit.source ? bit
                    set.bit(byte, bit.number, bit)
                  more.bits.expected & end.of.source ? CASE signal
                    more.bits.expected := FALSE
                  NOT more.bits.expected & SKIP
                    SKIP
              byte.sink ! byte
          end.of.source ? CASE signal
            more.bits.expected := FALSE
  :

  CHAN OF BYTE bytes :
  CHAN OF SIGNAL end.of.bytes :
  PAR
    SEQ
      pack.bits.into.bytes(bit.source, end.of.source, bytes)
      end.of.bytes ! signal
    pack.bytes.into.blocks(bytes, end.of.bytes, block.sink)
:
```

Process 8.22

```
BOOL FUNCTION get.bit(VAL BYTE byte, VAL INT bit.number) IS
                     (((INT byte) >> bit.number) /\ 1) <> 0 :
```

Turning seven-bit characters into a sequence of bits is also a simple task, since there is again no structure clash. The result of a call of *get.bit*, Process 8.22, is true or false according as the *bit.number*[th] bit of the representation of *byte* is one or zero, so the character code can be treated as

Process 8.23

```
INT VAL bits.in.a.character IS 7 :


PROC unpack.bits.from.chars(CHAN OF BYTE char.source,
                            CHAN OF SIGNAL end.of.source,
                            CHAN OF BIT bit.sink          )
  BOOL more.chars.expected :
  SEQ
    more.chars.expected := TRUE
    WHILE more.chars.expected
      ALT
        BYTE character :
        char.source ? character
          SEQ bit.number = 0 FOR bits.in.a.character
            bit.sink ! get.bit(character, bit.number)
        end.of.source ? CASE signal
          more.chars.expected := FALSE
  :
```

Process 8.24

```
PROC pack.chars.into.blocks(CHAN OF BYTE char.source,
                            CHAN OF SIGNAL end.of.source,
                            CHAN OF BLOCK block.sink      )
  CHAN OF BIT bits :
  CHAN OF SIGNAL end.of.bits :
  PAR
    SEQ
      unpack.bits.from.chars(char.source, end.of.source, bits)
      end.of.bits ! signal
    pack.bits.into.blocks(bits, end.of.bits, block.sink)
  :
```

though it were an array of seven bits:

```
VAL INT bits.in.a.character IS 7 :
SEQ bit.number = 0 FOR bits.in.a.character
  bit.sink ! get.bit(byte, bit.number)
```

Process 8.23, which turns a stream of characters into a stream of the bits which make up their codes, least significant bit of the character first, has exactly the same structure as the earlier unpacking process.

Packing seven-bit characters into half-kilobyte blocks is simply a matter of unpacking the characters into a stream of bits, and assembling the blocks from the stream of bits, the one activity in parallel with the other (Process 8.24). Substantially the same program structure can clearly be used to turn the stream of blocks back into a stream of seven bit character codes, since that is just another, similar packing problem.

The solution to each packing problem is of one of the three forms that we have shown here: grouping small objects to make larger ones; dividing large objects to make small ones; or a problem in which a structure clash requires that both the input data and the output data be divided into common sub-components. The parallel solution to the third kind of problem makes it no more complicated than the others.

Distributed implementation of buffers

It sometimes happens that it is necessary to communicate between processes where it is impracticable for them to share a channel. As mentioned earlier, the best that can be done is to implement a buffer between the processes. Consider, for example, two groups of processes executed by two distinct transputers. Each process in one group needs to communicate with the corresponding process in the other group, but the single serial link connecting the two transputers will only support a single channel in that direction. (At its simplest, a serial link between transputers does support exactly one channel in each direction.) The strategy in this case is to multiplex the use of the channel. Each output-producing process sends over the same channel, but identifies its message with its own name.

To be concrete, let each of the concurrent producers be identified by an INT index, and let the messages be counted arrays of characters

```
PROTOCOL MESSAGE IS INT::[]BYTE :

PROC producer(CHAN OF MESSAGE output)
  ... write some messages to output
:

PROC consumer(CHAN OF MESSAGE input)
  ... read some messages from input
:
```

The aim is to produce a program which behaves as nearly as possible like

```
CHAN OF MESSAGE left, right :
PAR i = 0 FOR width
  PAR
    producer(left)
    buffer(left, right)
    consumer(right)
```

where *buffer* is a buffer. For simplicity, assume that none of the producers or consumers ever terminates. The program must have the form

```
CHAN OF ... c :
PAR
  PAR
    PAR i = 0 FOR width
      producer(...)
    ...
  PAR
    ...
    PAR i = 0 FOR width
      consumer(...)
```

with only one channel global both to the array of producers and to the array of consumers.

Since a number of producers cannot use the same channel directly – only one process may write to a channel at a time – there must be a mediating process, and this process can add the tags identifying the source and consumer. Similarly there must be a mediating process directing the tagged messages to their ultimate destinations. Process 8.25 shows how these would be used.

Process 8.25

```
PROTOCOL TAGGED.MESSAGE IS INT; INT::[]BYTE :

PROC multiplex([]CHAN OF MESSAGE local,
               CHAN OF TAGGED.MESSAGE link )
  ...
:
PROC demultiplex(CHAN OF TAGGED.MESSAGE link,
                 []CHAN OF MESSAGE local    )
  ...
:
CHAN OF TAGGED.MESSAGE link :
PAR
  [width]CHAN OF MESSAGE local :
  PAR
    PAR i = 0 FOR width
      producer(local[i])
    multiplex(local, link)
  [width]CHAN OF MESSAGE local :
  PAR
    demultiplex(link, local)
    PAR i = 0 FOR width
      consumer(local[i])
```

The multiplexing process must continually arbitrate between the producers to decide which message is sent over the shared link, so should clearly

be a repeated alternative process, Process 8.26, and the demultiplexing process must dole out the received messages according to their tags, Process 8.27.

Process 8.26

```
PROC multiplex([]CHAN OF MESSAGE local,
               CHAN OF TAGGED.MESSAGE link )
  WHILE TRUE
    ALT source = 0 FOR SIZE local
      INT count :
      [longest.message]BYTE string :
      local[source] ? count::string
        link ! source; count::string
  :
```

Process 8.27

```
PROC demultiplex(CHAN OF TAGGED.MESSAGE link,
                 []CHAN OF MESSAGE local      )
  WHILE TRUE
    INT destination, count :
    [longest.message]BYTE string :
    SEQ
      link ? destination; count::string
      local[destination] ! count::string
  :
```

At a first glance it might appear that this is all that is needed. It is
relatively easy to show that any message which passes into the *multiplexer*
along an input channel and which passes out of the *demultiplexer* arrives on
the right channel. Similarly, the sequence of messages along corresponding
pairs of channels is the same, because no message can ever overtake another
with the same tag. However, this is not quite enough to be able to show that
the multiplexer and demultiplexer together implement an array of buffers.

There is a problem still, and one which could not have arisen in a
sequential program. Consider what might happen if one of the consumers,
say that indexed by one, were never to accept any input. If the multiplexer
were ever to accept input from the corresponding producer, that message
would never be delivered, so the demultiplexer would wait indefinitely to
perform an output on *local*[1]. This means that no further messages could
ever be delivered to any other consumer, for example that indexed by zero.
For that reason, the multiplexer and demultiplexer would not implement a
buffer between the processes with index zero, nor by symmetry between any
other pair.

The system with a multiplexer and demultiplexer has more opportunities to become deadlocked than the system with buffers, but since these are
all caused by a *consumer* refusing a message this is not a problem in a system

where each *consumer* is guaranteed eventually to consume each message sent to it, independently of the others. This would be the case if each consumer were always ready to receive any number of messages, or if there were some higher-level protocol that ensured that no producer ever sent any message that was not guaranteed to be accepted. In fact, it can be shown that this is the best that you can achieve with only one channel between the producers and consumers.

Whilst it is possible to avoid opportunities to become deadlocked by interposing another process which relieves the consumer of its responsibility to accept messages, to do so requires a second channel between the two parts of the program. A safe demultiplexer could provide a buffer between the link and the ultimate consumer; a safe multiplexer would accept and deliver over the link only those messages for which there was room in the demultiplexer's buffer. To code these requires a channel from the demultiplexer to the multiplexer indicating the state of the buffers.

An adequate buffer need contain room for only one message. An instance of Process 8.28 is always prepared to accept a message from *source* if it has sent more signals – one more signal, in fact – on *request* than it has received messages from *source*.

Process 8.28

```
PROC request.buffer(CHAN OF SIGNAL request,
                    CHAN OF MESSAGE source, sink )
  WHILE TRUE
    INT count :
    [longest.message]BYTE string :
    SEQ
      request ! signal
      source ? count::string
      sink ! count::string
  :
```

A possible coding of the demultiplexing process contains an array of these buffers driven by a naïve demultiplexing process, and an additional process to multiplex signals from the buffers onto the *back* channel, Process 8.29. On the assumption that the signals sent on the *back* channel are always accepted, it is easy to see that this process must, without blocking, accept from the *link* channel any message with an index that it has sent over the *back* channel. Moreover, it only sends a given index on the *back* channel once more than it has received messages with that index.

A similarly coded multiplexing process, Process 8.30, uses an array of buffers to throttle the input to a naïve multiplexing process. A message is only sent over the *link* channel if a corresponding index has been received over the *back* channel. Moreover, if messages are never blocked on the *link* channel this process is always prepared to receive indices from the *back* channel, so

Process 8.29

```
PROC safe.demultiplex(CHAN OF TAGGED.MESSAGE link,
                      CHAN OF INT back,
                      []CHAN OF MESSAGE local    )
  [width]CHAN OF SIGNAL ack :
  [width]CHAN OF MESSAGE fwd :
  PAR
    demultiplex(link, fwd)
    PAR i = 0 FOR width
      request.buffer(ack[i], fwd[i], local[i])
    WHILE TRUE
      ALT i = 0 FOR width
        ack[i] ? CASE signal
          back ! i
:
```

Process 8.30

```
PROC safe.multiplex([]CHAN OF MESSAGE local,
                    CHAN OF TAGGED.MESSAGE link,
                    CHAN OF INT back            )
  [width]CHAN OF SIGNAL ack :
  [width]CHAN OF MESSAGE fwd :
  PAR
    PAR i = 0 FOR width
      request.buffer(ack[i], local[i], fwd[i])
    multiplex(fwd, link)
    WHILE TRUE
      INT i :
      SEQ
        back ? i
        ack[i] ? CASE signal
:
```

Process 8.31

```
CHAN OF TAGGED.MESSAGE link :
CHAN OF INT back :
PAR
  [width]CHAN OF MESSAGE local :
  PAR
    PAR i = 0 FOR width
      producer(local[i])
    safe.multiplex(local, link, back)
  [width]CHAN OF MESSAGE local :
  PAR
    safe.demultiplex(link, back, local)
    PAR i = 0 FOR width
      consumer(local[i])
```

long as no index is received more than once more than a message with that index has been sent on the *link* channel.

Each half of the system has been shown to be safe, provided that it can rely on the safeness of the other half. Combining these arguments shows that a system built with 'safe' components, Process 8.31, is guaranteed not to become deadlocked.

Even this multiplexer and demultiplexer do not together implement an array of buffers. If one of the pairs of producer and consumer with a given index were to communicate an indefinitely long sequence of messages, the alternative processes might always be able to select the channels with that index. That would mean that although progress was always being made – the system did not become deadlocked – yet no messages would be transferred on any of the other virtual channels. In such a circumstance, the other processes are said to be *starved*. If a system of processes ignores its environment altogether – if it starves its environment – because it is busy with an infinite sequence of internal communications, the system is said by some to be *livelocked*.

The safe multiplexer and demultiplexer together cannot become livelocked, because they can never make an infinite sequence of communications without communication with a producer or consumer. If a producer and a consumer are added to them which communicate an infinite stream of messages, then that system is allowed to become livelocked.

In fact, this is a problem only if a group of the producers and consumers are able to keep the multiplexer and demultiplexer busy, to the exclusion of some others. Normally, it will be enough to observe that if the traffic does not exceed the bandwidth of the multiplexer and demultiplexer, starvation will not occur. If there is possibility of starvation, however, it is necessary to resort to asymmetric alternatives.

If the *multiplexer* component were *fair*, there should be no way that it could infinitely often decline to select any given channel which was ready. In fact, fairness is not particularly useful because a fair multiplexer could still take arbitrarily long to get around to noticing a particular channel. What is needed in practice is *short-term* fairness: a bound on the time for which a channel can be passed over.

The symmetric alternative constructor, ALT, is associative, commutative, and idempotent: all that determines the meaning of an alternative process is the *set* of guards which appear in it, not how they appear in nested alternatives, the order in which they appear, or indeed how often they appear. For that reason, we say that

```
ALT j = 0 FOR n
  c[j] ? ...
  ...j...
```

is the same process as

```
ALT
  c[i] ? ...
    ...i...
  ALT j = 0 FOR n
    c[j] ? ...
      ...j...
```

provided $0 \leq i < n$. Either would do in place of the other. An asymmetric alternative process on the other hand cannot pass over its first guard; so

```
WHILE TRUE
  SEQ i = 0 FOR n
    PRI ALT
      c[i] ? ...
        ...i...
      ALT j = 0 FOR n
        c[j] ? ...
          ...j...
```

cannot pass over any of the channels $c[i]$ for more than n consecutive iterations of the inner loop. To this extent it is a short-term fair implementation of the process

```
WHILE TRUE
  ALT j = 0 FOR n
    c[j] ? ...
      ...j...
```

If both of the alternatives in the system – one in the procedure *multiplex*, the other in *safe.multiplex* – are recoded in this way (see page 237) then the multiplexer and demultiplexer together implement an array of independent buffers. A system which could become neither deadlocked nor livelocked if connected by an array of buffers is also well behaved if connected by a safe, fair multiplexer and demultiplexer.

This rather lengthy discussion outlines a general strategy for demonstrating that a system is correct.

o It is important that the data values passed in messages and stored in variables cannot be incorrect.

o It must be shown that the system cannot become deadlocked: that there is always something that the system can do.

o It must be shown that the system cannot become livelocked: that by doing something that it can do, the system makes progress.

In a well structured system, it should be possible to demonstrate these three things independently, and in a modular fashion. For example, although *liveness* – a guarantee that a system cannot become deadlocked – is a global property of the whole system, in a well constructed system the liveness of the system should follow from demonstrable properties of the components.

Using parallelism to eliminate recursion

If a procedure has no free variables, and only value and variable parameters, a call to it can be thought of as a pair of communications; an output to send it the values of its parameters, and an input to receive in return the final values of its variable parameters.

To be precise,

```
PROC accumulate(INT x, VAL INT dx)
  x := x + dx
:
...
accumulate(acc, expr)
...
```

has the same effect on the value of the variable *acc* as

```
PROTOCOL int.pair IS INT; INT :
PROC server(CHAN OF INT.PAIR call, CHAN OF INT return)
  INT x, dx :
  SEQ
    call ? x; dx
    return ! x + dx
:
...
CHAN OF INT.PAIR call :
CHAN OF INT return :
PAR
  server(call, return)
  SEQ                    -- 'user' process
    call ! acc; expr
    return ? acc
...
```

A similar equivalence holds for a procedure or group of procedures which use and modify a free variable which is not used in any other way. In ALGOL, variables like this were called *own* variables, and they were difficult to use because of the problem of giving the variable an initial value. A

procedure with an own variable can be implemented by communicating with
a process which services a sequence of requests. Rather than write

```
INT accumulator :
PROC accumulate(VAL INT increment)
  accumulator := accumulator + increment
:
INT FUNCTION total() IS accumulator :
SEQ
  accumulator := 0
  ...
  accumulate(expr)
  ...
  use(total())
  ...
```

it would be natural in occam to write something like Process 8.32. Three
points are worth making about this program. Setting of the variable to an
initial value has been hidden away in the server, making it obvious that no
accesses can be made to the variable until after it has been given a value.
Not every call needs to be implemented as a pair of communications; since
calling *accumulate* returns no result, a single output will suffice. Thirdly,
termination of the server has to be caused by its user, so that their parallel
composition can terminate; in this case the termination is caused by an
explicit signal.

An array of mutually communicating processes can in this way be
used to implement what might have been written, were recursive procedures
allowed, as a recursive procedure. Consider implementing a process to maintain a set of at most n characters. There should be a way of adding a
character to the set, and a way of testing whether a particular character is
already in the set. To do this in the style of communication with a server
process, we would need a *byte.set* with the interface described by

```
PROTOCOL CALLS
  CASE
    add.element; BYTE
    is.element; BYTE
:
PROTOCOL RETURNS
  CASE
    is.element.return; BOOL
:
PROC byte.set(CHAN OF CALLS call, CHAN OF RETURNS return)
  ...
:
```

Process 8.32

```
PROTOCOL CALLS
  CASE
    accumulate; INT
    total
    terminate
  :

PROC server(CHAN OF CALLS call, CHAN OF INT return)
  BOOL more :
  INT accumulator :
  SEQ
    more, accumulator := TRUE, 0
    WHILE more
      call ? CASE
        INT dx :
        accumulate; dx                  -- accumulate(dx)
          accumulator := accumulator + dx
        total                           -- return total()
          return ! accumulator
        terminate                       -- done
          more := FALSE
  :

CHAN OF CALLS call :
CHAN OF INT return :
PAR
  server(call, return)
  SEQ
    ...
    call ! accumulate; expr
    ...
    INT x :
    SEQ
      call ! total
      return ? x
      use(x)
    ...
    call ! terminate
```

where sending *add.element*; *x* to an instance of the *byte.set* would add the
character *x* to it, and sending *is.element*; *x* to it would cause the return of
is.element.return; TRUE or *is.element.return*; FALSE from it according as *x*
was an element of it or not.

Suppose we had a procedure *small.set* which could itself handle up to
one element of a set, and which would pass on any other elements to a slave
process which would handle the rest of the set. Such a procedure would look
like Process 8.33. When the *small.set* is empty, it is prepared to accept an

Process 8.33

```
PROC singleton(VAL BYTE x,
               CHAN OF CALLS call, slave.call,
               CHAN OF RETURNS return, slave.return )
  -- represents the singleton set containing x
  WHILE TRUE
    call ? CASE
      BYTE y :
      add.element; y
        IF
          x = y
            -- y is already in the set
            SKIP
          x <> y
            -- add y to the slave set
            slave.call ! add.element; y
      BYTE y :
      is.element; y
        IF
          x = y
            -- y is in the set
            return ! is.element.return; TRUE
          x <> y
            -- y is in the set iff it is in the slave set
            BOOL found :
            SEQ
              slave.call ! is.element; y
              slave.return ? CASE is.element.return; found
              return ! is.element.return; found
:


PROC small.set(CHAN OF CALLS call, slave.call,
               CHAN OF RETURNS return, slave.return )
  WHILE TRUE
    call ? CASE
      BYTE x :
      add.element; x
        singleton(x, call, slave.call, return, slave.return)
      BYTE x :
      is.element; x
        return ! is.element.return; FALSE
:
```

add.element instruction and become a *singleton* set containing that element; at the same time, it is prepared to accept enquiries about set membership, and replies that the element is not in the set. The only element which can be added to a *singleton* is its member x; requests to add other elements to the set are passed on to the slave process which represents the rest of the set. A *singleton* process can tell that its own element is in the set; if asked about any other element it passes on the enquiry to the rest of the set, and passes the answer back.

If only we were allowed to write recursive procedures, we might implement the slave set as a *byte.set*, and implement a *byte.set* as a *small.set* in parallel with this, Process 8.34. Beware, this text would not define a recursive procedure in occam!

Process 8.34

```
PROC byte.set(CHAN OF CALLS call, CHAN OF RETURNS return)
  CHAN OF CALLS slave.call :
  CHAN OF RETURNS slave.return :
  PAR
    small.set(call, slave.call, return, slave.return)
    byte.set(slave.call, slave.return)
:
```

Now, if an instance of *byte.set* is required to store a set of up to n characters the slave set within it need store no more than $n - 1$ characters. If the programmer were to substitute the body of *byte.set* in place of the 'recursive' call of it

```
PAR                        -- set of up to n elements
  small.set(...)
  PAR                      -- set of up to n-1 elements
    small.set(...)
    byte.set(...)          -- set of up to n-2 elements
```

the new instance of *byte.set* would need to be able to deal with only $n - 2$ characters. The process of substitution can be repeated n times, until the problem has been reduced to one of implementing a process like *byte.set* which needs to be able to store no more than no characters at all. Since this particular instance of *byte.set* could be implemented by an instance of *small.set*, the task is done. Process 8.35 implements a set that can store up to n characters. Notice that there is only one process using each of the channels *calls*[n] and *returns*[n], but this does not matter because no communications are ever attempted on these channels.

In effect, this procedure uses an array of $(n + 1)$ *small.set* processes to implement a set of n elements: one process looks after the first element and communicates with the user; it uses an array of one fewer *small.set* processes as its slave. This sort of technique can be used to eliminate any linear recursions for which there is a known bound on the depth of the recursion. In Chapter 12 there is a slightly more complicated example which implements two recursive calls made in parallel with each other by using a tree-shaped network of processes.

Process 8.35

```
PROC byte.set(CHAN OF CALLS call, CHAN OF RETURNS return)
  -- a set of up to n characters
  [n+1]CHAN OF CALLS calls :
  [n+1]CHAN OF RETURNS returns :
  PAR
    small.set(call, calls[0], return, returns[0])
    PAR i = 1 FOR n
      small.set(calls[i-1], calls[i], returns[i-1], returns[i])
  :
```

Process farming

This chapter has been about the structures from which parallel programs are composed. You should think of things like buffers and multiplexers as being components in the parallel programmer's toolkit. They serve the same skeletal purpose in concurrent programs as are served by the familiar idioms of sequential programs, things like well-known sorting and searching algorithms. To close, here is an entirely unstructured scheme, which has turned out to be an unpredictedly simple way of using the parallel computers which have become available over the past few years.

There are some kinds of problems which are computationally expensive, but which can very easily be divided into a large number of small independent problems. You might call these 'embarrassingly parallel' problems, because almost any strategy for solving such a program on a multiprocessor machine will take some advantage of the parallelism in the machine. This is why such problems are often used in demonstrations of parallel machines.

For example a 'ray-traced' picture is constructed by performing, for each point on a screen, a lengthy calculation on a few data which describe the objects in the picture. The calculation follows the history of the ray of light which comes to the observer's eye through that point in the picture. By finding from which sources of light it has come, from which surfaces it has been reflected, and through which transparent bodies it has been transmitted, the colour and brightness of that ray can be constructed. The resulting pictures are startlingly realistic renderings of the non-existent scenes.

If the calculations at each point in the picture are treated as independent tasks, a ray tracing program can be executed more quickly by using more processors until the number of processors approaches the number of points on the screen, which is typically several millions.

A particularly simple general strategy, Process 8.36, is to run a *worker* process on each processor of the machine; each *worker*, Process 8.37, is a little sequential process accepting and processing a sequence of the small parts of the problem.

One additional process, Process 8.38, can then handle a pool of tasks

Process 8.36

```
PROTOCOL TASKS
  CASE
    new.task; INT; REAL64
    no.more.tasks
  :
PROTOCOL RESULTS IS INT; REAL64 :

[n]CHAN OF TASKS to.slave :
[n]CHAN OF RESULTS from.slave :
PAR
  farmer(tasks, to.slave, from.slave, results)
  PAR j = 0 FOR n
    worker(to.slave[j], from.slave[j])
```

Process 8.37

```
PROC worker(CHAN OF TASKS from.farmer, CHAN OF RESULTS to.farmer)
  BOOL more :
  SEQ
    more := TRUE
    WHILE more
      from.farmer ? CASE
        INT i :
        REAL64 task, result :
        new.task; i; task
          SEQ
            result := f(task)
            to.farmer ! i; result
        no.more.tasks
          more := FALSE
  :
```

and 'farm' them out to the workers. First a task is given to each of the n workers. Then whenever a worker finishes its present task, the result is recovered and a new task issued. This continues until all the tasks have been allocated, after which the farmer collects the remaining results and signals to the workers that they should terminate.

Provided that a calculation of f takes a long time, compared with the cost of communicating with the *farmer*, this program could be placed on n or $n + 1$ processors and would execute almost n times as quickly as the equivalent sequential program

```
SEQ i = 0 FOR SIZE tasks
  results[i] := f(tasks[i])
```

even though the calls of f might take widely different amounts of time. There is scope for tuning a farm like this, for example for each *worker* to keep a task in hand so that it never has to wait for the *farmer*.

Process 8.38

```
PROC farmer(VAL []REAL64 task,
                 []CHAN OF TASKS to.slave,
                 []CHAN OF RESULTS from.slave,
                              []REAL64 result )
  -- This process assumes n <= (SIZE task)
  SEQ
    PAR j = 0 FOR n
      to.slave[j] ! new.task; j; task[j]
    SEQ i = n FOR (SIZE task) - n
      ALT j = 0 FOR n
        INT k :
        from.slave[j] ? k; result[k]
          to.slave[j] ! new.task; i; task[i]
    SEQ i = 0 FOR n
      ALT j = 0 FOR n
        INT k :
        from.slave[j] ? k; result[k]
          to.slave[j] ! no.more.tasks
  :
```

Process 8.39

```
[number.of.workers + 1]CHAN OF ADDR.TASK.STREAM outgoing :
[number.of.workers + 1]CHAN OF ADDR.RESULT.STREAM incoming :
PAR
  farmer(task, outgoing[0], incoming[0], result)
  PAR i = 0 FOR number.of.workers
    work.detail(outgoing[i], outgoing[i+1],
                incoming[i+1], incoming[i] )
  farmers.boy(outgoing[number.of.workers],
              incoming[number.of.workers] )
```

More generally, all of the processors in a machine need not be directly connected, so it might not be possible to have a channel from the *farmer* to each *worker*. A farm can be constructed on any connected set of processors by grouping the workers into trees which are connected at their roots to the farmer. The *farmer* sees each of these trees as a worker which is capable of performing some number of tasks simultaneously. Each of the nodes of the tree must, in parallel with executing its own *worker*, farm tasks out to the sub-trees below it and recover their results.

Alternatively, the workers might be arranged in pipelines or rings, each node being additionally responsible for passing streams of tasks from the farmer to its successors, and streams of results from it predecessors to the farmer. The appendix contains a re-coding of the farm (page 241) to be executed on a row of processors each connected to its neighbours by a single pair of channels. In Process 8.39 each *work.detail* runs a single *worker*, but as well as dealing locally with a stream of tasks addressed to its worker, it also passes tasks to the sub-farm of processes with higher indices than its own. Each *work.detail* might be executed on a different transputer; each pair of channels *incoming*[*i*] and *outgoing*[*i*] could be implemented by a single link between an adjacent pair of processors.

9

Handling interrupts

It used to be that programmers met concurrently executing processes only if they had to code interrupt routines, or to write code which shared store with interrupt routines. An interrupt is a mechanism designed to make small amounts of processing power available at short notice to handle urgent tasks, when it would be unreasonably expensive to make that processing capability permanently available. To this extent, it separates two concerns: an applications programmer wanting to send characters to a lineprinter need only supply them to an interrupt handler; it is the responsibility of the interrupt handler to transmit them to the printer at the precise times that the printer indicates that it is ready for them. In this way, the programmer is relieved of the burden of making frequent checks on the state of the printer, and the structure of his program can be unaffected by the timing constraints imposed by the printer.

Interrupt routines are notoriously difficult to code and to use. In addition to assuming responsibilities of meeting real-time deadlines, the interrupt routine must maintain the programmer's illusion that the application program has exclusive use of the processor and store. This imposes rigorous discipline on the use of registers, and of store locations, both to avoid conflicts, and in the management of those shared variables by which program and interrupt routine communicate. Moreover, the interrupt routine has usually to be programmed as a 'subroutine' (rather than a 'coroutine') invoked once by each interrupt, which means that any state that is to persist from the handling of one interrupt to that of the next must be saved in store and reconstructed at the next interrupt. To make matters worse, high level programming languages are rarely able to offer convenient abstractions for coding interrupt handlers, which are inherently machine-dependent, and it is usual for interrupt routines to be written in machine code.

It is tempting to claim that the concurrently executed processes of occam are the right tools for writing interrupt routines. To do so would be misleading: concurrent processes are right for a task for which interrupt

96

routines have always been inadequate! The task is in two parts: that of writing code to meet real-time deadlines; and that of isolating their effects, so as to keep the rest of the program simple.

In occam, sustaining the illusion that the application program has exclusive use of the processor and store is easily done, since each and every process of every occam program operates under this very illusion. The illusion is sufficiently strong that a programmer need never know whether or not any particular process is executed on its own dedicated processor.

Meeting real-time deadlines remains a problem that must be solved by ensuring that each processor is fast enough, and that the code is short enough. Apart from this concern with urgency, an interrupt handler coded in occam can be written in exactly the same way as any other process, and communicates with the application program in the same way as any other processes communicate with each other.

Managing terminal input

To take a concrete example, consider managing the traffic to and from a terminal. Every time a key is struck at the keyboard, there will be a corresponding event (traditionally an interrupt) in the computer, and some action must be taken to read information about the key before the next key is struck, lest the information be lost. Quite often the action taken will be to store the character corresponding to the key in a buffer, from which it will subsequently be read at the leisure of the program which is consuming the terminal input. The capacity of the buffer determines how many characters can be 'typed ahead' of the demand from the program.

In occam, an 'event in the computer' is represented by a communication on a special channel which PLACE locates at some implementation-dependent address (such as that of the relevant peripheral controller).

```
CHAN OF BYTE keystroke.in :
PLACE keystroke.in AT keyboard.interface :
```

Programs use special channels just as they would use other channels, except that they use each channel only for input, or only for output, with the other half of the communication being performed by a process implemented in the hardware. On a transputer, this might be a 'link' to some other device.

In the case of the terminal example it would be possible, every time a key was struck, for the program to perform an input

```
keystroke.in ? char
```

so a reasonable interrupt handler might be

```
circular.buffer(keystroke.in, request, reply)
```

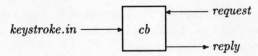

using the circular buffer, Process 8.8 from the preceding chapter. This process has the disadvantage that, were the buffer to become full through the coincidence of a fast typist and a slow program, the process would no longer be prepared to accept input from *keystroke.in*. Since there is (fortunately) no mechanism built into present-day terminals to suspend the execution of the typist while the computer is busy, this would mean that keystrokes made whilst the buffer was full would be lost, without warning.

An improved scheme would be to code the interrupt handler in such a way that it was always prepared to acknowledge the keystroke, and to take some remedial action in case there were no room left in the buffer.

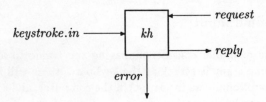

Process 9.1 will signal on the *error* channel if an attempt is made to overfill the type-ahead buffer; later, that signal will be used to cause the bell on the terminal to be rung. Notice that the *keyboard.handler* is written in such a way that, provided

o the outputs to *error* and *reply* are never delayed for more than a fixed time

o this process executes at a known rate within a known short time of becoming ready

then it is possible to put a bound on the length of time which can pass before the process next becomes ready to accept an input from *keystroke.in*. Bounds of this kind are what you would need to demonstrate that no interrupts were lost without trace.

Managing terminal output

For the purpose of this example, suppose that the outgoing traffic to the terminal screen consists of a sequence of bytes passing along the special channel

Process 9.1

```
VAL INT keyboard.interface IS ... :
                         -- some hardware address
VAL INT type.ahead IS ... :
                         -- number of characters that can
                         -- be typed ahead of being wanted
PROTOCOL SIGNAL
  CASE
    signal
:

PROC keyboard.handler(CHAN OF SIGNAL request,
                      CHAN OF BYTE reply,
                      CHAN OF SIGNAL error   )

  -- Characters typed at the keyboard can be read from
  -- reply. A signal is required on request before each
  -- item is read. If more than type.ahead are typed
  -- ahead, an error is signalled.

  CHAN OF BYTE keystroke.in :
  PLACE keystroke.in AT keyboard.interface :
  INT reader, writer, count :
  SEQ
    reader, writer, count := 0, 0, type.ahead

    [type.ahead]BYTE datum :
    WHILE TRUE
      ALT

        BYTE lost :
        count = 0 & keystroke.in ? lost
          error ! signal

        count > 0 & keystroke.in ? datum[writer]
          count, writer := count - 1, (writer + 1) \ type.ahead

        count < type.ahead & request ? CASE signal
          SEQ
            reply ! datum[reader]
            count, reader := count + 1, (reader + 1) \ type.ahead
:
```

screen.out to be displayed as characters on a screen, or acted upon in some other way by the terminal. The terminal may then become busy for some short time, before again being ready to accept output. The screen handling process has to accept characters from the user's program, and to pass them on; additionally, it must accept urgent error signals from the process handling the type-ahead buffer, and send a 'bell' character to the terminal when an error is flagged.

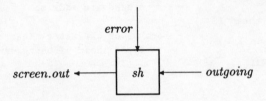

Process 9.2

```
PROC screen.handler(CHAN OF BYTE outgoing,
                    CHAN OF SIGNAL error  )
  CHAN OF BYTE screen.out :
  PLACE screen.out AT vdu.interface :
  VAL BYTE bell.character IS '*#07' :
  WHILE TRUE
    ALT
      BYTE char :
      outgoing ? char
        screen.out ! char
      error ? CASE signal
        screen.out ! bell.character
:
```

It might appear that there are no timing constraints on the behaviour of the screen handling process (Process 9.2), but recall that the performance of the *keyboard.handler* depends on its *error* signals not being unduly delayed. As written, the *error*-guard in the *screen.handler* might indeed be delayed indefinitely, even were it guaranteed that the *screen.handler* was executed immediately either of the guards became ready. It might be that the process that sends characters along the *outgoing* channel is able to send a new character in less time than it takes the *screen.handler* to execute the body of its WHILE loop once. In that case, the *outgoing*-guard would always be ready every time the alternative was executed, and since an alternative can choose any one of the ready guards, it is possible that the *error*-guard might be ignored indefinitely, even were it ready. Notice, particularly, that this behaviour is not caused by writing the *outgoing*-guard first: the order of the components of an alternative is immaterial to its meaning.

It is for just this reason that occam has the additional PRI ALT construct (see Chapter 7), which breaks the symmetry between its branches. Using this, the *screen.handler* can be re-written as Process 9.3 and then an *error* signal could not be delayed for longer than it takes to execute the body of the WHILE loop once. Discharging the responsibility to accept these signals in a fixed time reduces to showing that o the outputs to *screen.out* are never delayed for more than a fixed time

o this process executes at a known rate within a known short time of becoming ready

The first requirement is met by the terminal, by assumption; the second will be discussed later. Notice that there is no constraint on the timing of transactions on the *outgoing* channel; the aim is to build a firewall around the terminal, beyond which meeting real-time deadlines will no longer be a concern.

Process 9.3

```
PROC screen.handler(CHAN OF BYTE outgoing,
                    CHAN OF SIGNAL error  )
  CHAN OF BYTE screen.out :
  PLACE screen.out AT vdu.interface :
  VAL BYTE bell.character IS '*#07' :
  WHILE TRUE
    PRI ALT
      error ? CASE signal
        screen.out ! bell.character
      BYTE char :
      outgoing ? char
        screen.out ! char
  :
```

A particular program that uses the terminal may contain a large number of processes, each needing to send characters to the terminal screen. Since the *outgoing* channel is now the only way out to the terminal, and since only one process is able to send along that channel, a process must be written to interleave the many output streams, and send their interleaving along *outgoing*.

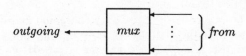

Process 9.4 interleaves messages (sequences of characters) from each of the *from* channels, in an arbitrary order, each message being terminated by the *release* value. (One could use on each *from* channel a BYTE.STREAM protocol, like INT.STREAM except for bytes, or an integer type into which the data bytes can be coerced, using −1, say, for the *release* value. Our solution avoids the extra complexity and overheads at the expense of the − probably correct − assumption that nobody is going to want to output an ASCII null character.) The most interesting property of this process, for our present purpose, is that

Process 9.4

```
VAL BYTE release IS 0(BYTE) :

PROC output.multiplexer([]CHAN OF BYTE from,
                        CHAN OF BYTE outgoing )
  WHILE TRUE
    ALT selected.process = 0 FOR SIZE from
      BYTE char :
      from[selected.process] ? char
        WHILE char <> release
          SEQ
            outgoing ! char
            from[selected.process] ? char
  :
```

it is outside the firewall: there are no constraints on the speed with which it executes, nor on the times at which other processes communicate with it.

Managing echoing

The time-dependency firewall is not yet complete: there remains the problem of reading from the type-ahead buffer. Recall that, having issued a *request* signal, the reader assumes a responsibility to accept the reply from the *reply* channel within a fixed time. That means the reader must be within the firewall.

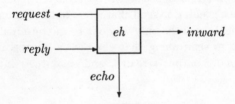

Process 9.5 reads each character from the type-ahead buffer by signalling a *request* and accepting a *reply*. The character is passed on to the *inward* channel to the user. This process is given the additional job of 'echoing' the printable characters to the terminal screen as and when they are read by the program using the keyboard input. The only timing constraint on this process is that it execute sufficiently rapidly that the input from *reply* is accepted within a permissible time of acceptance by the *keyboard.handler* of the preceding *request*. There being no constraints on communication on the *echo* and *inward* channels, these may cross the firewall: the *echo* channel is to be one of the array *from* going to the *output.multiplexer*, and the *inward* channel can be used directly by the process that consumes keyboard input.

Process 9.5

```
PROC echo.handler(CHAN OF SIGNAL request,
                  CHAN OF BYTE reply, echo, inward )
  VAL BYTE enter IS '*c' :
  WHILE TRUE
    BYTE char :
    SEQ
      request ! signal
      reply ? char
      inward ! char    -- Transmit character to user
      IF
        ('*s' <= char) AND (char <= '~')
          echo ! char         -- Echo visible input to screen
        char = enter
          SEQ
            echo ! '*c'        -- Echo carriage return ...
            echo ! '*n'        -- ... and newline
            echo ! release     -- Release screen at end of line
        TRUE
          SKIP                 -- No action on other characters
:
```

Thus Figure 9.1 represents the completed scheme for the terminal handling processes, showing the firewall. The starred processes are those that have to execute at a known rate within a known time of being ready.

Figure 9.1 The firewall in place

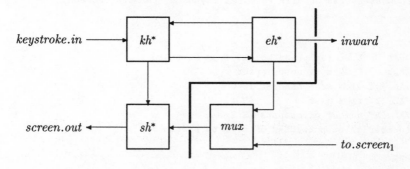

Notice that the screen sharing strategy is implemented by an 'ordinary' process not subject to any timing constraints. Since each line of echoed characters from the type-ahead buffer is sent to the screen as an indivisible message, there is no problem about input characters being mixed in with output, but neither is there any need for the *echo.handler* to be concerned with screen allocation. The user process must ensure that it releases its channels to the multiplexer before accepting keyboard input, and that it consumes whole

lines of input before attempting further output. If the program that used the
terminal were written as the procedure *user*, then the whole could be put
together with the terminal handler to form Process 9.6.

Process 9.6

```
VAL INT keyboard.interface IS ... : -- hardware address
VAL INT vdu.interface      IS ... : -- hardware address

VAL INT type.ahead IS ... :  -- size of buffer
VAL BYTE release IS 0(BYTE) :

PROC keyboard.handler(CHAN OF SIGNAL request,
                      CHAN OF BYTE reply,
                      CHAN OF SIGNAL error   )
  ...
:
PROC echo.handler(CHAN OF SIGNAL request,
                  CHAN OF BYTE reply, echo, inward )
  ...
:
PROC output.multiplexer([]CHAN OF BYTE from,
                        CHAN OF BYTE outgoing )
  ...
:
PROC screen.handler(CHAN OF BYTE outgoing,
                    CHAN OF SIGNAL error  )
  ...
:
PROC user(CHAN OF BYTE terminal.keyboard, terminal.screen)
  ...
:


CHAN OF BYTE reply, outgoing, from.keyboard :
CHAN OF SIGNAL request, error :
VAL INT from.echo.handler IS 0 :
VAL INT from.user         IS 1 :
VAL INT number.of.outputs IS 2 :
[number.of.outputs]CHAN OF BYTE to.screen :

PAR
  keyboard.handler(request, reply, error)      --*
  echo.handler(request, reply,
               to.screen[from.echo.handler],
               from.keyboard                 ) --*
  output.multiplexer(to.screen, outgoing)
  screen.handler(outgoing, error)              --*
  user(from.keyboard, to.screen[from.user])
```

Configuring the program

Ignoring, for the moment, the timing constraints imposed by the proper handling of the terminal interrupts, checking the correctness of this program can be done in two parts. First of all, there are properties of individual processes that can be checked in isolation from the other processes: for example, that the *echo.handler* performs a cycle of communications in a fixed order, behaviour that is unaffected by the other processes. Secondly, there are some properties that are inherently global, notably freedom from deadlock, which may depend on the behaviour of every one of the processes.

The same is the case with the timing constraints: the argument thus far has been about each of the component processes, more or less in isolation. If we had in mind a particular implementation of occam on a particular computer, and with a particular set of terminal characteristics, then we could calculate the 'fixed times' within which actions must occur as so many seconds of processor time, so much communication time, and so on. It remains, however, to be demonstrated that there will always be sufficient processor time available when it is required.

One way of achieving this would be to dedicate a processor to the execution of each of the five components of the program. This is where the PLACED PAR variant of the parallel constructor, introduced in Chapter 7, would be useful. To indicate such a division of labour, a placed parallel could be used instead of the PAR in the present program, together with other housekeeping annotations such as assigning processor numbers and fixing the inter-processor channels onto hardware communication links with PLACE. The result would be that the processor occupancy times calculated for the three starred processes would be actual elapsed times, each independent of the processor loading of the other processes. In this particular case, such a solution seems excessive, since the tasks are each fairly simple, and the traffic is light. It would be a more reasonable way of dealing with, say, the traffic to and from a fast disk, where a whole transputer might be allocated to managing the large volumes of data, and the potentially intricate calculations required to make efficient accesses to the disk.

More realistically, this particular program would probably be run on a single processor, say one transputer. As it stands, in order to be able to guarantee sufficient speed of execution in the starred processes, it is necessary to know details of the behaviour of the unstarred processes: for example, that the *user* process does not require more than a known proportion of the processor's time. This being unsatisfactory, we can use the other PAR variant from Chapter 7: PRI PAR, which distinguishes more and less urgent tasks. In occam programs to be executed on current transputers, asymmetric parallel constructs can have no more than two components, corresponding to the two process-queues in the transputer. For that machine, the right way to organize the terminal handler would be Process 9.7.

Process 9.7

```
PRI PAR

  PAR                            -- High priority process
    keyboard.handler(request, reply, error)
    echo.handler(request, reply,
                 to.screen[from.echo.handler],
                 from.keyboard            )
    screen.handler(outgoing, error)

  PAR                            -- Low priority process
    output.multiplexer(to.screen, outgoing)
    user(from.keyboard, to.screen[from.user])
```

Now it cannot matter what the *user* or *output.multiplexer* processes do: if any of the urgent processes is able to execute, then one of them will do so within a very short time. This latency will be determined and guaranteed by the implementation, so again, with a particular implementation in mind, this would be known. The total waiting time, for any of the 'interrupt' processes, between becoming ready and beginning to execute, is bounded by the sum of one latency time and the sum of the longest execution time of each of the other interrupt processes.

That completes the analysis of the timing of the program. All that is needed in the case of a particular implementation is to calculate the times, a matter of counting instructions, which task could and should be delegated to the compiler. Substituting the figures for the waiting and execution times allows a check to be made that the required response times are achieved.

10
Formatted input and output

One of the things you will probably miss in occam if you are used to writing programs in a conventional high-level language is the support for input and output of text. There are usually either language constructs or predefined routines which take the data from your program – that is, bit patterns representing strings, integers, floating-point numbers, and so on – and translate them into appropriate sequences of characters sent to terminals, printers or files. In the same way, there are usually built-in ways of analysing input from keyboard, file or card-reader and interpreting, for example, sequences of digits as the integer value to be stored in some variable. It is almost always possible to write input and output routines of your own but those provided for you will usually do very well.

Since occam is designed to be usable for applications where the program may be required to run in a 'stand-alone' environment, possibly on many processors, there can be no assumption of a standard operating system; the program must perform its own input and output translations. The *Reference Manual* describes a number of standard libraries of procedures and functions that an implementation will normally make available, including one providing low-level support for such conversions. This consists of a number of procedures which essentially take either a value and a string buffer in which to return a formatted representation, or a string and a variable into which to place the result of parsing the string as the representation of an object of some particular data type.

This chapter explores a possible implementation of these input and output translations, taking the alternative approach of converting directly between values and sequences of bytes communicated along a channel. Some procedures are introduced which are used in programs later in the book, including a higher-level routine which does multiple output translations according to a programmer supplied format.

Simple output

This section describes a number of procedures which convert the bit patterns of each of the primitive data types into canonical sequences of characters sent down a channel with the BYTE protocol. The particular representation chosen will result in a fixed number of characters being sent for every value of a given type. This is perhaps not the natural representation for everyday use, although it may simplify the tabulation of data; but it will be shown below how the fixed format of output can be massaged to fit one desired by the user.

The procedure for sending a single character (Process 10.1) is so simple that it is hardly worth writing.

Process 10.1

```
PROC write.character(CHAN OF BYTE output, VAL BYTE character)
  output ! character
:
```

Of course, a BYTE can also be interpreted as a numeric value, which you may wish to display as a decimal numeral, or indeed in hexadecimal notation. In this case, however, it is redundant to invest any mental effort or program code on the details of generating such a representation, since one may as well produce the same characters for a number in the range 0 to 255 – say, 137 – whether it is encoded internally as 137(BYTE), 137(INT) or 137(INT64). The definitions of Process 10.2 and Process 10.3 become very simple once the routines for dealing with INT64 values have been written.

Process 10.2

```
PROC write.decimal.byte(CHAN OF BYTE output, VAL BYTE number)
  write.decimal.int64(output, (INT64 number))
:
```

Process 10.3

```
PROC write.hexadecimal.byte(CHAN OF BYTE output, VAL BYTE bits)
  write.hexadecimal.int64(output, (INT64 bits))
:
```

A similar argument disposes of the other integer types, and the definition of the decimal output routines for these is as simple as in the BYTE case, provided the bit patterns are to be interpreted as signed, twos-complement numbers. In representing the unsigned value corresponding to the bit pattern, as is probably desirable for the hexadecimal case, a complication arises. If #FFFF(INT16) is to produce only four 'F's, no matter how many digits are displayed, then it must be treated differently from (INT64 #FFFF(INT16)), which is, of course, #FFFFFFFFFFFFFFFF(INT64). Indeed, it should be treated like #FFFF(INT64) instead. In order to effect this transformation the range of bits which are significant in the longer data type must be restricted; the sign-extended value must be trimmed by a BITAND with the mask which has as many low-order bits set as fit into the shorter type.

How should this mask be denoted? In each integer type the bit pattern with all bits set represents −1; but the operands of BITAND must be of the same type, and it is precisely −1 in the shorter type that we have seen to change bit pattern when it is coerced to the longer. The bit pattern could be hand-coded into each routine, or could be generated by shifting -1(INT64) right by the difference in lengths of the two types; but these are *ad hoc* solutions. Neither, for instance, would allow a machine-independent expression for the correct mask in the INT case. It is preferable to let sign extension, which causes the problem, also solve it: MOSTNEG INT16 has only the sign bit set, so INT64 (MOSTNEG INT16) has all the bits that are not wanted set, and also the next most significant. Thus shifting this left gives the complement of the mask needed for Process 10.4.

Process 10.4

```
PROC write.hexadecimal.int16(CHAN OF BYTE output, VAL INT16 bits)
  VAL INT64 mask IS (INT64 (MOSTNEG INT16)) << 1 :
  write.hexadecimal.int64(output, (INT64 bits) /\ (BITNOT mask))
:
```

The other integer types can be dealt with after the same fashion.

This leaves us with the task of converting INT64 values into decimal and hexadecimal representations. The hexadecimal case is very straightforward: Process 10.5 transmits the representation of each four bits in turn.

Process 10.5

```
PROC write.hexadecimal.int64(CHAN OF BYTE output, VAL INT64 bits)
  VAL []BYTE hex.digit IS "0123456789abcdef" :
  SEQ i = 1 FOR 64 / 4
    VAL nibble IS INT ((bits >> (64 - (4 * i))) /\ #F(INT64)) :
    output ! hex.digit[nibble]
:
```

A standard technique for outputting a decimal number relies on the observation that, for a positive n and a power of ten *tens*, the value of $(n/tens)\backslash 10$ is the coefficient of *tens* in the decimal expansion of n. This can be converted to the corresponding digit either by subscripting a string or by the arithmetic trick of Process 10.6, which relies on the digit characters having consecutive codes.

Process 10.6

```
BYTE FUNCTION decimal(VAL INT d) IS BYTE (d + (INT '0')) :
```

This gives rise to an algorithm which performs the digit calculation for each power of ten not exceeding n, and the results are produced in sequence in decreasing order of their weight.

```
INT64 tens :
SEQ
  tens := 1(INT64)
  WHILE (n / tens) >= 10(INT64)
    tens := 10(INT64) * tens
  WHILE tens <> 0(INT64)
    SEQ
      output ! decimal(INT ((n / tens) \ 10(INT64)))
      tens := tens / 10(INT64)
```

This carefully calculates the minimum power of ten required, and so yields the shortest possible sequence of bytes along *output*. For a fixed length sequence of bytes, to simplify further manipulations, it suffices to replace the first occurrence of n by MOSTPOS INT64 – or, as the effect of the first WHILE is then constant, just to initialize *tens* to the appropriate power of ten, which calculation shows to be 10^{18}.

That process works for all positive n and, as a special case, for zero. To extend it to output negative numbers as well, it is tempting to try changing the sign first; but this is wrong, because to change the sign of MOSTNEG INT64 with normal arithmetic negation is an error, and MINUS (MOSTNEG INT64) is just MOSTNEG INT64 again. The standard, if perhaps confusing, solution is to treat positive numbers as special cases which are best output by making them negative, or equivalently to change the sign of *tens* so that the result of dividing by *tens* is consistently negative. This gives us Process 10.7. Notice that it is a matter of the definition of the division and remainder operators in occam that changing the sign either of *tens* or of *number* just changes the sign of the expression $(number/tens)\backslash 10$. The division of *tens* by ten always gives an exact answer, excepting the final occasion, when *tens* is one, and the result of the division is zero.

A procedure which sends the characters of a string down a channel (Process 10.8) has already been seen, in Chapter 5. This can be used to send appropriate representations of the Boolean values with Process 10.9.

There remains the task of producing representations of floating-point values. This is a problem of much greater complexity than for the discrete data types, and it is quite possible to write at great length on algorithms for producing the right sort of accuracy. The difficulties arise from the fact that to represent an N-bit binary mantissa *exactly* takes N decimal digits (as two is not a factor of five), but mantissas differing only in their least significant bit differ in their decimal representation in about the $(N/\log_2 10)^{\text{th}}$ digit, so over two-thirds of the exact representation's apparent accuracy is illusory.

Process 10.7

```
PROC write.decimal.int64(CHAN OF BYTE output, VAL INT64 number)

  -- Write a signed decimal representation of number
  -- to the output channel

  VAL INT64 ten.to.the.eighteen IS 1000000000000000000(INT64) :
  INT64 tens :
  SEQ
    IF
      number < 0(INT64)
        SEQ
          output ! '-'
          tens := ten.to.the.eighteen
      number >= 0(INT64)
        SEQ
          output ! '+'
          tens := -ten.to.the.eighteen
    WHILE tens <> 0(INT64)
      SEQ
        output ! decimal(INT (-((number / tens) \ 10(INT64))))
        tens := tens / 10(INT64)
:
```

Process 10.8

```
PROC write.string(CHAN OF BYTE output, VAL []BYTE string)
  SEQ i = 0 FOR SIZE string
    output ! string[i]
:
```

Process 10.9

```
VAL []BYTE true.string  IS "true" :
VAL []BYTE false.string IS "false" :

PROC write.bool(CHAN OF BYTE output, VAL BOOL condition)
  IF
    condition
      write.string(output, true.string)
    NOT condition
      write.string(output, false.string)
:
```

The floating-point number is, after all, only approximating the 'correct' real value to within about half a least significant bit.

Analysis identifies the accuracy to aim for, but this cannot always be attained using the same format of floating-point arithmetic to scale the mantissa associated with a power-of-two exponent to obtain one corresponding to a power-of-ten exponent. This problem can be solved; see for example [15]. Although we could code the arithmetic in occam, the necessary algorithms are both long and intricate and not central to our presentation, so are omitted from this book. The following code assumes the existence of functions

```
INT, INT64 FUNCTION split.real32(VAL REAL32 r)
  ...
:

INT, INT64 FUNCTION split.real64(VAL REAL64 r)
  ...
:
```

which when applied to a floating-point number r of the appropriate type return a pair $\langle exponent, mantissa \rangle$ such that

$$r = m \times 10^{exponent} \text{ and } m = exponent = 0 \ \lor \ 0.1 \le |m| < 1.0$$

$$mantissa \simeq m \times 10^N \text{ where } N = \begin{cases} 9, \text{ if } r \text{ is a REAL32} \\ 17, \text{ if } r \text{ is a REAL64} \end{cases}$$

for some real number m. It is then a simple matter to output the *exponent* and *mantissa* as integers, with suitable punctuation.

Simple input

Constructing a data object from its textual representation is slightly more difficult because, in general, not all sequences of characters will be legal representations. For example, a process to read a numeral might expect some spaces, perhaps a sign and some more spaces, and then a sequence of digits, followed by something else. If there are no digits, or if the number represented is too large to be encoded as a bit pattern of the appropriate type, then an error has occurred.

The particular action to be taken to recover from an error depends on the circumstances of the conversion: for example, whether the digits are being read from a terminal keyboard, or a magnetic tape, whether the process is running in a desk-top microcomputer or in aircraft autopilot equipment. For a general purpose routine, it is reasonable to return a Boolean indication of whether the conversion was successful. (Other indications might be possible, for example, a communication on a channel laid aside for indicating errors.)

Ignoring, for the present, the matter of the sign, and the possibility of error, a sequence of digits can be converted into a bit pattern representing the same number by

```
BYTE char :
SEQ
  n := 0
  input ? char
  WHILE ('0' <= char) AND (char <= '9')
    SEQ
      n := (10 * n) + ((INT char) - (INT '0'))
      input ? char
```

The arithmetic is essentially dual to that in the output routine. If *char* is the character code of a digit, then it lies between the codes of the characters zero and nine, and (*char* − '0') is its value as a digit, having interpreted the BYTE values as integers in order to perform arithmetic on them.

As in the case of output, it is necessary to be careful with the most negative integer: it will not do to read negative numerals by reading the digits as if they were those of a positive numeral and then changing the sign of the result. Furthermore, to avoid overflow the new value of n must be compared with either the most positive or the most negative bit pattern, again being careful to keep all the arithmetic in the expressible range

```
VAL INT digit IS (INT char) - (INT '0') :
IF
  (sign = '+') AND (n <= (((MOSTPOS INT) - digit) / 10))
    n := (10 * n) + digit
  (sign = '-') AND ((((MOSTNEG INT) + digit) / 10) <= n)
    n := (10 * n) - digit
  otherwise
    ok := FALSE      -- an error has occurred
```

A possible solution to the problem of errors would be to omit the third branch of the conditional entirely, so that the routine would stop in case of an overflow. This more general solution postpones the decision, giving the caller of the process the option of ignoring the error, or of acting on it in any way he chooses, including the option of stopping.

The appendix contains a routine complementary to the decimal output routines which has the following specification:

```
PROC read.signed(CHAN OF BYTE input, INT n, BOOL ok)
  -- Read an (optionally signed) decimal numeral from
  -- the input returning the corresponding value in n,
  -- and TRUE in ok precisely if the conversion succeeded
  ...
:
```

In many programming languages a routine like *read.signed* could only be used for conversion of a numeral being read from a peripheral device. In PASCAL, for example, such a routine would be reading from a file, but an entirely different routine would be needed to convert a numeral stored in an array of characters. In occam, there is nothing to stop you doing this by putting input and output routines together in parallel. The process

```
CHAN OF BYTE internal :
PAR
  write.string(internal, "-137*C")
  read.signed(internal, n, ok)
```

sets *n* to −137. This might not look very useful for constant strings, but the same can be done with variable arrays of characters. This means, for example, that it is easy to separate the business of line construction, editing and echoing when reading from a terminal, from whatever data conversion you might want to perform on the input.

For completeness, the appendix also contains a coding of a line construction process suitable for input from a VDU

```
PROC read.line(CHAN OF BYTE keyboard, echo, []BYTE s, INT n)
  -- Construct a string in [s FROM 0 FOR n] from the
  -- printable characters read from keyboard and sent
  -- back on the echo channel.
  ...
:
```

As it reads characters from the *keyboard* stream, this process packs them into the byte array *s* and copies them to the *echo* stream, allowing the usual sort of line editing. For example, if the *char* typed on *keyboard* is backspace the last character in the line is cancelled, and its echo is removed from the screen by writing a blank in its place:

```
CASE char
  ...
  backspace
    IF
      n > 0
        SEQ
          echo ! backspace
          echo ! '*s'
          echo ! backspace
          n := n - 1
      n = 0                -- nothing to delete
        echo ! bell
  ...
```

Multiple output

Most high-level languages provide some way of combining the output of various pieces of data into a single command. In PASCAL this leads to an exceptional violation of the language's rules that all procedures have a fixed number of arguments of fixed types: rather than requiring the sequence of commands

```
BEGIN
    write_string(output, 'the square root of ');
    write_integer(output, n);
    write_string(output, ' is ');
    write_real(output, sqrt(n))
END
```

the first relaxation is that all the procedures are called *write*, and then you are allowed to substitute a single procedure call

```
write(output, 'the square root of ', n, ' is ', sqrt(n))
```

There are rightly no such exceptions in occam.

The C language is another which makes output formatting easy by providing a routine *printf* which takes as one of its arguments a control string that describes how to interpret the bit patterns of the other parameters. A call like

```
printf("The square root of %5d is %E", n, sqrt((float) n));
```

says that n is to be interpreted as an integer, and output in a field of width five characters, and $sqrt((float)\,n)$ is a floating-point number to be output in a default exponential format. If n is an integer which has the value 1936 then the resulting output will be

```
The square root of   1936 is 4.400000E+01
```

(If n happened to be a floating-point variable the first number printed would be that obtained in occam by VAL INT n RETYPES n!) This section develops the full expressive power of *printf* within the safe, restrictive occam philosophy.

In occam, a procedure certainly cannot have a variable number of arguments; so how can the required flexibility be obtained? It would be possible, but inelegant, to declare a procedure which took as many arguments as we can imagine ever possibly wanting to use, and supplying zero or some other value as the actual parameter in the places not needed by a particular call. Another possibility would be to build the arguments into a table, and allow the body of the procedure to work out how many there were using SIZE. But neither of these allows objects of more than one type to be passed: the formal parameter specifier fixes the type of each individual argument in the first case, and of all the arguments *en masse* in the second. To pass items of different type would need some kind of variant record or union type, which is not provided in occam. But as was remarked in Chapter 3 there is an occam 2 analogue, the discriminated protocol; moreover, a variable and unbounded number of items may be communicated along a channel. The solution, therefore, is to declare a protocol DATA.ITEM and write a procedure *write.formatted* with three parameters:

```
PROC write.formatted(CHAN OF BYTE output,
                     VAL []BYTE control,
                     CHAN OF DATA.ITEM data )
  ...
:
```

What are the variants that DATA.ITEM must allow? One tag is required for each primitive type, if we want to be able to set different default field widths for the different length data types; *printf* also allows strings, which would naturally correspond to a counted-array protocol. One other item that may prove useful, especially if we use the same protocol in an input filter, is a tag to mark abnormal termination of the formatting operation.

```
PROTOCOL DATA.ITEM
  CASE
    data.bool;    BOOL
    data.byte;    BYTE
    data.int;     INT
    data.int16;   INT16
    data.int32;   INT32
    data.int64;   INT64
    data.real32;  REAL32
    data.real64;  REAL64
    data.string;  INT::[]BYTE
    data.abort
:
```

Using this procedure and protocol, the earlier example can be coded as

```
CHAN OF DATA.ITEM data :
PAR
  write.formatted(output,
                  "The square root of %5d is %E", data)
  SEQ
    data ! data.int; n
    data ! data.real32; sqrt(REAL32 ROUND n)
```

The control string, to follow the model of *printf* reasonably closely, will be an array of characters most of which will simply be sent down the *output* channel. At every place in the sequence where a '%' is encountered, a number of characters taken together will describe the formatting to apply to an item input along *data*, and the result of this conversion will be inserted into the output stream. If the hard work is abstracted into a procedure, *process.item*, the required routine is then Process 10.10.

Process 10.10

```
PROC write.formatted(CHAN OF BYTE output,
                     VAL []BYTE control,
                     CHAN OF DATA.ITEM data )

  PROC process.item(CHAN OF DATA.ITEM data,
                    VAL []BYTE control, INT i,
                    CHAN OF BYTE output          )
    -- interpret characters from [control FROM i FOR ...]
    -- read and format item accordingly from data and send
    -- along output; set i beyond last character of format
    ...
  :
  INT i :
  SEQ
    i := 0
    VAL INT size IS SIZE control :
    WHILE i < size
      IF
        control[i] <> '%'
          SEQ
            output ! control[i]
            i := i + 1
        control[i] = '%'
          SEQ
            i := i + 1
            process.item(data, control, i, output)
:
```

The individual format descriptions are analysed into four parts, most of which can be omitted to obtain default values. They are: flag characters, determining whether the field should be left-justified, whether positive numbers should appear preceded by a '+', or by an extra space; a decimal numeral representing the minimum field width; a dot followed by a decimal numeral denoting some notion of *precision*, which varies according to the type of format; and a non-optional character defining the type of format.

As an extra sophistication either numeral in the format description may be replaced by an asterisk, which causes another item (which must be an INT) to be input first, to supply the number required. The coding of *process.item* will require the format parameters to be passed to subsidiary routines. In order to avoid having to supply a large number of arguments to each routine, the information will be packaged as a pair of arrays, with named constants to index them:

```
VAL INT left.justify IS 0 :
VAL INT     sign.plus IS 1 :
VAL INT     sign.blank IS 2 :
VAL INT number.of.flags IS 3 :
[number.of.flags]BOOL flag :

VAL INT   get.flag IS -1 :
VAL INT      width IS  0 :
VAL INT precision IS  1 :
VAL INT field.numbers IS 2 :
[field.numbers]INT field :
```

The body of the procedure is then a WHILE loop which scans through the control string, keeping track of which of the first three parts of the format it has already found present or omitted, and processing characters which make sense as a component of one of the remaining ones. When it reaches some other character – or runs off the end of the string – the loop terminates and the procedure tries to interpret the latest character as a format type (Process 10.11).

The actual acceptance of data from the source stream and transmission of the textual representation along *output* is delegated to a routine

```
PROC formatted.output(VAL BYTE format,
                      VAL []BOOL flag, []INT field,
                      CHAN OF DATA.ITEM data,
                      CHAN OF BYTE output            )
  ...
:
```

Process 10.11 always invokes this routine, even when errors have been detected. It would not have been unreasonable to omit the final branches of each of the IF processes in *process.item*, and so cause the whole to stop at any of those errors in the control string. Falling out of the WHILE loop, however, with *format.char* containing the offending character, which cannot be valid as a format designator, gives the option of generating a message explaining the error. It would be possible to handle the other tagged variants on the input for a '*' similarly, setting *this.format* false or coercing the value to an INT where possible; but the user process could still cause a deadlock by refusing to communicate. In this example, for simplicity, erroneous communication will cause the natural deadlock.

Before proceeding to the details of the *formatted.output* procedure, there remain one or two other gaps in Process 10.11 which are straightforward

Process 10.11

```
PROC process.item(CHAN OF DATA.ITEM data,
                  VAL []BYTE control, INT i,
                  CHAN OF BYTE output     )
  ... declare arrays, constants and PROC formatted.output
  INT which.field :
  BOOL this.format :
  BYTE format.char :
  VAL INT size IS SIZE control :
  SEQ
    flag := [FALSE, FALSE, FALSE]
    field := [-1, -1]
    which.field, this.format := get.flag, TRUE
    format.char := '*#00' -- not a valid format type
    WHILE this.format AND (i < size)
      SEQ
        format.char := control[i]
        CASE format.char
          '-', '+', '*s'
            IF
              which.field = get.flag
                ... set appropriate flag
              which.field > get.flag
                this.format := FALSE  -- error case
          '.'
            IF
              which.field < precision
                which.field, field[precision] := precision, 0
              which.field >= precision
                this.format := FALSE  -- error case
          '**'
            IF
              (which.field < width) AND (field[width] < 0)
                SEQ
                  which.field := width
                  data ? CASE data.int; field[width]
                  this.format := field[width] >= 0  -- error?
              (which.field = precision) AND (field[precision] < 0)
                SEQ
                  data ? CASE data.int; field[precision]
                  this.format := field[precision] >= 0  -- error?
              otherwise
                this.format := FALSE  -- error case
          '0', '1', '2', '3', '4', '5', '6', '7', '8', '9'
            ... accumulate number for width or precision
          ELSE
            this.format := FALSE  -- parsed format successfully
        i := i + 1
    formatted.output(format.char, flag, field, data, output)
:
```

to fill in. These are setting the flags, which is a simple case discrimination on the flag character

```
-- set appropriate flag
CASE format.char
  '-'
    flag[left.justify] := TRUE
  '+'
    flag[sign.plus] := TRUE
  '*s'
    flag[sign.blank] := TRUE
```

and accumulating the numbers, taking care to ensure arithmetic overflow does not occur

```
-- accumulate number for width or precision
VAL INT digit IS (INT format.char) - (INT '0') :
CASE which.field
  get.flag
    which.field, field[width] := width, digit
  width, precision
    INT parameter IS field[which.field] :
    IF
      parameter <= (((MOSTPOS INT) - digit) / 10)
        parameter := (parameter * 10) + digit
      parameter > (((MOSTPOS INT) - digit) / 10)
        this.format := FALSE  -- error case
```

The bulk of the remaining work is in the code to implement recognized formats. This can be separated into at least two tasks: accepting an appropriate value from *data* and converting it into a sequence of bytes; and massaging that sequence into the one specified by the values of *flag* and *field*. In some cases the default values to supply for the *field* settings and so on depend on the type of value input: for instance the hexadecimal output for an INT16 is 'naturally' made up of four digits, while that of an INT64 needs all sixteen; so a channel is required to transfer miscellaneous information. This gives the scheme

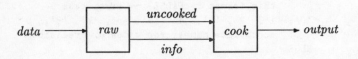

for the non-error case of Process 10.12. The capital letter format characters represent the same formatting instructions as the corresponding lower-case

Process 10.12

```
PROC formatted.output(VAL BYTE format,
                      VAL []BOOL flag, []INT field,
                      CHAN OF DATA.ITEM data,
                      CHAN OF BYTE output            )

  PROC raw.output(CHAN OF DATA.ITEM data,
                  VAL BYTE format,
                  CHAN OF INT info,
                  CHAN OF BYTE uncooked )
    ...
  :

  PROC cook.output(CHAN OF BYTE uncooked,
                   CHAN OF INT info,
                   VAL BYTE format,
                   VAL []BOOL flag, []INT field,
                   CHAN OF BYTE cooked          )
    ...
  :

  VAL BYTE format.type IS lower.case(format) :
  CASE format.type
    '%', 'b', 'c', 'd', 'e', 'f', 'x'
      CHAN OF BYTE uncooked :
      CHAN OF INT info :
      PAR
        raw.output(data, format.type, info, uncooked)
        cook.output(uncooked, info, format, flag, field, output)
    ELSE  -- unrecognized format character
      SEQ
        write.string(output, "<format error>")  -- e.g.
        STOP
  :
```

ones, but with any alphabetic characters in the output forced into capitals.
(This affects the larger hexadecimal digits and the exponent sign, as well
as the strings for the Boolean values and character output.) The same raw
output will be generated for both, and the translation will form part of the
cooking process. This explains the use of the function *lower.case*, which is
given in Process 10.13; the function *upper.case* (Process 10.14), which we
will need later, is similar except that it modifies lower-case letters.

   The production of the basic character sequence by the *raw.output*
routine (Process 10.15) is a matter of a case discrimination on the format
character, in each case performing a discriminating input on *data*, converting
appropriate variants to the canonical sequence of characters along *uncooked*,
preceeded by size information along *info* where needed. The one exception

Process 10.13

```
BYTE FUNCTION lower.case(VAL BYTE char)
  BYTE result :
  VALOF
    IF
      ('A' <= char) AND (char <= 'Z')
        result := BYTE ((INT char) >< ((INT 'A') >< (INT 'a')))
      (char < 'A') OR ('Z' < char)
        result := char
    RESULT result
:
```

Process 10.14

```
BYTE FUNCTION upper.case(VAL BYTE char)
  BYTE result :
  VALOF
    IF
      ('a' <= char) AND (char <= 'z')
        result := BYTE ((INT char) >< ((INT 'A') >< (INT 'a')))
      (char < 'a') OR ('z' < char)
        result := char
    RESULT result
:
```

to this is where a repeated '%' stands for itself. Any type-dependent size information that is needed, for instance the number of significant figures produced by the *split.real*— functions or the number of hexadecimal characters required for a value of some type

```
VAL INT real32.precision IS 9 :
VAL INT real64.precision IS 17 :
VAL INT nibbles.in.a.byte IS 2 :
```

is sent along *info* to act as default values for the *field* parameters. The canonical sequence of characters corresponding to the input value is then sent along *uncooked*.

The *raw.output* process does not generate any explicit termination signal for the cooking process. Instead, the latter must know how many characters to expect. By the construction of the simple routines, the canonical raw text in most cases has a length determined purely by the format character:

```
VAL INT decimal.raw IS 1+19 : -- sign and digits from decimal
VAL INT hexadecimal.raw IS 16 : -- and hexadecimal raw output
```

Only in the Boolean case is the length of the character sequence dependent on the actual value to be represented, as *true.string* and *false.string* will in

Process 10.15

```
PROC raw.output(CHAN OF DATA.ITEM data, VAL BYTE format,
               CHAN OF INT info, CHAN OF BYTE uncooked )
  CASE format
    '%' -- percent sign
      write.character(uncooked, '%')
    'b' -- Boolean
      ... accept data.bool for write.bool after 'info'
    'c' -- character
      BYTE character :
      SEQ
        data ? CASE data.byte; character
        write.character(uncooked, character)
    'd' -- decimal (signed) integer
      ... as for 'x' using write.decimal.<type> and no 'info'
    'e' -- exponential form of real
      INT exponent :
      INT64 mantissa :
      SEQ
        data ? CASE
          REAL32 float :
          data.real32; float
            SEQ
              exponent, mantissa := split.real32(float)
              info ! real32.precision
          REAL64 float :
          data.real64; float
            SEQ
              exponent, mantissa := split.real64(float)
              info ! real64.precision
        write.decimal.int64(uncooked, mantissa)
        write.decimal.int(uncooked, exponent)
    'f' -- positional form of real
      ... as 'e' but write mantissa and 'info ! exponent' in PAR
    'x' -- hexadecimal (unsigned) integer
      data ? CASE
        BYTE number :
        data.byte; number
          SEQ
            info ! nibbles.in.a.byte
            write.hexadecimal.byte(uncooked, number)
        ... similarly for INT16, INT32 and INT64
        INT number :
        data.int; number
          SEQ
            VAL []BYTE count.bytes RETYPES number :
            info ! (SIZE count.bytes) * nibbles.in.a.byte
            write.hexadecimal.int(uncooked, number)
  :
```

general have different lengths. But with only two values, and the *info* channel available, this causes no difficulty:

```
-- accept data.bool for write.bool after 'info'
BOOL condition :
SEQ
  data ? CASE data.bool; condition
  IF
    condition
      info ! SIZE true.string
    NOT condition
      info ! SIZE false.string
  write.bool(uncooked, condition)
```

Notice that should some other textual representation of the Boolean values be required throughout, then it is sufficient to change the two definitions

```
VAL []BYTE true.string  IS "gwir" :
VAL []BYTE false.string IS "gau"  :
```

and the rest of the code automatically adapts to compensate.

Arranging the text

The output-cooking process has several jobs to do, the precise selection depending on the format type and the values of the flags. The tasks potentially required for the integer formats are typical:

o the number of characters to expect must be determined, and unspecified values of the *field* array filled in; in the hexadecimal case the default must be input from the *info* channel even if the precision has been specified

o those leading zeros not demanded by the *field*[*precision*] must be suppressed, and the remaining digits (preceded by a sign, if required) must be fitted, right-justified, into a sequence of no less than *field*[*width*] number of bytes

o if *flag*[*left.justify*] is set, the result must be left-justified, perhaps by counting leading spaces and retransmitting them after the significant text

o in an 'X' format, letters in the hexadecimal representation must be translated to upper case

o *flag*[*sign.blank*] may require a plus sign to be replaced by a blank.

The main difference in the other formats is the meaning attached to the *precision* field: this specifies the minimum number of digits for the integer formats, but the maximum number of significant digits for floating-point numbers, and the maximum number of characters to print from the textual representation of Boolean values.

The first two of the listed tasks naturally coalesce; the one establishes the boundaries within which the second operates. Conceptually, therefore, there might be a chain of processes

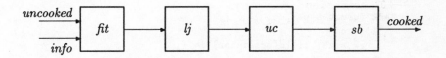

each passing on the result of its modifications to the next. There are a number of disadvantages to this scheme, however.

If for instance, as will often be the case, none of the three later features is selected, then all the processes bar the first will be acting as simple buffers, with no benefit in exchange for the consequent overhead of frequent rescheduling. This could be overcome by setting up the pipeline including just those elements required, although the resulting procedure would be relatively complex and hard to comprehend. Moreover, since the *field*[*width*] specification is only the minimum number of bytes to generate for this item – neither truncation nor replacing with '*'s seems an adequate way of dealing with 'format overflow' when the channel can accept a stream of unlimited length – the output from the field-fitting stage would be of unpredetermined length; and so there would be the added complexity of organizing the distributed termination of the parallel components.

It will therefore be desirable to collapse the pipeline (distributed in 'space') into a sequential process (distributed in time). The following remark suggests that this is possible without having to read all the data from *uncooked* before producing any on *cooked*: in each numeric format the sign character and ultimate spacing are all determinable at the moment that the first non-zero digit, if any, is received on the *uncooked* channel; and the only state required to determine them is the sign and the position of that digit in the stream. For since the input stream is of known length, by construction, and the punctuation for the format is fixed, it is easy to tell how many significant characters there will be; and thence how many spaces and zeros are required to meet the specification of *field* and *flag*. Any initial text can then be sent, the remaining characters copied (with translation if requested), and finally any left-justifying spaces complete the output for that item. Each character of the non-numeric formats is significant, and so the number of significant characters is already known and the same argument applies.

Process 10.16

```
PROC cook.output(CHAN OF BYTE uncooked, CHAN OF INT info,
                 VAL BYTE format, VAL []BOOL flag, []INT field,
                 CHAN OF BYTE cooked                                )

  VAL BYTE format.type IS lower.case(format) :

  INT raw.size, text.size :
  BOOL signed :
  BYTE sign.char, first :
  SEQ
    CASE format.type
      '%', 'c'
        raw.size, field[precision] := 1, 1
      'b'
        ... set up Boolean
      'd'
        raw.size := decimal.raw
      'e', 'f'
        ... set up approximate real
      'x'
        ... set up hexadecimal


    CASE format.type
      '%', 'b', 'c'
        SEQ
          text.size, signed := raw.size, FALSE
          uncooked ? first
      'd', 'e', 'f'
        VAL BOOL plus  IS flag[sign.plus] :
        VAL BOOL blank IS flag[sign.blank] :
        ... signed numeral
      'x'
        ... unsigned numeral


    VAL BOOL left  IS flag[left.justify] :
    VAL BOOL right IS NOT left :
    VAL BOOL upper IS format <> format.type :
    INT zero.pad, space.pad, copy, truncate :
    CASE format.type
      '%', 'b', 'c', 'd', 'x'
        ... straightforward cases
      'e'
        ... send exponent before final spaces
      'f'
        ... may need leading or trailing zeros
  :
```

Since the formatting tasks differ for different format characters, the body of *cook.output* could be written as a case discrimination on the format type. There are, however, some tasks which can be done the same way for a number of formats, but the sharing differs from task to task. This can be exploited by placing three case discriminations in sequence (Process 10.16). The first determines the number of characters to be expected; the second determines the number of significant digits, reading the first, and also decides about any sign; the last performs the actual output.

The three elided cases in the first discrimination all share a need to accept a default value on the *info* channel and set the precision if it has been left unspecified. As to require no characters at all would be bizarre, a precision specified as zero will be taken as an explicit request for the default. Process 10.17 performs the conditional assignment.

Process 10.17

```
PROC set.unless.specified(INT parameter, VAL INT default)
  IF
    parameter > 0  -- already specified
      SKIP
    parameter <= 0  -- left to default
      parameter := default
:
```

Using this routine, the initialization task for the Boolean case is

```
-- set up Boolean
INT max.chars IS field[precision] :
INT default.precision :
SEQ
  info ? default.precision
  set.unless.specified(max.chars, default.precision)
  raw.size, max.chars :=
      default.precision, min(max.chars, default.precision)
```

The other two cases are similar, setting *raw.size* to either *decimal.raw* or *hexadecimal.raw*. In the cases where the precision is an upper limit, the default is the maximum value it may take; for hexadecimal numerals it may cause padding with leading zeros, so the restriction of *field[precision]* to at most *default.precision* is omitted.

At the start of the second case discrimination *raw.size* characters representing the item being processed remain to be read from *uncooked*. By the end of it, *text.size* contains the number of significant characters, including a *first* which has been read already; that a *sign.char* is to be displayed is separately encoded by *signed* being true. In the non-numeric formats there is no sign, and all characters are significant, so this is simply established by reading *first* and setting the variables as shown in Process 10.16.

Process 10.18

```
PROC get.first.significant(CHAN OF BYTE input,
                           INT number.of.digits, BYTE digit )
  SEQ
    input ? digit
    WHILE (number.of.digits > 1) AND (digit = '0')
      SEQ
        input ? digit
        number.of.digits := number.of.digits - 1
  :
```

For numerals insignificant leading zeros must be discarded. If the *number.of.digits* parameter to *get.first.significant* (Process 10.18) is initially the number of digits to come, each time round the loop it is the number left to read plus one for the cached *digit*; at the end these are the values required for *text.size* and *first*. The loop ensures the return of a count of one and the character '0', respectively, in the case of a stream representing zero.

The decimal numerals are preceded by their sign which must be input from *uncooked*. This sign will eventually be printed if it is minus, or if it is explicitly requested by *plus* or *blank* flags. The integer format must also ensure that no significant figures are discarded by the requested precision.

```
-- signed numeral
SEQ
  uncooked ? sign.char
  signed := (sign.char = '-') OR plus OR blank
  IF
    signed AND blank AND (sign.char = '+')
      sign.char := '*s'  -- replace '+' by space
    otherwise
      SKIP
  text.size := raw.size - 1  -- sign dealt with already
  get.first.significant(uncooked, text.size, first)
  IF
    format.type = 'd'
      field[precision] := max(text.size, field[precision])
    format.type <> 'd'
      SKIP
```

The code for the unsigned hexadecimal case simply replaces the sign manipulation by an assignment of FALSE to *signed*, and again adjusts the precision.

The third phase of *cook.output* uses the accumulated information to produce output on *cooked*. The precision now represents how many ordinary characters (excluding extras such as sign and decimal point) are to be displayed. Comparing this with the number of significant characters available determines the requisite number of padding zeros to insert or characters to discard according as the precision is greater or less than that number, and the number of characters to copy from *uncooked* to *cooked*; comparing with the field width gives the number of spaces needed to pad out the result. The necessary calculations are performed by *set.padding* (Process 10.19).

Process 10.19

```
PROC set.padding(VAL []INT field, VAL BOOL signed,
                 VAL INT significant.chars,
                 INT pad.zeros, pad.spaces, wanted, unwanted )
  VAL INT total.width IS field[width] :
  VAL INT displayed IS field[precision] :
  SEQ
    VAL INT discrepancy IS displayed - significant.chars :
    IF
      discrepancy >= 0  -- not enough uncooked text
        pad.zeros, wanted, unwanted :=
                   discrepancy, significant.chars, 0
      discrepancy <= 0  -- too much
        pad.zeros, wanted, unwanted :=
                   0, displayed, -discrepancy
    pad.spaces := total.width - displayed
    IF
      signed
        pad.spaces := max(0, pad.spaces - 1)
      NOT signed
        pad.spaces := max(0, pad.spaces)
  :
```

Notice that space is reserved for a sign character when one is required. The final IF in Process 10.19 could have been collapsed into a single line: since INT TRUE is one, whereas INT FALSE yields zero, the conditional pair of assignments are entirely equivalent to

```
pad.spaces := max(0, pad.spaces - (INT signed))
```

but the amount of explanation required by this coding would have more than made up the four lines saved by using it!

It now remains only to transmit the various batches of characters in the correct order. For all except the approximate real formats, these are a selection from the same sequence: right-justifying spaces; sign; leading zeros; characters from *uncooked*; and left-justifying spaces. Of course, not all of these will be present in displaying a single item; the spaces can only appear at one end, that determined by the *left.justify* flag. A Boolean never has a sign or leading zeros, but even a decimal numeral by default requires only the significant characters, if it is non-negative.

Rather than producing the optional material by a sequence of conditionals of the form

```
IF
  need.this.batch
    ... send this batch along cooked
  NOT need.this.batch
    SKIP
```

it is far neater to observe that each of the optional batches consists of a
known number of a fixed character, and so abstract Process 10.20.

Process 10.20

```
PROC conditionally.repeat(VAL BOOL condition,
                         VAL INT count, VAL BYTE char,
                         CHAN OF BYTE output           )
  IF
    condition
      SEQ i = 1 FOR count
        output ! char
    NOT condition
      SKIP
:
```

The significant characters of the raw output must be copied, forcing
letters to be capitals if the format character was itself one. This can be
encapsulated in Process 10.21.

Process 10.21

```
PROC copy.translating(VAL BOOL change, CHAN OF BYTE source,
                      VAL INT count, VAL BYTE first,
                      CHAN OF BYTE sink                    )
  -- send first, then count-1 bytes from source along sink
  BYTE char :
  IF
    change       -- letters must be made capital
      SEQ
        sink ! upper.case(first)
        SEQ i = 2 FOR count - 1
          SEQ
            source ? char
            sink ! upper.case(char)
    NOT change   -- send unchanged
      SEQ
        sink ! first
        SEQ i = 2 FOR count - 1
          SEQ
            source ? char
            sink ! char
:
```

Finally, if the output sequence is truncated by the specified precision there remain characters unread from *uncooked*. These must be thrown away by Process 10.22.

Process 10.22

```
PROC discard.input(CHAN OF BYTE input, VAL INT unwanted)
  SEQ i = 0 FOR unwanted
    BYTE discard :
    input ? discard
:
```

These procedures fit together as follows in the common case of the third phase of Process 10.16:

```
-- straightforward cases
SEQ
  set.padding(field, signed, text.size,
                    zero.pad, space.pad, copy, truncate )
  conditionally.repeat(right, space.pad, '*s', cooked)
  conditionally.repeat(signed, 1, sign.char, cooked)
  conditionally.repeat(TRUE, zero.pad, '0', cooked)
  copy.translating(upper, uncooked, copy, first, cooked)
  discard.input(uncooked, truncate)
  conditionally.repeat(left, space.pad, '*s', cooked)
```

Again, the two remaining cases are quite similar, although more complex; the same component processes are used, but the exponent and decimal point come into the space calculations. The complete listings can be found in the appendix (page 250).

That more or less concludes the development of *write.formatted*. One or two loose ends remain to be tied up: the DATA.ITEM protocol includes a variant for strings, but this routine makes no provision for them. There is a reason for this; one of the design criteria of this suite has been that it should operate individually on the characters of the stream representing the objects to be displayed, with an absolute minimum of buffering. The only occam 2 protocol (as opposed to any higher-level protocol which the programmer may build out of sequences of communications) which allows the transfer of a message of undetermined length as one of the variants of a discriminated protocol is a counted-array protocol like that used in the *data.string* case above. But the target of a counted-array input must itself be an array, and so a buffer must be declared somewhere. Moreover, there is no means of specifying as part of the protocol the size of the largest segment that may be sent, so an arbitrarily large buffer is required.

It would not be particularly difficult to add a clause to *raw.output* to accept a string into a local buffer, of some size declared to be 'big enough' by arbitrary fiat. The size of the string could be passed over *info*, and then each byte in turn along *uncooked*, to be treated in the established way by *cook.output*, as the Boolean strings are. This would of course fail, irremediably, if a user process tried to send a string that was 'too big'.

An alternative, which would give full flexibility to the caller of such a 'library' routine, at the expense of increasing the complexity of the interface, would be to require a buffer to be passed as one of the arguments to *write.formatted*, and for this ultimately to be passed to *raw.output*. It would then be the user's responsibility to ensure that enough space was reserved for the largest string that might be sent. Indeed, one can always transform something of the form

```
PROC uses.buffer(...)                    PROC needs.buffer([]BYTE buf, ...)
  [large.fixed]BYTE buf :
                                           ...
                                           :
  ...
                                 into  ...
  :
                                         [just.right]BYTE user.buf :
  ...                                     needs.buffer(user.buf, ...)

  uses.buffer(...)
                                           ...
  ...
```

or *vice versa*, depending on the particular relative weights attached to these two concerns.

Output into buffers

There are other circumstances, apart from counted-array protocols, where buffering is required: one is where output from two sources is to be combined into packets to be sent down a channel with a sequential protocol. Here, because there must be a single output process for each packet, even though the number and size of the items is fixed they must be stored and then retransmitted.

This buffering of, for instance, the digits representing a number can be done by a process executed in parallel with an instance of *write.formatted*; but packing digits into a fixed-size buffer is a task which does not require the full flexibility of that routine. It can be done more simply by a process like *make.decimal.string.int* (Process 10.23). If there is no room for all the digits, or for any minus sign required by a negative number, the buffer is filled with *length* asterisk characters. As always, other error indications would have been possible; but the 'field width' for this translation is given implicitly by the size of *buffer*, and to exceed it really is an error.

Process 10.23

```
PROC make.decimal.string.int([]BYTE buffer, VAL INT number)
  CHAN OF BYTE internal :
  PAR
    write.decimal.int(internal, number)
    BYTE sign, digit :
    INT size :
    VAL INT length IS SIZE buffer :
    SEQ
      internal ? sign
      size := decimal.raw - 1  -- sign already read
      get.first.significant(internal, size, digit)
      IF
        (size < length) OR ((size = length) AND (sign = '+'))
          -- put blanks, sign, and digits in correct place
          VAL INT spaces IS length - size :
          SEQ
            SEQ i = 0 FOR spaces
              buffer[i] := '*s'
            CASE sign
              '-'
                buffer[spaces - 1] := sign  -- there is room
              '+'
                SKIP
            buffer[spaces] := digit
            SEQ i = spaces + 1 FOR size - 1 -- remaining digits
              internal ? buffer[i]
        (size > length) OR ((size = length) AND (sign = '-'))
          -- too large to fit, so fill with '*' characters
          SEQ
            SEQ i = 0 FOR length
              buffer[i] := '**'
            discard.input(internal, size - 1)  -- discard digits
  :
```

Having a buffer available in fact makes the translation of a number
into a sequence of bytes simpler even than this last example, were we starting
from scratch without a battery of components to re-use. You might want
to try coding *make.decimal.string.int* directly, remembering that a buffer,
unlike a channel, can be filled in reverse order.

11

Parallel matrix multiplication

In systems which manipulate and display geometrical data, one of the common routine tasks is the application of linear transformations to the data. A system containing a representation of a three-dimensional object may need to rotate or displace that representation so as to select a point of view from which to project a two-dimensional picture of the object onto the plane of a terminal screen, or a plotter. If the positions of the parts of the object are represented by a vector of Cartesian co-ordinates, encoded as floating-point numbers, then these rotations and displacements can be achieved by matrix multiplication and vector addition. For each point $\mathbf{u}$, with co-ordinates $\langle u_0, u_1, u_2 \rangle$, it is necessary to calculate the corresponding vector $\mathbf{v}$ of transformed co-ordinates $\langle v_0, v_1, v_2 \rangle$ given by

$$v_i = \sum_{j=0}^{2} a_{ij} u_j + k_i$$

This requires nine multiplications and nine additions for each point in the representation of the object.

If the transformation is being applied once to an object with a view to printing an image on a slow, hard copy device such as a pen plotter, then the time taken to do the transformation is probably not important, and it does not matter much how the matrix multiplication is organized. On the other hand, if the image is being displayed on a graphics screen and the observer is allowed to change his point of view from the console, then speed is important. Ideally, the transformation should be applied to every relevant point of the object as the position of that point is required for refreshing the display, so that the observer sees the effect of a change in the transformation as soon as possible.

If there are of the order of a thousand points in the representation of the image, then this means something of the order of a hundred thousand matrix multiplications in a second. For practical purposes, this requires that

134

special hardware be dedicated to performing the matrix multiplications on a stream of co-ordinates on its way to the display. In such an arrangement, the time taken to perform the nine individual multiplications will dominate the time taken by all of the communications and additions involved. There is therefore an advantage in arranging that as many as possible of the multiplications can happen at once.

Figure 11.1 shows a natural configuration of processors to perform this task: a square array, mimicking the matrix a, one processor being responsible for each element of the matrix, and performing the multiplication by that element. Successive values of each co-ordinate of the vector **u** are poured

Figure 11.1   Design layout for the matrix multiplier

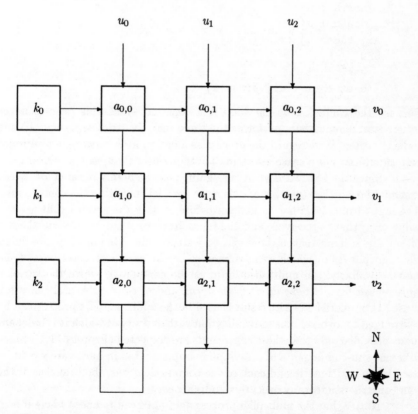

into the array from the top, passing down along the north-to-south channels, and successive values of the transformed co-ordinates of **v** emerge from the west-to-east channels at the right of the array. In this diagram, each processor is labelled with the parameter for which it takes responsibility. For simplicity, the transformation is assumed to be constant: a mechanism for changing the parameter values might involve a further array of channels at right angles to the plane of the array of processes. These would connect each relevant processor to a controlling process.

Each multiplier cell has three tasks to perform during each complete matrix multiplication: getting the next co-ordinate u_j from its northern neighbour and passing it on to its southern neighbour; performing its own multiplication; getting a partial sum from its western neighbour, adding its own contribution and passing the sum on to the east. These tasks might be performed sequentially:

```
REAL32 uj, aij.times.uj, vi :
WHILE TRUE
  SEQ
    SEQ
      north ? uj
      south ! uj
      aij.times.uj := aij * uj
    SEQ
      west ? vi
      east ! vi + aij.times.uj
```

Because the condition on the loop is a constant TRUE, this process never terminates; it repeatedly performs the three tasks in strict sequence. This is to be expected, if we regard the process as a design for hardware; a multiplier chip should no more cease operation autonomously than, say, an and-gate.

Since the hardware we are designing is to be highly parallel for speed, it should be worth extracting a little more parallelism within the components. The input from *north* has to happen before each of the actions that use the value of *uj* that is received, and the input from *west* has to precede the use of *vi*. There is no reason, however, to wait for the value of *vi* before doing the multiplication (which was assumed to be the most expensive part of the task). Similarly, the multiplication must be completed before the variable *uj* is reused for the next input from *north*, and of course the multiplication must be complete before its result is used in the addition. The process can be rearranged to 'overlap' the multiplication with activity of which it is independent, provided only that these constraints are respected (Process 11.1). Since different sub-components of a *multiplier* implemented in hardware would be used by the arithmetic and each of the communications, the branches of the PAR constructs naturally execute simultaneously.

Notice that the multiplier process does not need to know where it is in the array – it is independent of i and of j. This means that an implementation in hardware could use nine identical circuits.

In order to complete the matrix multiplier, a source of the k_i offset values is needed along the western border (Process 11.2) – again, for simplicity, we take these to be constant – and a sink must be provided at the southern end of each column of multipliers to receive the redundant u_j from

Process 11.1

```
PROC multiplier(VAL REAL32 aij,
                CHAN OF REAL32 north, south, west, east )
  REAL32 uj, aij.times.uj, vi :
  SEQ
    north ? uj
    WHILE TRUE
      SEQ
        PAR
          south ! uj
          aij.times.uj := aij * uj
          west ? vi
        PAR
          east ! vi + aij.times.uj
          north ? uj
:
```

Process 11.2

```
PROC offset(VAL REAL32 ki, CHAN  OF REAL32 east)
  WHILE TRUE
    east ! ki
:
```

Process 11.3

```
PROC sink(CHAN OF REAL32 north)
  WHILE TRUE
    REAL32 discard :
    north ? discard
:
```

the southernmost multiplier processes (Process 11.3). Although the *sink* does nothing with the values received, its input actions are necessary so that the corresponding output can happen in its neighbouring *multiplier*. A row of *sink* processes yields a simpler solution than one which involves two kinds of multiplier process, one for the north of the array, and another for the southernmost row.

Connecting these components to form the matrix multiplier is a matter of using CHAN arrays, suitably indexed. Two arrays are used, one for north-to-south traffic and one for west-to-east. As channel arrays can be two-dimensional, one obvious solution to the indexing would be to have the process handling a_{ij} served by input channels subscripted first by i and then by j, and output channels with the appropriate index incremented by one. This has the disadvantage that each one-dimensional sub-array of the west-to-east channel array comprises the four channels that carry some particular k_i through, accumulating terms, until it emerges as v_i; thus it is a collection of channels which are used sequentially, as far as any particular calculation is concerned, and it is not useful to be able to refer to it as a whole. If, however, the order of the subscripts to this array is reversed, each one-dimensional sub-array carries all the results at some point in the calculation, and in particular the easternmost carries the final answers. The preferred solution is therefore that of Figure 11.2, and so the channels connected to a typical multiplier process are as shown in Figure 11.3, while the matrix a naturally corresponds to the elements of an **occam 2** two-dimensional array.

Figure 11.2 Channel indices for the matrix multiplier

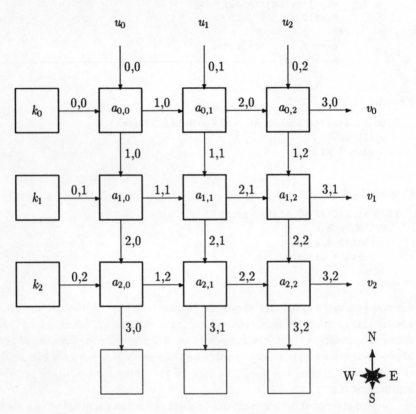

The whole multiplier is thus described by Process 11.4. It is the task of the *produce.u* process to output the three co-ordinates of successive values of **u** in parallel, and that of the *consume.v* process to input the three transformed co-ordinates of successive values of **v**.

Having supplied suitable definitions of the two processes *produce.u* and *consume.v*, this program can be run with any **occam 2** implementation as a simulation of the parallel matrix multiplier hardware. Of course, if it is executed on a single-processor computer, then it will be very much slower than a simpler sequential program, because of the additional work

Figure 11.3 A typical multiplier cell

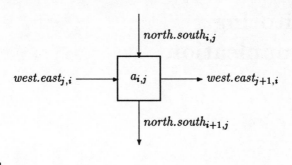

Process 11.4

```
VAL INT n IS 3 :
VAL [n][n]REAL32 a IS
          ... values of the matrix :
VAL [n]REAL32 k IS
          ... values of the offsets :

[n+1][n]CHAN OF REAL32 north.south, west.east :
PAR
  produce.u(north.south[0]) -- producer of co-ordinates u[j]

  PAR                       -- the matrix multiplier
    PAR i = 0 FOR n
      offset(k[i], west.east[0][i])
    PAR i = 0 FOR n
      PAR j = 0 FOR n
        multiplier(a[i][j],
                   north.south[i][j], north.south[i+1][j],
                   west.east  [j][i], west.east  [j+1][i] )
    PAR j = 0 FOR n
      sink(north.south[n][j])

  consume.v(west.east[n])   -- consumer of co-ordinates v[i]
```

in communicating and scheduling. On the special hardware for which it is designed, however, it will be very much faster. The longest data path from input to output is that traversed by u_0 on the way to contributing to v_2. This path involves six communications, three additions, and a single multiplication, all of which must happen in sequence. The program is designed on the assumption that the time taken for the multiplication would dominate all others, under which assumption it would be almost nine times faster than a sequential implementation.

The matrix multiplier example appears in essentially this form as an example in [7].

12

Monitoring communication

Sorting is a candidate problem for parallel solution because many algorithms have an element of divide-and-conquer. That means the task is carried out by dividing it into some number of smaller, simpler tasks each of which is repeatedly divided until only trivial tasks remain. Such a strategy rapidly discovers independent parts of the original problem which can be tackled concurrently.

This chapter describes a tree-shaped parallel sorting program, and a way of observing it whilst it is running. No claims are made for the sorting algorithm used, beyond its simplicity, because the real subject is how to observe a parallel program in operation. With very small changes to the sorting program itself, its activity can be displayed on a VDU screen, turning the program into a simulator of its own behaviour.

The example: a sorter

The program developed here will work equally well *mutatis mutandis* for sorting a collection of any type of object which has a less-than relation computable on it. In occam 2 any particular coding of the program can operate on only one data type; for definiteness and simplicity the program in this chapter deals with INT data with the ordinary comparison operations. The program consists of a number of simple processes linked together in a tree-shaped structure. As in the case of the matrix multiplier, no process need ever know where it is in the tree. There will be only two types of process: leaves, and internal nodes. Each process is also independent of the size of the problem, and need never store more than two values and some flags, no matter how many values are being sorted. Any particular tree will sort collections which are no larger than some fixed size; a bigger problem demands a bigger tree, but the components are unchanged.

The strategy is to distribute the numbers upwards from the root of

140

the tree, until they are spread out, at most one to each leaf. Each process is then responsible for sending back to its parent the sequence of numbers which it has received, but sorted into ascending order. For a leaf, the task is simple, since its one number, if it has one, already constitutes a sequence in ascending order. Each internal node, relying on the fact that the sub-sequences which it will receive from its children will be sorted, merges two ascending sequences to generate its output sequence.

The number of data items that must be accepted by a node depends on the position of the node in the tree, and as this is not known to the process an indication of the end of the data stream must be communicated to it. A protocol for just such an indefinitely long sequence of integers was suggested in Chapter 8:

```
PROTOCOL INT.STREAM
  CASE
    another.int; INT
    no.more.ints
:
```

Each leaf process needs two-way communication with its parent,

```
PROC leaf(CHAN OF INT.STREAM from.parent, to.parent)
  ...
:
```

and each internal node needs six channels, two to provide two-way communication with its parent, and two each to and from each of its children:

```
PROC fork(CHAN OF INT.STREAM from.parent, to.parent,
                            from.left.child,
                            to.left.child,
                            from.right.child,
                            to.right.child          )
  ...
:
```

The root of the tree has both to manage its children and to interact with the outside world; we may separate these concerns by supplying one process which behaves as an internal node, and a virtual root process which takes the place of the parent of the root

```
PROC driver(CHAN OF INT.STREAM up.to.tree, down.from.tree)
  ...
:
```

and acts as a driver to control the activity of the tree.

To connect these processes, they have to be indexed, so as to correspond to arrays of channels. For simplicity, let us assume we want to be able to sort collections of size up to some power of two, and so program a complete balanced tree of depth *depth.of.tree*. Although any tree can be drawn in two dimensions, this does not map comfortably onto a two-dimensional array; there are exponentially, not quadratically, many nodes compared with the depth of the tree. The desired structure can be built within linear arrays, effectively using array indices in the place of the pointers of a language like PASCAL – a method easily extended to model any tree. First define

```
VAL INT number.of.leaves    IS 1 << depth.of.tree :
VAL INT number.of.forks     IS number.of.leaves - 1 :
VAL INT number.of.processes IS
                  number.of.forks + number.of.leaves :
VAL INT number.of.channels  IS number.of.processes :
```

then, numbering the processes breadth-first, upwards from the root

```
VAL INT root      IS 0 :
VAL INT first.fork IS root :
VAL INT first.leaf IS first.fork + number.of.forks :
```

the children of the internal node process i are indexed $2i + 1$ and $2i + 2$; Figure 12.1 shows the enumeration of a particular size of tree.

Figure 12.1　Enumeration of the process tree, *depth.of.tree* = 3

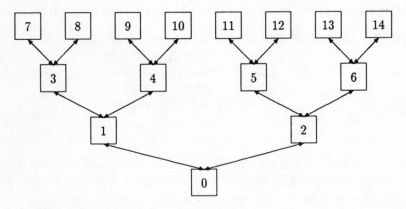

If channels indexed i are used to connect process i to its parent, these same formulae will give the indices of the channels to and from the children of internal node process i, so the program fits together as Process 12.1. Notice that the channels passed to a *fork* as *to.left.child* and *to.right.child* are consecutive elements of the *up* array, and similarly the *from.—.child* are consecutive in *down*. Since the *fork* process will deal with its children quite

Process 12.1

```
[number.of.channels]CHAN OF INT.STREAM up, down :
PAR
  driver(up[root], down[root])
  PAR i = first.fork FOR number.of.forks
    VAL INT left  IS (2 * i) + 1 :
    VAL INT right IS (2 * i) + 2 :
    fork(up[i], down[i],
         down[left], up[left],
         down[right], up[right] )
  PAR i = first.leaf FOR number.of.leaves
    leaf(up[i], down[i])
```

symmetrically, it will pay to exploit this fact by passing those two-element segments sliced from the whole, rather than the individual channels, for communication with the children; for this will allow FOR loops which range over the children.

This decision means that the interface to the *fork* process must be changed, and its arguments must now be specified as

```
PROC fork(CHAN OF INT.STREAM from.parent, to.parent,
          [2]CHAN OF INT.STREAM from.children, to.children )
  ...
:
```

and with the corresponding call the program becomes Process 12.2.

Process 12.2

```
[number.of.channels]CHAN OF INT.STREAM up, down :
PAR
  driver(up[root], down[root])
  PAR i = first.fork FOR number.of.forks
    VAL INT first.born IS (2 * i) + 1 :
    fork(up[i], down[i],
         [down FROM first.born FOR 2],
         [up   FROM first.born FOR 2] )
  PAR i = first.leaf FOR number.of.leaves
    leaf(up[i], down[i])
```

Components of the sorter

There are two phases of activity in the tree: first the sequence of numbers is distributed; then sorted sequences are gathered and merged. Each component process passes through the same two phases, so the *fork* procedure can be decomposed into a sequence of these two phases, as in Process 12.3.

Process 12.3

```
PROC fork(CHAN OF INT.STREAM from.parent, to.parent,
          [2]CHAN OF INT.STREAM from.children, to.children )
  SEQ
    fork.distribute(from.parent, to.children)
    fork.gather(to.parent, from.children)
:
```

During the distribution phase, each internal node receives a sequence of numbers from its parent. The simplest way of distributing the sequence amongst the children, without foreknowledge of its length, is to send one-for-left, one-for-right, alternately (Process 12.4). Notice that the termination signal is eventually broadcast to the children, whether the distributing process has zero, one or more values to share out.

Process 12.4

```
PROC fork.distribute(CHAN OF INT.STREAM from.parent,
                     [2]CHAN OF INT.STREAM to.children )
  VAL INT left IS 0 :
  VAL INT right IS 1 :
  INT child :
  BOOL more :
  SEQ
    child, more := left, TRUE
    WHILE more
      from.parent ? CASE
        INT number :
        another.int; number
          SEQ
            to.children[child] ! another.int; number
            child := child >< (left >< right)
        no.more.ints
          more := FALSE
    PAR child = left FOR 2
      to.children[child] ! no.more.ints
:
```

Since the component processes are to serve in an arbitrarily large tree, they should not count the numbers as they pass upwards. This means that during the merging phase there are again sequences of unknown length to be read, and it is correct to use the same protocol.

To preserve the ordering during the merge, numbers must be compared, and this requires that each process have at least two registers holding numbers. Since each child sends its sequence in ascending order, the head of each sequence is the minimum of those to come. The merging

Process 12.5

```
PROC fork.gather(CHAN OF INT.STREAM to.parent,
                 [2]CHAN OF INT.STREAM from.children )
  VAL INT left IS 0 :
  VAL INT right IS 1 :
  [2]BOOL more :
  [2]INT minimum :
  SEQ

    PAR child = left FOR 2
      from.children[child] ? CASE
        another.int; minimum[child]
          more[child] := TRUE
        no.more.ints
          more[child] := FALSE

    WHILE more[left] OR more[right]
      IF child = left FOR 2
        VAL INT other IS child >< (left >< right) :
        more[child] AND
                ((NOT more[other]) OR
                 (minimum[child] <= minimum[other]))
          SEQ
            to.parent ! another.int; minimum[child]
            from.children[child] ? CASE
              another.int; minimum[child]
                SKIP
              no.more.ints
                more[child] := FALSE

    to.parent ! no.more.ints
  :
```

process compares the heads, passes on the smaller, and draws one more value
from the selected sequence, continuing until the sequences are exhausted
(Process 12.5). If there are less than *number.of.leaves* values to sort then
one or more children of some *fork* will be sorting an empty sequence, so both
cases of the initial discriminated input may arise.

The leaf process (Process 12.6) must be designed to simulate the behaviour of an internal node that handles a sequence of at most one number.

Finally, the driver process must generate and absorb sequences of
numbers, stuffing and stripping the protocol. The sections of code missing
from Process 12.7 control the behaviour of the whole program. They might,
for example, read numbers from the terminal keyboard, and write them back,
in ascending order, to the terminal screen.

That completes the sorting program which, whilst it may look over-
complex for a single processor implementation, would look better on an array

Process 12.6

```
PROC leaf(CHAN OF INT.STREAM from.parent, to.parent)
  SEQ
    from.parent ? CASE
      INT number :
      another.int; number
        SEQ
          from.parent ? CASE no.more.ints
          to.parent ! another.int; number
      no.more.ints
        SKIP
    to.parent ! no.more.ints
  :
```

Process 12.7

```
PROC driver(CHAN OF INT.STREAM up.to.tree, down.from.tree)
  SEQ
    BOOL more.output :
    INT i :
    SEQ
      i := 0
      ... initialize more.output
      WHILE (i < number.of.leaves) AND more.output
        INT number :
        SEQ
          ... think of a number, and whether any more
          up.to.tree ! another.int; number
          i := i + 1
      up.to.tree ! no.more.ints
    BOOL more.input :
    SEQ
      more.input := TRUE
      WHILE more.input
        down.from.tree ? CASE
          INT number :
          another.int; number
            ... do something with the number
          no.more.ints
            more.input := FALSE
  :
```

of *number.of.processes* simple processors. Notice, particularly, that once the numbers have started to emerge from the tree in ascending order, each is available only one comparison time after its predecessor. This advantage would be more obvious were the sorter managing more complex data, where the comparison time might be very large.

Monitoring strategy

The program as it stands can be run on a single processor to simulate the
activity of the ideal multi-processor implementation. By writing the missing
code in the driver, you could observe numbers going into and coming out of
the tree, checking that the program sorts particular sequences of numbers.
That tells you nothing about what goes on inside the tree. To get a better
idea of *how* the program sorts sequences you might also want to be able to
watch the activity in the branches of the tree.

By analogy with the testing of electronic circuits, the idea is to probe
the components of the circuit, rather than just watching the signals that
pass into and out of the terminals. There are two techniques: breaking
connections to measure the current flowing through them corresponds to
tapping the channels to watch the traffic; attaching probes to measure the
potential at various points in a circuit corresponds to noting the state in each
process.

In order to observe the traffic on a channel, a process must be added
which duplicates the traffic along a monitoring channel. Suppose for instance
that the data stream passing along a channel between a *producer* and a
consumer process

```
CHAN OF INT channel :
PAR
  producer(channel)
  consumer(channel)
```

is to be sampled. Then coding a *duplicate* process after the fashion of
Process 12.8 allows a copy of the communications to be passed on to a third
party, a process *monitor*, say

```
VAL INT collect IS 0 :
VAL INT deliver IS 1 :
[2]CHAN OF INT channel :
CHAN OF INT test.data :
PAR
  producer(channel[collect])
  duplicate(channel[collect], channel[deliver], test.data)
  consumer(channel[deliver])
  monitor(test.data)
```

Of course, the observation is not perfect: it may affect the behaviour of the
program. First of all, the *duplicate* process acts as an additional buffer in the
data stream. In this example it cannot matter, but were there some other
communication, possibly mediated by another process, between the *producer*
and *consumer*, it might matter that the output from the *producer* could

Process 12.8

```
PROC duplicate(CHAN OF INT source, sink, copy)
  WHILE TRUE
    INT datum :
    SEQ
      source ? datum
      PAR
        copy ! datum
        sink ! datum
  :
```

proceed, despite the corresponding demand not being made in the *consumer*. Secondly, the *duplicate* process, as written, does not terminate, so unless it is used to observe an infinite data stream, the program will eventually become deadlocked, even had it previously terminated correctly.

In both of these ways you must be careful to design monitoring code that does not interfere excessively with the activity being observed. In general, it is necessary for the behaviour of the monitoring processes to depend on the data passing through them, and this in-stream technique should be avoided if there are many parallel data paths between pairs of processes in the program being observed. Also, whatever care is taken, the performance of the program is almost certain to change; so one cannot hope to successfully monitor time-dependent behaviours.

The other form of observation, making internal state visible, requires additional code inserted into the processes being observed. Just as observing traffic involves adding new output processes in parallel with the observed program, so observing state requires that new output processes be set in sequence with the code being observed.

```
PROC p(...)              PROC p(..., CHAN OF INT test.data)
  INT x :                  INT x :
  SEQ                      SEQ
    ...                      ...
                             SEQ
    x := e                     x := e
             becomes           test.data ! x
    ...                        ...
                             SEQ
    c ? x                      c ? x
                               test.data ! x
    ...                        ...
  :                        :
```

In order to observe the changing value of a variable each assignment to that variable should be followed by an output process signalling the change on a channel which passes out to the monitoring code. Again, the observation is invasive: you must be aware that the observed process may be delayed by executing the new output processes.

In the example of the parallel sorter, we will use both types of monitoring: the explanation of the behaviour of the merging is in terms of the sequences of values passing along channels, so the traffic along the channels will be watched; the leaves are used as storage locations, so it is appropriate to observe their state. The result of adding this monitoring code is a number of channels emerging from the tree. Messages from each will be treated similarly: to write a number to, or to remove it from, a position on the screen which will represent the place in the program which is being watched. Since changes to the screen must be made in sequence, it is appropriate to multiplex the test data from the tree, and process each new test signal in sequence.

In order to get around the problem of termination, and to show the delivery as well as the collection of values sent along tapped channels, we will adopt a slightly more complex scheme. There are three types of message to be sent along the monitoring channels: messages indicating the arrival of a number, messages indicating the departure of a number, and a final termination message. These will conform to the protocol

```
PROTOCOL DISPLAY.STREAM
  CASE
    display.number; INT
    display.empty
    display.stop
:
```

This protocol will serve equally for the intrusive probes in the leaves. The output of the multiplexer will also carry the same kinds of message, but the data must be accompanied by a note of which probe it comes from:

```
PROTOCOL MULTIPLEX.STREAM
  CASE
    multiplex.number; INT; INT   -- probe; data
    multiplex.empty; INT         -- probe
    multiplex.stop               -- all probes stopped
:
```

Putting this all together leads to the changed program structure of Process 12.9. Each *monitor* process copies data from its *collect* channels to its *deliver* channels, duplicating the activity along the corresponding *probe*. Every leaf is modified to indicate its state with similar messages. All of these messages are multiplexed onto a single channel, and then translated into sequences of instructions to display the changing state of the program on the terminal screen.

Process 12.9

```
VAL INT collect IS 0 :
VAL INT deliver IS 1 :
VAL INT number.of.probes IS number.of.channels+number.of.leaves :
VAL INT first.channel.probe IS 0 :
VAL INT first.leaf.probe   IS number.of.channels :

[2][number.of.channels]CHAN OF INT.STREAM up, down :
[number.of.probes]CHAN OF DISPLAY.STREAM probe :
CHAN OF MULTIPLEX.STREAM all.probes :
PAR
  driver(up[collect][root], down[deliver][root])
  PAR
    PAR i = first.fork FOR number.of.forks
      VAL INT first.born IS (2 * i) + 1 :
      fork(up[deliver][i], down[collect][i],
           [down[deliver] FROM first.born FOR 2],
           [up[collect] FROM first.born FOR 2]   )

    []CHAN OF DISPLAY.STREAM leaf.probe IS
         [probe FROM first.leaf.probe FOR number.of.leaves] :
    PAR i = first.leaf FOR number.of.leaves
      leaf(up[deliver][i], down[collect][i],
                               leaf.probe[i - first.leaf] )

    []CHAN OF DISPLAY.STREAM channel.probe IS
         [probe FROM first.channel.probe FOR number.of.channels] :
    PAR i = root FOR number.of.channels
      monitor(up[collect][i], down[collect][i],
                 up[deliver][i], down[deliver][i], channel.probe[i] )

  multiplex(probe, all.probes)
  display(all.probes, terminal.screen)
```

Component processes

The monitoring processes will guarantee that the communications on a *probe*
will be a sequence in which *display.number* and an accompanying number alternates with *display.empty*, the whole sequence ending in a single
display.stop. Sending an explicit termination signal insulates the monitoring
code from changes to the protocol operated in the sorter.

To start with the *leaf* process, all that is needed is to indicate the
arrival and departure of the stored number. There are three things which the
monitoring code must do: display a number arriving while the tree is filled;
clear the display when that number is unloaded; and indicate the end of the
leaf's activity. The modified *leaf* is implemented by Process 12.10. Notice
that if a *leaf* has no number to sort, because the input stream is smaller than

Process 12.10

```
PROC leaf(CHAN OF INT.STREAM from.parent, to.parent,
          CHAN OF DISPLAY.STREAM probe                 )
  SEQ
    from.parent ? CASE
      INT number :
      another.int; number
        SEQ
          probe ! display.number; number
          from.parent ? CASE no.more.ints
          to.parent ! another.int; number
          probe ! display.empty
      no.more.ints
        SKIP
    to.parent ! no.more.ints
    probe ! display.stop
  :
```

Process 12.11

```
PROC monitor(CHAN OF INT.STREAM up.collect, down.collect,
                                up.deliver, down.deliver,
             CHAN OF DISPLAY.STREAM probe                 )
  PROC copy.monitoring(CHAN OF INT.STREAM collector, deliverer,
                       CHAN OF DISPLAY.STREAM probe                 )
    BOOL more :
    SEQ
      more := TRUE
      WHILE more
        collector ? CASE
          INT number :
          another.int; number
            SEQ
              probe ! display.number; number
              deliverer ! another.int; number
              probe ! display.empty
          no.more.ints
            more := FALSE
      deliverer ! no.more.ints
    :
  SEQ
    copy.monitoring(up.collect, up.deliver, probe)
    copy.monitoring(down.collect, down.deliver, probe)
    probe ! display.stop
  :
```

the size of the tree, it nonetheless carries on the same conversation with its parent as do all children. The monitoring code abstracts away from this, and displays no transactions for such a process.

The *monitor* process must copy the sequences of numbers passing first up and then down the tree. The necessary monitoring code is just what you would need to record changes of state in this buffering process. The activity of the *monitor*, Process 12.11, falls into three stages: being a monitored buffer for a sequence of upward communications; being a monitored buffer for a sequence of communications returning downwards; and finally marking the end of the monitoring signals on its *probe*.

Each of the probes coming out of the sorter carries a sequence of display instructions, the last of which is a *display.stop*, so they can all be treated uniformly from now on. The *multiplex* process, Process 12.12, simply gathers together all of the probe signals, tagging them with the corresponding index number for later identification. Once a *display.stop* is received from a particular probe, no more signals are read from it, and the multiplexer terminates when all probes have been shut off.

Process 12.12

```
PROC multiplex([]CHAN OF DISPLAY.STREAM probe,
               CHAN OF MULTIPLEX.STREAM all.probes )
  INT active.probes :
  [number.of.probes]BOOL more.from :
  SEQ
    active.probes := number.of.probes
    SEQ i = 0 FOR number.of.probes
      more.from[i] := TRUE
    WHILE active.probes > 0
      ALT i = 0 FOR number.of.probes
        more.from[i] & probe[i] ? CASE
          INT number :
          display.number; number
            all.probes ! multiplex.number; i; number
          display.empty
            all.probes ! multiplex.empty; i
          display.stop
            active.probes, more.from[i] :=
                                  active.probes - 1, FALSE
    all.probes ! multiplex.stop
:
```

Managing the output from the simulation

It remains only to translate the stream of probe messages into a stream of terminal-screen control messages. The first thing to do is to translate the probe numbers into positions on the screen. This happens in two stages: first the numbers are translated into positions in a terminal-independent space; those positions and the data to display are then passed to a process which maps that space onto a particular type of terminal screen. So the *display* process decomposes as Process 12.13.

Process 12.13

```
PROC display(CHAN OF MULTIPLEX.STREAM source,
             CHAN OF BYTE sink          )
  CHAN OF TERMINAL.STREAM internal :
  PAR
    independent(source, internal)
    dependent(internal, sink)
  :
```

The terminal-independent space has right-handed co-ordinates, with the leaves evenly spread across the top, and the root at the middle of the bottom line, as in Figure 12.2.

Figure 12.2 The abstract screen layout

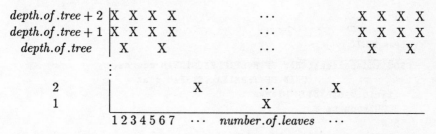

Messages from probes with indices less than *number.of.channels* are from probes within the tree, and those with higher indices are from the leaves. The top line, representing the states of the leaves, is clearly not a part of the pattern in the rest of the tree, so is dealt with differently.

For the internal probes, the simplest solution is to count up from the root. There are $2^{line} - 1$ probes represented on the bottom *line* lines of the display, so the line for a particular probe is the first for which its index lies below this number. The column is calculated by discounting the $2^{line-1} - 1$ probes displayed lower down and multiplying by a factor to account for the exponentially greater separation of nodes at greater depths. The *make.cartesian* function, Process 12.14, translates a channel probe index into an $\langle x, y \rangle$ pair satisfying

$$1 \leq x \leq ((2 \times number.of.channels) - 1)$$
$$1 \leq y \leq depth.of.tree + 1$$

and places leaf probes on the line above the leaves

$$1 \leq x \leq ((2 \times number.of.channels) - 1)$$
$$y = depth.of.tree + 2$$

each one immediately above the corresponding channel.

Process 12.14

```
INT, INT FUNCTION make.cartesian(VAL INT index)
  INT x, y :
  VALOF
    IF
      IF line = 1 FOR depth.of.tree + 1
        index < ((1 << line) - 1)
          VAL INT column IS index - ((1 << (line - 1)) - 1) :
          VAL INT spread IS number.of.leaves >> (line - 1) :
          x, y := ((2 * column) + 1) * spread, line
      index >= number.of.channels
        VAL INT column IS index - number.of.channels :
        x, y := (2 * column) + 1, depth.of.tree + 2
    RESULT x, y
:
```

Process 12.15

```
PROC independent(CHAN OF MULTIPLEX.STREAM source,
                 CHAN OF TERMINAL.STREAM sink   )
  [field.width]BYTE blanks :
  BOOL running :
  SEQ
    SEQ i = 0 FOR field.width
      blanks[i] := '*s'
    running := TRUE
    WHILE running
      source ? CASE
        INT index, number :
        multiplex.number; index; number
          INT x, y :
          [field.width]BYTE buffer :
          SEQ
            x, y := make.cartesian(index)
            make.decimal.string.int(buffer, number)
            sink ! terminal.item; x; y; buffer
        INT index :
        multiplex.empty; index
          INT x, y :
          SEQ
            x, y := make.cartesian(index)
            sink ! terminal.item; x; y; blanks
        multiplex.stop
          running := FALSE
    sink ! terminal.stop
:
```

The TERMINAL.STREAM protocol could be very similar to the others, indicating the presence (and value) or absence of a number; but in order to keep the terminal-dependent part of the translation as simple as possible the actual characters to display are generated here. If a number is present it must be turned into digits, otherwise blanks must be sent. All the numbers are to be written in a fixed-width field, and so the output from *independent* consists of a sequence of packets, each beginning with an ⟨x, y⟩ pair, followed by the *field.width* characters to be displayed there. Each packet is preceded by a *terminal.item* tag, and the whole sequence is terminated with a *terminal.stop*. So the protocol TERMINAL.STREAM is, in fact,

```
PROTOCOL TERMINAL.STREAM
  CASE
    terminal.item; INT; INT; [field.width]BYTE
    terminal.stop
:
```

and the terminal-independent process will then be Process 12.15.

Displaying the output on a screen

If the terminal has general cursor addressing, then the task is almost complete. For example, we will assume an ANSI standard terminal which can clear the screen, Process 12.16, and move the cursor around the screen, Process 12.17.

Process 12.16

```
PROC clear.screen(CHAN OF BYTE terminal)
  -- clear screen sequence for an ANSI terminal
  write.string(terminal, "*#1B[2J")
:
```

Process 12.17

```
PROC move.cursor(CHAN OF BYTE terminal, VAL INT x, y)
  -- left-handed co-ordinates, origin 0,0 at top left
  CHAN OF DATA.ITEM c :
  PAR
    write.formatted(terminal, "*#1B[%d;%dH", c)
    SEQ
      c ! data.int; y + 1
      c ! data.int; x + 1
:
```

The terminal-independent co-ordinate space has a size which depends only on the depth of the tree

```
VAL INT virtual.height IS depth.of.tree + 1 :
VAL INT virtual.width  IS (2 * number.of.leaves) - 1 :
```

but the terminal screen has a fixed size

```
VAL INT screen.height IS 24 :
VAL INT screen.width  IS 80 :
```

If the picture of the tree is to be fitted onto the screen, it must be scaled

```
VAL INT height.scale  IS
                   (screen.height - 1) / virtual.height :
VAL INT width.scale   IS
                   (screen.width - field.width) / virtual.width :
```

and translated into the left-handed co-ordinate system of the terminal. The necessary terminal-dependent part of the display process is Process 12.18.

Process 12.18

```
PROC dependent(CHAN OF TERMINAL.STREAM source,
               CHAN OF BYTE terminal           )
  -- terminal-dependent code for driving ANSI terminal
  BOOL more :
  SEQ
    clear.screen(terminal)
    more := TRUE
    WHILE more
      source ? CASE
        INT x, y :
        [field.width]BYTE buffer :
        terminal.item; x; y; buffer
          SEQ
            move.cursor(terminal, (x - 1)  * width.scale,
                (virtual.height - (y - 1)) * height.scale )
            write.string(terminal, buffer)
        terminal.stop
          more := FALSE
    move.cursor(terminal, 0, screen.height - 1)
  :
```

The division of work between *independent* and *dependent* is such that, if it is at all reasonable to draw such pictures on a particular terminal, the program can be modified to do so simply by writing the appropriate *dependent* process. Even should the terminal not have full cursor control, but only the ability to move the cursor in small steps, *dependent* can be made to keep track of the position of the cursor.

Driving the simulation

For the purpose of the simulator, a simple coding of the driver process invents a random sequence of numbers for input to the tree, and discards the sorted sequence which is returned by the tree.

A common way of generating an unpredictable sequence of numbers is to use a linear feedback shift register, Process 12.19, with an uncontrolled initial state. An arbitrary initial state can be obtained by reading the real-time clock. Since the state of the shift register can never change if it is zero, the time has its bottom bit set to guarantee a non-zero initial state.

Process 12.19

```
VAL INT mask IS BITNOT ((BITNOT 0) << 9) :

PROC shift(INT state)
  SEQ i = 1 FOR 9
    state := ((state << 1) /\ mask) \/
             (((state >> 4) >< (state >> 8)) /\ 1)
:
```

Process 12.20

```
PROC driver(CHAN OF INT.STREAM up.to.tree, down.from.tree)
  TIMER clock :
  SEQ
    INT event, number :
    SEQ
      clock ? event
      number :=  (event /\ mask) \/ 1
      SEQ i = 0 FOR number.of.leaves
        SEQ
          event := event PLUS second
          shift(number)
          up.to.tree ! another.int; number
          clock ? AFTER event
      up.to.tree ! no.more.ints
    INT event :
    SEQ
      clock ? event
      SEQ i = 0 FOR number.of.leaves
        SEQ
          event := event PLUS second
          INT discard :
          down.from.tree ? CASE another.int; discard
          clock ? AFTER event
      down.from.tree ? CASE no.more.ints
:
```

The *driver*, Process 12.20, can discard the result of the sort, because all the information has already been displayed as it passes out of the root process. This coding of the driver completely fills the tree with a known number of values, and removes the same number, so the inputs on *down.from.tree* are guaranteed to have the expected tag.

The driver pauses after injecting each number into the tree and after removing each number from the tree, so as to allow time to see what is happening. There is nothing scientific about the choice of a one second delay; it was adjusted to give an acceptable display on a particular implementation.

13

Conway's game of Life

Lest you be misled by the name, *Life* is neither a competitive game between several players, nor yet a solitaire game in which a player competes against the collusion between the rules and the roll of the dice. The game is more a simulation, in which the evolution of a system is fully determined by a set of rules.

To be precise, Life is played on an infinite square board: that means that there are a number of squares, or *cells*, each of which has four immediate neighbours and four diagonal neighbours, in the fashion of a chess board. That the board is infinite means simply that every cell in which you will be interested is one with a full complement of neighbours, so that you need never worry about what happens at the edges. There will be only a finite number of interesting cells to think about at any one time. Each cell may be in one of two states: occupied (*alive*) or unoccupied (*dead*), and only finitely many will be alive at any time.

The rules describe the succession of states of each cell in terms of earlier states of that cell and of its eight near neighbours. Each cell passes through a sequence of generations, with the state of the cell in the next generation being determined by its state in this generation, and by the number of cells adjacent to it which are alive in this generation. If a cell is currently alive, and if it has less than two live neighbours, it is deemed to die of loneliness, and will be dead in the next generation. A live cell with two or three neighbours alive in the same generation survives into the next generation, but if it has four or more contemporaries, it will be dead from overcrowding by the next generation. A dead cell with exactly three live neighbours in this generation will give birth and be alive in the next generation, otherwise it will remain barren.

Notice that the rules determine the state of the whole board in the next generation in terms of its state in the present generation. Moreover, the rules are expressed in purely local terms, and the property of Life that makes it interesting is that these local rules can control the evolution of global structures. A number of patterns of live cells are known to pass through cycles of growth and decline, some are known to grow without limit, whilst others die out.

Although the rules of evolution are simple, applying them to a pattern large enough to be interesting, for more than one or two generations, is a tedious business. Machine assistance makes it possible to watch the long-term development of substantial colonies, and Life was once a popular way of consuming otherwise unused machine cycles! More practically, a Life board is a particularly simple and symmetrical example of a systolic cellular array. These are studied by VLSI designers seeking algorithms with fast but simple implementations in highly parallel hardware. A systolic array is characterized by the achievement of global co-operation through many simultaneous calculations organized by local communications. Ideally, the components of the array are, like the cells of a Life board, all of a few basic types, have a small finite amount of state, and need never know where they are in the array.

The program described here is, like the parallel sorter of Chapter 12, a simulation in two parts: there is a plane of parallel processes in which the cells of a Life board are represented, one cell to a process; added to this is an essentially sequential mechanism for guiding and watching the evolution of the colony. Perhaps it is worth pointing out at the outset that the resulting program, run on a single processor, is far from the fastest way of playing Life. There are, for example, a number of optimizations that require each process to have a more global view of the state of the board, and naturally give rise to a sequential program. This program is here for two reasons: firstly as an intricate example of the interconnection of processes, showing how to separate this from the workings of the processes themselves; secondly, it is an example of a general method of adding global synchronization to a loosely coupled system in order to observe its behaviour.

The Life board

There is no problem in selecting a representation the board. Each cell of the board has a state, and is represented by a process which administers the variable in which that state is stored. There is no reason why each of these processes should not be identical. Each cell is distinguished only by the particular eight other cells which are close enough to influence its state in the next generation. The neighbours of a cell process are connected to it, each by a pair of channels along which to exchange information about states, one in each direction.

The first problem that arises is one of representing an infinite board on what must necessarily be a finite array of processes. As suggested earlier, the requirement of an infinite board is made so that the behaviour of a cell will not be influenced by its being at an edge of the board. Unless a colony grows without limit, or moves *en masse* in some direction, a finite board will do, since the evolution of a colony is unaffected by any amount of dead space around it.

One solution, and the one that is adopted here, is to take a finite sized board and wrap it around a torus, so that the cells on the top edge have neighbours on the bottom edge, and those on the right have neighbours on the left, as in Figure 13.1. There are now no edges about which to worry.

Figure 13.1   A toroidal board with circumference 3

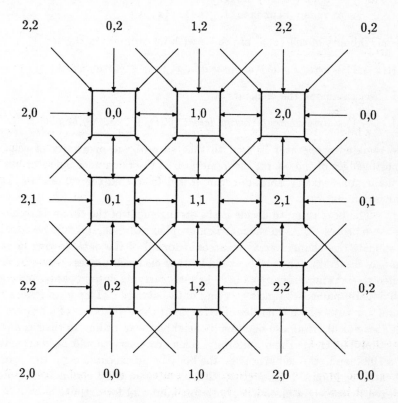

You can think of this toroidal board in either of two ways. Looking at it as a flat board with tricky edges, it correctly implements the rules of healthy living until one or more of the edge cells gives birth, from which point on it is possible for things to go wrong, with miraculous conceptions and unexplained deaths happening in ways not predicted by the rules. Another way of thinking about it is that the toroidal board behaves as if it were a fragment of a truly infinite flat board on which the real finite colony that you can see is repeated, in the fashion of a wallpaper pattern, at regular intervals in the horizontal and vertical directions. The boundary effects are now explicable, since they are the effects (predicted by the rules) of a neighbouring copy of the colony coming close enough to influence the visible part of the board.

To be more definite about the program, it consists of a rectangular array of cell processes in parallel

```
VAL INT array.width IS ... :
VAL INT array.height IS ... :


PAR x = 0 FOR array.width
  PAR y = 0 FOR array.height
    ... process representing cell (x, y)
```

The neighbours of cell $\langle x, y \rangle$ are those with an ordinate in the set

$$\{((x - 1) + array.width)\backslash array.width, \; x, \; (x + 1)\backslash array.width\}$$

and abscissa among the elements of

$$\{((y - 1) + array.height)\backslash array.height, \; y, \; (y + 1)\backslash array.height\}$$

The remainder operator is used to take care of the proximity of cells at opposite edges of the board; the numerator of the remainder operator has to be made non-negative, since in occam it is defined that the value of $(-1) \backslash n$ is always minus one.

The next thing to decide is the arrangement of the channels connecting these processes. As in the matrix multiplier example, it would be possible to allocate one channel array to account for all of the data flowing in each compass direction. The result would be that each cell process would be connected to eight individually named channels carrying data inwards, and eight individually named channels carrying data outwards. This is to ignore the symmetry with which the rules of living treat the neighbours of a process. A cell does not discriminate between its neighbours according to their compass direction, but treats them uniformly. This symmetry should be represented by a FOR loop in the cell processes, the body being executed eight times, once for each neighbour. That suggests that an array of eight channels is needed, indexed by the eight directions, both for input and for output.

However, since the channels need to be shared with a number of the other component processes, and it is not possible to produce a table of channels drawn from different sources, this can be achieved for only one type of communication. Each process may 'own' the channels on which it outputs, but it would then have to listen to those 'belonging' to the eight neighbours. A single large three-dimensional array, indexed by the x and y co-ordinates of the transmitting cell and by the eight directions, is ideal for allocating output channels; some arithmetic is required to determine which component of which sub-arrays are allocated to each process for input.

Consistent usage of shared arrays requires that this arithmetic selects distinct channels in each process. You should certainly be able to check this disjointness yourself, although it might be too tricky for a mechanical checker, a part of an occam 2 compiler. The identifiers involved are either constants (*array.width*, *array.height*) or will be the bound variables of constant-bounded FOR loops (*x*, *y* and the direction *d*), but a compiler which attempts to check the definition and the calls of *cell* independently of each other will almost certainly fail.

Rather than recalculate the indices of the neighbours in each direction each time, which would dominate the rest of the calculations involved, it is preferable to build them into tables *nx* and *ny* for each process, as in Process 13.1.

Process 13.1

```
VAL INT radius     IS 1 :   -- of the 'sphere of influence'
VAL INT diameter   IS (2 * radius) + 1 :
VAL INT neighbours IS (diameter * diameter) - 1 :

VAL INT number.of.cells IS array.height * array.width :
VAL INT number.of.links IS neighbours * number.of.cells :

PROC cell([][][]CHAN OF STATE link,
          VAL INT x, y, VAL []INT nx, ny )
  -- cell using link[x][y][d] for output
  --          and link[nx[d]][ny[d]][d] for input
  ...
:

[array.width][array.height][neighbours]CHAN OF STATE link :
PAR x = 0 FOR array.width
  PAR y = 0 FOR array.height
    VAL [neighbours]INT nx IS ... :
    VAL [neighbours]INT ny IS ... :
    cell(link, x, y, nx, ny)
```

The remaining question is which are the correct subscripts to use to select the incoming links. First numbers between 0 and *neighbours* − 1 must be assigned to the directions. The precise enumeration does not particularly matter; that adopted here is to number them clockwise from top-left.

Incoming links at ⟨*x*, *y*⟩ are, if looked at from the other end, the outgoing links from its neighbours. If the output of each cell is to be sent in direction *d* along a channel with final index *d*, then it is not the cell in direction *d* to which this cell must listen on the input channel with final index *d*; rather, as can be seen from Figure 13.2, it is the diametrically opposite cell. Indeed, precisely because the outgoing channel array $link_{x,y}$ will be treated uniformly by *cell*, it is really the selection of the incoming channels

Figure 13.2   The numbering of directions

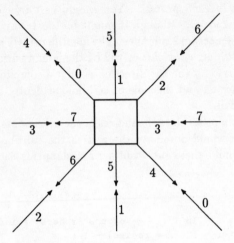

which fixes the meaning of the direction numbers.

Having calculated the indices of the adjacent rows and columns, the tabulation of *nx* and *ny* is really no more than reading the appropriate horizontal and vertical displacements for each *d* corresponding to the outer ring of arrows on the diagram. This gives us Process 13.2 as the body of the program.

Process 13.2

```
PAR x = 0 FOR array.width
  PAR y = 0 FOR array.height
    VAL INT left  IS ((x - 1) + array.width)  \ array.width :
    VAL INT right IS  (x + 1)                  \ array.width :
    VAL INT up    IS  (y + 1)                  \ array.height :
    VAL INT down  IS ((y - 1) + array.height) \ array.height :
    VAL [neighbours]INT nx IS
         [ right, x,    left, left, left, x,  right, right ] :
    VAL [neighbours]INT ny IS
         [ down, down, down, y,    up,   up, up,    y     ] :
    cell(link, x, y, nx, ny)
```

With the framework now fixed, the code of the *cell* process is quite simple. It records the state of the cell, whether it is dead or alive, and controls the evolution of the state between generations. Since the state has only two possible values, it may as well be modelled with a variable of type BOOL, using the following definitions to give Process 13.3:

```
PROTOCOL STATE IS BOOL :
VAL BOOL alive IS TRUE :
VAL BOOL dead IS NOT alive :
```

Process 13.3

```
PROC cell([][][]CHAN OF STATE link,
          VAL INT x, y, VAL []INT nx, ny )
  PROC broadcast.present.state([][][]CHAN OF STATE link,
                                VAL INT x, y, VAL BOOL state )
    ... tell neighbours about the state of this cell
  :
  PROC calculate.next.state([][][]CHAN OF STATE link,
                             VAL []INT nx, ny,
                             VAL BOOL state, BOOL next.state )
    ... evolve in keeping with the rules
  :
  BOOL state :
  SEQ
    ... set the state to some appropriate value
    WHILE TRUE
      BOOL next.state :
      SEQ
        PAR
          broadcast.present.state(link, x, y, state)
          calculate.next.state(link, nx, ny,
                                        state, next.state )
        state := next.state
:
```

The initial value given to the cell's *state* variable determines the type of colony being watched. A later section will describe an editor that allows the user to set an initial configuration from the keyboard.

In each generation, each *cell* must learn the state of each of its neighbours. There is a corresponding obligation on a *cell* to tell each of its neighbours about its own current state (Process 13.4).

Process 13.4

```
PROC broadcast.present.state([][][]CHAN OF STATE link,
                              VAL INT x, y, VAL BOOL state )
  PAR d = 0 FOR neighbours
    link[x][y][d] ! state
:
```

To calculate its next state, the *cell* counts the number of adjacent cells which have told it they are occupied, and applies the local rule, as in Process 13.5. Notice that although the input processes are written in a parallel FOR loop, the counting of live neighbours has to be sequential, since the *count* variable must not be shared. Whilst the array *state.of.neighbour* is shared between parallel processes, it is clear that no element of the array is shared, and this can be checked by the compiler as *d* is a bound variable in a FOR loop with constant bounds.

Process 13.5

```
PROC calculate.next.state([][][]CHAN OF STATE link,
                          VAL []INT nx, ny,
                          VAL BOOL state, BOOL next.state )
  INT count :        -- number of living neighbours
  SEQ
    [neighbours]BOOL state.of.neighbour :
    SEQ
      PAR d = 0 FOR neighbours
        link[nx[d]][ny[d]][d] ? state.of.neighbour[d]
      count := 0
      SEQ d = 0 FOR neighbours
        IF
          state.of.neighbour[d] = alive
            count := count + 1
          state.of.neighbour[d] = dead
            SKIP
    IF
      count < 2       -- death from isolation
        next.state := dead
      count = 2       -- this cell is stable
        next.state := state
      count = 3       -- stable if alive, a birth if dead
        next.state := alive
      count > 3       -- death from overcrowding
        next.state := dead
:
```

Observation and control

As in Chapter 12, having completed the highly parallel part of the program, it remains to design a means for controlling and watching what happens. The observation will impose more synchronization on the array of cells: there is, so far, nothing to prevent widely separated processes from working on as widely separated generations, but the display should be capable of showing the state of one generation at a time, across the whole of the board.

There are three instructions that the controlling process will need to issue to each cell on the board: it may ask for the cell to assume a new state, so as to initialize, and subsequently edit, the state of the board; it may instruct the cell to evolve for one generation; and it may tell the cell process to terminate. In response to instructions to evolve, the cell should yield up its new state. In fact, at the end of each generation, the *cell* process will send not only its new state, but also an indication of whether the state has changed in this generation. That makes the task of the controlling process simpler. To carry these messages, a channel is needed into each cell, and one from each cell, and the *cell* process must be recoded to expect and comply with the instructions received on its *control* channel (Process 13.6). This coding of *cell* expects a sequence of instructions, each of which is either a *set.state* followed by a new state to be assumed, or is an *evolve* which causes the cell to evolve and report its new state. The whole sequence is followed by a single instruction to terminate.

Process 13.6

```
PROTOCOL COMMAND
  CASE
    set.state; BOOL
    evolve
    terminate
:

PROTOCOL RESPONSE IS BOOL; BOOL :


PROC cell([][][]CHAN OF STATE link,
         VAL INT x, y, VAL []INT nx, ny,
         CHAN OF COMMAND control,
         CHAN OF RESPONSE sense        )
  BOOL state, not.finished :
  SEQ
    state := dead     -- the whole board starts off dead
    not.finished := TRUE
    WHILE not.finished
      control ? CASE

        set.state; state
          SKIP        -- state has been set to the new value

        evolve
          BOOL next.state :
          SEQ
            PAR
              broadcast.present.state(link, x, y, state)
              SEQ
                calculate.next.state(link, nx, ny,
                                     state, next.state )
                sense ! (state <> next.state); next.state
            state := next.state

        terminate
          not.finished := FALSE
:
```

Since there is only one terminal keyboard and one terminal screen involved, the *controller* is essentially a sequential process, with all of the *control* and *sense* channels connected to it. The new program has the structure shown in Process 13.7.

Process 13.7

```
[array.width][array.height][neighbours]CHAN OF STATE link :
[array.width][array.height]CHAN OF COMMAND control :
[array.width][array.height]CHAN OF RESPONSE sense :
PAR
  controller(keyboard, screen, control, sense)
  PAR x = 0 FOR array.width
    PAR y = 0 FOR array.height
      ... declarations of nx and ny :
      cell(link, x, y, nx, ny, control[x][y], sense[x][y])
```

The *controller* (Process 13.8) is written as a state machine; its state may be represented by a variable of type INT, and set to values determined by characters typed on the keyboard

```
INT FUNCTION new.activity(VAL BYTE char)
  ... select a new activity
:
```

Under the control of input from the terminal keyboard, the *controller* calls procedures either to modify the state of cells on the board by issuing *set.state* instructions

```
PROC editor(CHAN OF BYTE keyboard, screen,
            [][]CHAN OF COMMAND control  )
  ... modify the colony on the board
:
```

or to drive the whole board through the evolution of a single generation by scanning the board, issuing *evolve* instructions, and reading back the new states

```
PROC generation(CHAN OF BYTE screen,
                [][]CHAN OF COMMAND control,
                [][]CHAN OF RESPONSE sense,
                BOOL active                )
  ... cause the colony on the board to move on a step
:
```

The *active* parameter returns an indication of whether any changes have happened during the generation.

Process 13.8

```
VAL INT idle         IS 0 :   -- controller activity values
VAL INT editing      IS 1 :
VAL INT single.step  IS 2 :
VAL INT free.running IS 3 :
VAL INT terminated   IS 4 :

PROC controller(CHAN OF BYTE keyboard, screen,
                [][]CHAN OF COMMAND control,
                [][]CHAN OF RESPONSE sense    )
  INT activity :
  SEQ
    activity := idle
    initialize.display(screen)
    WHILE activity <> terminated
      SEQ
        display.activity(screen, activity)
        BYTE char :
        PRI ALT
          (activity <> editing) & keyboard ? char
            activity := new.activity(char)
          (activity <> idle) & SKIP
            CASE activity
              editing
                SEQ
                  editor(keyboard, screen, control)
                  activity := idle
              free.running, single.step
                BOOL changing :
                SEQ
                  generation(screen, control, sense, changing)
                  IF
                    (activity = single.step) OR (NOT changing)
                      activity := idle
                    (activity = free.running) AND changing
                      SKIP
    display.activity(screen, activity)
    PAR x = 0 FOR array.width
      PAR y = 0 FOR array.height
        control[x][y] ! terminate
    clean.up.display(screen)
:
```

The normal activity of the controller, *free.running*, is to cause a sequence of invocations of *generation* so that the colony is continually evolving. The alternative has to be asymmetric, because a sequence of calls to *generation* might otherwise go on indefinitely without ever allowing pending keyboard input to be accepted. As it is, between any two generations the keyboard is given an opportunity to change to the *new.activity* which Process 13.9 associates with the character typed.

Process 13.9

```
INT FUNCTION new.activity(VAL BYTE char)
  INT activity :
  VALOF
    CASE char      -- typed on the keyboard ...
      'q', 'Q'           -- ... Q to finish program
        activity := terminated
      's', 'S'           -- ... S to halt evolution
        activity := idle
      'e', 'E'           -- ... E to start editing
        activity := editing
      'r', 'R'           -- ... R to start evolution
        activity := free.running
      ELSE   -- ... or anything else for one generation
        activity := single.step
    RESULT activity
:
```

The *single.step* activity, entered by typing almost anything on the keyboard, causes an evolution of precisely one generation. This makes it easier to follow the details of a history. Notice that the code of the board is entirely unaffected by the detailed design of the single stepping mechanism, and even of the details of the editor.

Recall that each cell starts a step of its evolution in response to an *evolve* instruction on its *control* channel. It cannot complete the advance unless its neighbours also move, so the *generation* process, Process 13.10, starts each cell on the board, and only then collects a new state from each of the cells. When the new states are gathered, any changes are notified on the display. Note is also kept of whether any of the cells has changed state, because a colony which does not change in one generation has become stable, and never changes again. If the colony becomes stable, the *active* parameter to *generation* is returned as FALSE and the controller becomes *idle*.

The details of the display are all contained in the procedures to set up the screen, to display the state of a cell, to display the activity of the controller, and to clear up the screen after the program has terminated. Assuming that the board is some tens of cells on a side, it is reasonable to allocate consecutive screen locations to adjacent cells, and so use the co-ordinates of the cell as those of its representation on the screen (Process 13.11). A live cell shows as an asterisk, and a dead cell as a blank space.

To make the initial screen consistent with the initial state of the board, which is entirely dead, it suffices to clear the screen (Process 13.12), and to clean up at the end of the program, the cursor is moved to the left of the line below the image of the board (Process 13.13). Assuming that there is some

Process 13.10

```
PROC generation(CHAN OF BYTE screen,
                [][]CHAN OF COMMAND control,
                [][]CHAN OF RESPONSE sense,
                BOOL active                  )
  SEQ
    PAR x = 0 FOR array.width
      PAR y = 0 FOR array.height
        control[x][y] ! evolve
    active := FALSE
    SEQ x = 0 FOR array.width
      SEQ y = 0 FOR array.height
        BOOL changed, next.state :
        SEQ
          sense[x][y] ? changed; next.state
          IF
            changed
              SEQ
                display.state(screen, x, y, next.state)
                active := TRUE
            NOT changed
              SKIP
:
```

Process 13.11

```
PROC display.state(CHAN OF BYTE screen,
                   VAL INT x, y, VAL BOOL state )
  SEQ
    move.cursor(screen, x, y)
    IF
      state = alive
        screen ! '**'
      state = dead
        screen ! '*s'
:
```

Process 13.12

```
PROC initialize.display(CHAN OF BYTE screen)
  -- display an entirely dead board
  clear.screen(screen)
:
```

Process 13.13

```
PROC clean.up.display(CHAN OF BYTE screen)
  move.cursor(screen, 0, array.height)
:
```

Process 13.14

```
PROC display.activity(CHAN OF BYTE screen,
                      VAL INT activity   )
  SEQ
    move.cursor(screen, array.width+1, array.height/2)
    CASE activity
      idle
        write.string(screen, "Idle")
      editing
        write.string(screen, "Edit")
      single.step
        write.string(screen, "Step")
      free.running
        write.string(screen, "Busy")
      terminated
        write.string(screen, "Done")
  :
```

Process 13.15

```
PROC move.cursor(CHAN OF BYTE screen, VAL INT x, y)
  -- move to column x of line y (of an ANSI terminal screen)
  CHAN OF DATA.ITEM c :
  PAR
    write.formatted(screen, "*#1B[%d;%dH", c)
    SEQ
      c ! data.int; x+1
      c ! data.int; y+1
  :
```

Process 13.16

```
PROC clear.screen(CHAN OF BYTE screen)
  -- clear the whole of the screen (of an ANSI terminal)
  write.string(screen, "*#1B[2J")
  :
```

spare room on the screen to the right of the image of the board, the activity of the controller can be displayed there (Process 13.14).

The terminal-specific declarations are just those of the procedures invoked to alter the screen. Process 13.15 and Process 13.16 are suitable definitions for an ANSI terminal.

All that remains is to supply an editor. Process 13.17 is a simple process that allows a cursor to be moved around the board image, and allows the state of the cell under the cursor to be set. Editing continues until the 'Q' key is typed. The cursor control keys move the cursor vertically and horizontally over the board, the space bar kills the occupant of a cell, and the asterisk key plants a new occupant. For simplicity, any other character or an attempt to pass over the boundary of the board image is ignored without comment. This means that although ANSI cursor keys generate a control sequence – for example the down-arrow key sends escape and open bracket (or an equivalent eight-bit control character), and 'B' – it is sufficient to interpret only the terminating character ('A' to 'D').

Process 13.17

```
PROC editor(CHAN OF BYTE keyboard, screen,
            [][]CHAN OF COMMAND control   )
  INT x, y :
  BOOL editing :
  SEQ
    -- initialize co-ordinates to centre of board
    x, y := array.width / 2, array.height / 2
    editing := TRUE
    WHILE editing
      BYTE char :
      SEQ
        move.cursor(screen, x, y)
        keyboard ? char
        CASE char
          'A'          -- move up, if possible
            y := max(y - 1, 0)
          'B'          -- move down, if possible
            y := min(y + 1, array.height - 1)
          'C'          -- move right, if possible
            x := min(x + 1, array.width - 1)
          'D'          -- move left, if possible
            x := max(x - 1, 0)
          '*s', '**'
            VAL BOOL state IS (char = '**') = alive :
            PAR
              control[x][y] ! set.state; state
              display.state(screen, x, y, state)
          'q', 'Q'
            editing := FALSE
          ELSE
            SKIP     -- ignore anything else
  :
```

Life

A brief word seems to be in order about the history of *Life* itself. It first became widely known through Martin Gardner's column *Mathematical Games* in the *Scientific American* magazine[16, 17]. The former article explains the rules, and introduces some of the jargon of the subject: for example, the speed of light, which is one cell width per generation, the greatest rate at which information can pass across the board; and the glider, a small, fixed-size, moving colony (Figure 13.3).

Figure 13.3   The glider

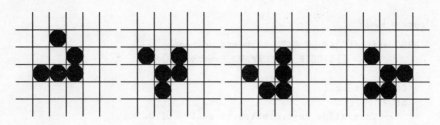

The glider is one of the small, simple colonies whose evolution is fully known: it moves across the board in the direction in which it appears to be pointing, at a quarter of the speed of light, passing through the fixed sequence of four distinct forms.

The second article describes more complicated examples, drawn from the readers' experience of wasting both machine cycles and mathematical ingenuity. Here you will find the curiosities of the subject: Garden of Eden colonies, which are ones that cannot possibly have come about as a result of an evolutionary advance from a former state; the glider gun, a huge structure which grows without limit, by firing off an unending stream of gliders; and a glider-gobbler which, although stable in itself, can also swallow a stream of gliders such as that given off by the gun, to no ill effect. There are viruses, which disrupt regular structures, and regular structures which can recover their symmetry after withstanding a virus infection.

14

Huffman minimum redundancy coding

It has become usual to store data and transmit messages using codes of fixed length such as ASCII. The character set is represented by some number of codewords, each of the same length, which in the case of ASCII is seven binary digits. The result is that it takes the same number of bits to store, or the same bandwith to transmit, all messages with the same number of characters. Of course, if you know in advance that your message is in, say, English, then you know that it is much less likely to contain letter 'z's than letter 'e's. This means that if you use a shorter codeword to represent 'e' than that used for 'z', you can expect to use less store, or bandwidth, for the average message.

In ASCII, the message 'message' is encoded

```
1101101 1100101 1110011 1110011 1100001 1100111 1100101
   m       e       s       s       a       g       e
```

requiring forty-nine bits, whereas by using a code made up of the following representations

a	$\mapsto$	0 0 0
e	$\mapsto$	1
g	$\mapsto$	0 0 1 0
m	$\mapsto$	0 0 1 1
s	$\mapsto$	0 1

the same message can be encoded

```
0 0 1 1 1 0 1 0 1 0 0 0 0 0 1 0 1
  m       e s   s   a     g       e
```

in only seventeen bits. The codewords must be chosen in such a way that none is a prefix of any of the others, to ensure that there can be only one way of decoding a particular coded text.

In a classic paper, published in 1952, David Huffman described an algorithm to find the set of codes that would minimize the expected length of a message, given that the probability of each character's occurring were known. Essentially, his method decides the lengths of codewords, giving the longest to the least likely characters. It then remains to create an arbitrary unambiguous code with codewords of the right lengths.

The terminology of Huffman's paper is a little different from that in use today. He uses the term 'message' to mean an individual character. First of all, the ensemble [= character set], which has size N, is numbered in decreasing order of probability. $L(n)$ is defined to be the (unknown) length of the code for the nth most probable message; it is shown to be required that $i < j \Rightarrow L(i) \leq L(j)$:

> [It is] necessary that the two least probable messages have codes of equal length ... $L(N)$ which are identical except for their last digits. The final digits of these two codes will be one of the two binary digits, 0 and 1. It will be necessary to assign these two message codes to the Nth and $(N-1)^{\text{st}}$ messages since at this point it is not known whether or not other codes of length $L(N)$ exist. Once this has been done, these two messages are equivalent to a single composite message. Its code (as yet undetermined) will be the common prefixes of order $L(N) - 1$ of these two messages. Its probability will be the sum of the probabilities of the two messages from which it was created. The ensemble containing this composite message in the place of its two component messages ... contains one less message than the original. Its members should be rearranged if necessary so that the messages are again ordered according to their probabilities. It may be considered exactly as the original ensemble was. ...
>
> The procedure is applied again and again until the number of messages in the most recently formed auxiliary ensemble is reduced to two. One of each of the binary digits is assigned to each of these two composite messages. These messages are then combined to form a single composite message with probability unity, and the coding is complete. ...
>
> Since each combination of the two messages ... is accompanied by the assigning of a new digit to each, then the total number of digits which should be assigned to each original message is the same as the number of combinations [undergone by] that message.
>
> Having now decided proper lengths of code for each message, the problem of specifying the actual digits remains. Since the combining of messages into their composites is similar to the successive confluences of trickles, rivulets, brooks, and creeks into a final large river, the procedure thus far described might be considered analogous to the placing of signs by a water-borne insect at each of these junctions as he journeys downstream. ... The

code we desire is that one which the insect must remember in order to work his way back upstream.

A method for the construction of minimum-redundancy codes,

David A. Huffman [19]

Restated more prosaically, the final paragraph identifies the unambiguous set of codewords with a (binary) tree. Each leaf of the tree corresponds to one of the characters. The depth of that leaf, that is its distance from the root, is the length of that character's codeword. The digits of the codeword are the 'address' of the leaf, that is a sequence of instructions for getting to the leaf from the root, say 0 for 'go to the left' and 1 for 'go to the right'.

Representing a coding tree

As usual, the task of representing a data structure in occam amounts to choosing an enumeration for the component parts, so as to map the structure onto an array. The structure in question this time is a binary tree similar to that in Chapter 12, but this tree may be severely imbalanced, and is of unpredictable depth. This means that the simple fixed enumeration, with the children of node i being nodes $2i + 1$ and $2i + 2$, would be unreasonably wasteful of store, so is unsuitable. A better representation, in this case, roots the tree at node zero

```
VAL INT root IS 0 :
```

and uses an array *eldest* to record the index of the leftmost offspring of a node, so that the children of node i are indexed *eldest*$[i]$ and *eldest*$[i] + 1$.

Since the root is by definition not the child of any node, the test

$$eldest[node] = root$$

can be used to signify that *node* is a leaf of the tree. In the case of the leaves, it will be necessary to know to which character they correspond. This is most readily recorded in another array of the same size as *eldest* in which the value of *character*$[node]$ is the character corresponding to that node, if it is a leaf.

The array *eldest* makes it easy to pass 'upstream' from the root of the tree to the leaves. In order to make the 'downstream' journey as efficient, it will be useful to record the inverse of *eldest*, in an array *parent*, such that

$$parent[eldest[node]] = parent[eldest[node] + 1] = node$$

for each non-leaf node, and the inverse of *character* in an array *representative*, which records the index of the leaf corresponding to each character.

It remains to be decided how big these arrays must be. This, of course, depends on the size of the character set being encoded. For the purposes of this example, the (unencoded) character set will be signed, eight-bit significant values, $-128 \leq char < 128$. This allows room for the normal seven-bit characters in the non-negative half range, and room for another, negative, character set which can be used for control information, indicating such things as the end of a message. Since we are admitting negative values, BYTE is not the appropriate type for the characters here; we are also going to want to create subscripts into the array *representative* from them, so INT is convenient. This is also the natural type to use in the other arrays, as they will store subscripts. In this case, the relevant definitions to make are

```
VAL INT bits.in.character    IS 8 :
VAL INT number.of.characters IS 1 << bits.in.character :
VAL INT number.of.codes      IS number.of.characters :
VAL INT character.mask IS
                    BITNOT ((BITNOT 0) << bits.in.character) :
INT FUNCTION index(VAL INT char) IS char /\ character.mask :
```

The *character.mask* has ones as its *bits.in.character* least significant bits, and zeros elsewhere, and is used by *index* to map signed characters onto non-negative array indices, so that

$$char = character[representative[index(char)]]$$

Now if there are *number.of.codes* leaves in a binary tree, then there will be one less than that number of non-leaf nodes, so the total number of nodes is given by

```
VAL INT size.of.tree IS (2 * number.of.codes) - 1 :
```

and the declarations of the arrays for representing the tree could be

```
[size.of.tree]INT eldest, parent, character :
[number.of.characters]INT representative :
```

As these four arrays constitute the representation of a single data structure, it is convenient to group them together in a single two-dimensional array which can be passed as a complete entity to procedures, and to use abbreviation to give the descriptive names to the component arrays

```
VAL INT number.of.arrays IS 4 :
VAL INT eldest.index IS 0 :
VAL INT parent.index IS 1 :
VAL INT character.index IS 2 :
VAL INT representative.index IS 3 :

[number.of.arrays][size.of.tree]INT tree :
```

```
[]INT eldest IS tree[eldest.index] :
[]INT parent IS tree[parent.index] :
[]INT character IS tree[character.index] :
[]INT representative IS
          [tree[representative.index] FROM
                              0 FOR number.of.characters] :
```

This wastes a certain amount of space, since the *representative* array is not as large as the others, but this is unlikely to be significant.

Constructing a coding tree

Huffman's algorithm proceeds in two stages. First the character set is sorted into descending order of probability of the character's occurrence. Each of the characters will correspond to a leaf of the tree, so you can think of this stage of the process as constructing *number.of.codes* number of leaves. These leaves will be sub-trees of the final coding tree. Since each is just a leaf, they are disjoint, in the sense that they share no nodes with each other, and they are maximal, in the sense that there is not yet any bigger tree of which any is a member.

The second stage of the algorithm repeatedly reduces the size of the collection of maximal disjoint sub-trees, by combining the two lightest trees to make one new composite tree – 'lightest' meaning of least *weight*, where the weight of a leaf is the probability of the corresponding character, and the weight of a larger tree is the sum of the weights of its leaves. Notice that during this second stage, it is guaranteed that any two siblings – children of a common parent – are already adjacent in descending order of weight. This observation, which is taken from Robert Gallager

> A prefix condition code is a code with the property that no codeword is a prefix of any other codeword. A binary tree has the sibling property if each node (except the root) has a sibling, and if the nodes of the tree can be arranged in order of non-increasing probability with each node being adjacent to its sibling. A binary prefix condition code is a Huffman code iff the code tree has the sibling property.

> Variations on a Theme by Huffman, Robert G. Gallager [20]

is in fact a non-algorithmic characterization of Huffman codes. It also shows that in the representation chosen for the coding tree, which allocates adjacent elements of the arrays to siblings, it is possible to keep the arrays sorted in descending order of weight. Gallager's proof that this property holds is, essentially, an informal proof of correctness of Huffman's algorithm.

Process 14.1

```
PROC construct.tree([][]INT tree, VAL []REAL32 probability)
  INT left.limit, right.limit :
  [size.of.tree]REAL32 weight :

  PROC construct.leaves([][]INT tree,
                        INT left.limit, right.limit,
                        []REAL32 weight,
                        VAL []REAL32 probability    )
    ... build the leaves of the tree
  :

  PROC construct.other.nodes([][]INT tree,
                             INT left.limit, right.limit,
                             []REAL32 weight             )
    ... join pairs of sub-trees until only one remains
  :

  PROC invert.representation([][]INT tree)
    ... set parent[] and representative[]
  :

  SEQ
    left.limit   := size.of.tree
    right.limit  := size.of.tree

    -- left.limit = size.of.tree
    -- (right.limit - left.limit) = 0

    construct.leaves(tree,
                     left.limit, right.limit, weight,
                     probability                      )

    -- left.limit = number.of.codes
    -- (right.limit - left.limit) = number.of.codes

    construct.other.nodes(tree, left.limit, right.limit, weight)

    -- left.limit = root
    -- (right.limit - left.limit) = 1

    invert.representation(tree)
  :
```

Keeping the arrays sorted by weight of node in this way simplifies the finding of the two lightest sub-trees, and if the arrays are filled from the high-index, light, end towards the root, then sub-trees once constructed need not be moved again.

The algorithm is divided into three parts (Process 14.1). Throughout, the collection of maximal disjoint sub-trees consists of those trees rooted at nodes for which

$$left.limit \leq node < right.limit$$

The initialization of the limits makes this collection empty. The process *construct.leaves* introduces a new sub-tree into the collection for each of the characters of the character set, setting its weight according to the probability of the character, maintaining the arrangement of the leaves in descending order, so that

$$left.limit \leq i \leq j < size.of.tree \quad \Rightarrow \quad weight[i] \geq weight[j]$$

The process *construct.other.nodes* combines the two lightest leaves, which are those nearest to *right.limit*. It introduces a new node with the combined weight of these two, adjusting the limits of the collection, and filling in the shape of the tree in *eldest*. Finally, the process *invert.representation* constructs the arrays *parent* and *representative*.

Both *construct.leaves* and *construct.other.nodes* repeatedly create a new node of some given weight, and insert it into the right place between the limits to maintain the weight ordering of the nodes. The determination of this right place and the consequent adjustment of the lighter nodes is done by Process 14.2. Recall that the roots of the collection of maximal disjoint sub-trees of the coding tree constructed so far lie at or to the right of *left.limit* and to the left of *right.limit* and that they are in descending order of weight. This means that the conditional

```
IF
    IF node = left.limit FOR right.limit - left.limit
    weight[node] <= weight.of.new.node
        weight.limit := node
    TRUE
        weight.limit := right.limit
```

sets the *weight.limit* so that

$$left.limit \leq node < weight.limit \Rightarrow weight[node] > weight.of.new.node$$
$$weight.limit \leq node < right.limit \Rightarrow weight.of.new.node \geq weight[node]$$

The sequential loop then displaces each of the heavier nodes one place to the left to make room for the *new.node*, and the *left.limit* of the collection is adjusted to compensate. The shapes of the sub-trees remain the same, so that apart from being shifted up by one no changes are necessary to the values in *eldest*. This is because only nodes to the left of the *weight.limit* are moved, but

$$node < weight.limit \quad \Rightarrow \quad node < right.limit$$

Process 14.2

```
PROC insert.new.node([][]INT tree,
                     INT left.limit,
                     VAL INT right.limit,
                     INT new.node,
                     []REAL32 weight,
                     VAL REAL32 weight.of.new.node )
  INT weight.limit :
  SEQ
    IF
      IF node = left.limit FOR right.limit - left.limit
        weight[node] <= weight.of.new.node
          weight.limit := node
      TRUE
        weight.limit := right.limit
    []INT eldest IS tree[eldest.index] :
    []INT character IS tree[character.index] :
    SEQ node = left.limit FOR weight.limit - left.limit
      character[node-1], eldest[node-1], weight[node-1] :=
        character[node],   eldest[node],   weight[node]
    left.limit, new.node := left.limit - 1, weight.limit - 1
    weight[new.node] := weight.of.new.node
:
```

Process 14.3

```
PROC construct.leaves([][]INT tree,
                      INT left.limit, right.limit,
                      []REAL32 weight,
                      VAL []REAL32 probability     )
  VAL INT minimum.character IS -(number.of.characters / 2) :
  SEQ char = minimum.character FOR number.of.characters
    INT new.node :
    SEQ
      insert.new.node(tree, left.limit, right.limit,
                      new.node, weight, probability[index(char)] )
      []INT eldest IS tree[eldest.index] :
      []INT character IS tree[character.index] :
      eldest[new.node], character[new.node] := root, char
:
```

and the construction guarantees

$$(eldest[node] = root) \lor (eldest[node] \geq right.limit)$$

so that no node which is moved is yet a child.

The *insert.new.node* procedure performs the bulk of the work required for the process that creates the leaf nodes (Process 14.3). This inserts a new leaf into the collection, increasing the size of the collection by decreasing the *left.limit.* Process 14.4 then combines the leaves into a tree; it first removes the two lightest sub-trees from the collection, by decreasing *right.limit*, then joins them under a parent whose weight is the sum of their individual weights. Notice that the assignment to *eldest[new.node]* maintains the property that there are no children to the left of the *right.limit*. The process is complete when only one tree remains.

Inverting the representation of the tree is a simple task, which involves assigning to *representative* the indices of the leaf nodes, and to *parent* the indices of the nodes that are not leaves, as in Process 14.5.

That completes the code to construct a coding tree from a given probability distribution.

Process 14.4

```
PROC construct.other.nodes([][]INT tree,
                           INT left.limit, right.limit,
                           []REAL32 weight                )
  WHILE (right.limit - left.limit) <> 1
    INT new.node :
    REAL32 new.weight :
    SEQ
      right.limit := right.limit - 2
      new.weight := weight[right.limit] + weight[right.limit + 1]
      insert.new.node(tree, left.limit, right.limit,
                      new.node, weight, new.weight )
      []INT eldest IS tree[eldest.index] :
      eldest[new.node] := right.limit
  :
```

Process 14.5

```
PROC invert.representation([][]INT tree)
  ... abbreviate eldest, parent, character, representative
  SEQ node = root FOR size.of.tree
    IF
      eldest[node] = root
        representative[index(character[node])] := node
      eldest[node] <> root
        SEQ child = eldest[node] FOR 2
          parent[child] := node
  :
```

Encoding and decoding using a coding tree

The encoding of any given character *char* is the sequence of 'go left' and 'go right' instructions that Huffman's insect must follow to pass upstream from the root node to the representative node of that character. It is easy enough to construct this code backwards, since floating downstream involved passing from *node* to *parent*[*node*] in succession from the representative node until the root is reached.

Since the result of the encoding should be a sequence of bits, the natural occam 2 type to use is BOOL. In what follows the value TRUE will mean that the insect should turn to the right, and FALSE to the left. As *eldest* records the leftmost offspring of its subscript, *node* is reached by a right turn precisely when it is the younger child of its parent; that is, when it is not *eldest*[*parent*[*node*]]. Therefore the process

```
SEQ
  length := 0
  node   := representative[index(char)]
  WHILE node <> root
    SEQ
      encoding[length] := node <> eldest[parent[node]]
      length           := length + 1
      node             := parent[node]
```

establishes the condition that

$$\bigwedge_{0 \le i < length} node_i = \begin{cases} eldest[node_{i+1}] + 1 & \text{if } encoding[i] \\ eldest[node_{i+1}] & \text{otherwise} \end{cases}$$

where

$$node_0 = representative[index(char)]$$
$$node_{length} = root$$

so that the encoding of *char* can be transmitted in the right order by

```
SEQ i = 1 FOR length
  output ! encoding[length - i]
```

It remains only to decide how much room needs to be allocated to store the *encoding* whilst it is being constructed. Consider the situation when decoding a Huffman encoded character. Before you receive the first bit of the encoding, there are *number.of.codes* possible codes that you might be about to receive. Each bit that you receive divides the set of possible characters into two non-empty subsets: those that are still possible, and those that are now precluded. This means that at most *number.of.codes* − 1 bits will suffice. In fact, in the worst case, this limit is achieved: if each character is more than twice as probable as the next most likely, then the Huffman codes are, in decreasing order of probability

0,   10,   110,   1110,   11110,   ...

with encodings that are *number.of.codes* − 1 bits long for each of the two
least probable characters. With this bound on the size of the encoding we
can write *encode.character* (Process 14.6).

Process 14.6

```
PROTOCOL BIT IS BOOL :

PROC encode.character(CHAN OF BIT output,
                      VAL [][]INT tree,
                      VAL INT char          )
  -- Transmit the encoding of char in tree along output
  ... abbreviate values of eldest, parent, etc. from tree
  VAL INT size.of.encoding IS number.of.codes - 1 :
  [size.of.encoding]BOOL encoding :
  INT length, node :
  SEQ
    length := 0
    node   := representative[index(char)]
    WHILE node <> root
      SEQ
        encoding[length] := node <> eldest[parent[node]]
        length := length + 1
        node   := parent[node]
    SEQ i = 1 FOR length
      output ! encoding[length - i]
  :
```

Decoding a stream of bits to determine the character consists of following the 'go left' and 'go right' instructions as they arrive; remembering
that TRUE means 'go right' this is achieved by

```
SEQ
  input ? go.right
  IF
    go.right
      node := eldest[node] + 1
    NOT go.right
      node := eldest[node]
```

Enough bits must be accepted to pass upstream, starting from the root node
until a leaf is reached. That leaf indicates the decoded character, and so
Process 14.7 decodes a single *char*.

Process 14.7

```
PROC decode.character(CHAN OF BIT input,
                      VAL [] []INT tree,
                      INT char           )
  ... abbreviate values of eldest and character from tree
  INT node :
  SEQ
    node := root
    WHILE eldest[node] <> root
      BOOL go.right :
      SEQ
        input ? go.right
        IF
          go.right
            node := eldest[node] + 1
          NOT go.right
            node := eldest[node]
    char := character[node]
:
```

Process 14.8

```
PROC copy(CHAN OF INT source,
          CHAN OF SIGNAL end.of.source,
          CHAN OF INT sink             )
  -- Copy characters from source to sink until a
  -- signal is received from end.of.source
  BOOL more.characters.expected :
  SEQ
    more.characters.expected := TRUE
    WHILE more.characters.expected
      ALT
        INT char :
        source ? char
          sink ! char
        end.of.source ? CASE signal
          more.characters.expected := FALSE
:
```

Having once fixed on a coding tree, the encoding process can be applied repeatedly to a sequence of characters to produce a sequence of bits. This, in turn, by repeated application of the decoding process, can be turned back into the original sequence of characters.

These procedures can be combined in a pair of processes that when executed in parallel duplicate the behaviour of a buffer like Process 14.8, but which transmit the minimum number of bits necessary to communicate the information contained in the sequence of characters.

Assume for the moment that the probabilities of the characters are fixed in advance, perhaps by considering an average over many messages of the type to be sent.

```
VAL [number.of.characters]REAL32 probability IS
                                                ... :
```

If it is possible to read the message through before sending it, then you can count actual character frequencies, and produce an optimal Huffman code for the message, but of course you will then have to transmit a description of the code with your message!

If one of the character codes is laid aside to indicate the end of a transmission,

```
VAL INT end.of.message IS -1 :
```

then that can be transmitted after the last real character of the message. That means that the end of the message is marked within the sequence of Huffman encodings of the characters.

Process 14.9

```
PROC copy.encoding(CHAN OF INT source,
                   CHAN OF SIGNAL end.of.source,
                   CHAN OF BIT sink              )

  -- Read characters from source, sending their
  -- encodings along sink, until a signal is received
  -- along end.of.source.

  BOOL more.characters.expected :
  [number.of.arrays][size.of.tree]INT tree :
  SEQ
    construct.tree(tree, probability)
    more.characters.expected := TRUE
    WHILE more.characters.expected
      ALT
        INT char :
        source ? char
          encode.character(sink, tree, char)
        end.of.source ? CASE signal
          more.characters.expected := FALSE
    encode.character(sink, tree, end.of.message)
  :
```

Process 14.9 translates a stream of characters into a stream of bits representing their Huffman encodings, and marks the end of the stream by

Process 14.10

```
PROC copy.decoding(CHAN OF BIT source,
                   CHAN OF INT sink   )

  -- Read a bit stream from source, decoding it
  -- into characters and send these along sink
  -- until end.of.message is decoded

  BOOL more.characters.expected :
  [number.of.arrays][size.of.tree]INT tree :
  SEQ
    construct.tree(tree, probability)
    more.characters.expected := TRUE
    WHILE more.characters.expected
      INT char :
      SEQ
        decode.character(source, tree, char)
        IF
          char <> end.of.message
            sink ! char
          char = end.of.message
            more.characters.expected := FALSE
:
```

Process 14.11

```
PROC copy.over.serial.medium(CHAN OF INT source,
                             CHAN OF SIGNAL end.of.source,
                             CHAN OF INT sink             )

  -- Copy characters from source to sink until a
  -- signal is received from end.of.source

  CHAN OF BIT serial.medium :
  PAR
    copy.encoding(source, end.of.source, serial.medium)
    copy.decoding(serial.medium, sink)
:
```

sending the encoding of *end.of.message*. Process 14.10 accomplishes the corresponding decoding, terminating when the encoded *end.of.message* value is received and decoded.

These processes can be used at the opposite ends of a serial communications medium where each communication on *serial.medium* is the transmission of a single bit. The process *copy.over.serial.medium* (Process 14.11) is a buffer: provided a sequence of bytes is communicated on *source* which does not include *end.of.message* (if for example they are all seven-bit character codes) either *copy* or *copy.over.serial.medium* can be substituted for the other in any program without affecting the behaviour of the program.

Many communications media are most efficiently used by sending fixed-sized messages, each consisting of a large number of bits. You already have most of the components necessary to implement a process like *copy* which makes efficient use of such a medium. Encoding characters and packing the bits into blocks can be done by executing *copy.encoding* concurrently with the process *pack.bits.into.blocks* (Process 8.20) from Chapter 8 (Process 14.12).

Process 14.12

```
PROC encode.into.blocks(CHAN OF INT source,
                        CHAN OF SIGNAL end.of.source,
                        CHAN OF BLOCK sink           )
  CHAN OF BIT bit.stream :
  CHAN OF SIGNAL end.of.bit.stream :
  PAR
    SEQ
      copy.encoding(source, end.of.source, bit.stream)
      end.of.bit.stream ! signal
    pack.bits.into.blocks(bit.stream, end.of.bit.stream, sink)
  :
```

Decoding the characters from the stream of blocks is a slightly trickier task, since the end of the message is determined from the decoded data. The most elegant solution, as seems common in parallel programs, involves a process that throws away unwanted information (Process 14.13). This inputs successively from *source*, ignoring the values that it receives, until a signal is sent to it on *end.of.source*.

Process 14.13

```
PROC discard(CHAN OF BIT source, CHAN OF SIGNAL end.of.source)
  BOOL more.expected :
  SEQ
    more.expected := TRUE
    WHILE more.expected
      ALT
        BOOL bit :
        source ? bit
          SKIP
        end.of.source ? CASE signal
          more.expected := FALSE
  :
```

With this, Process 14.14 decodes the bits in a stream of blocks. When *copy.decoding* decodes an *end.of.message* it terminates, causing a signal to be offered for output on *end.of.block.stream*, which is a feed-back path to the block unpacking process. At the same time, *discard* absorbs any bits that

Process 14.14

```
PROC decode.from.blocks(CHAN OF BLOCK block.source,
                        CHAN OF INT sink            )
  CHAN OF SIGNAL end.of.block.source, end.of.bit.stream :
  CHAN OF BIT bit.stream :
  PAR
    SEQ
      unpack.bits.from.blocks(block.source,
                              end.of.block.source, bit.stream)
      end.of.bit.stream ! signal           -- 'feed-forward'

    SEQ
      copy.decoding(bit.stream, sink)
      PAR
        end.of.block.source ! signal       -- 'feed-back'
        discard(bit.stream, end.of.bit.stream)
:
```

Process 14.15

```
PROC copy.over.blocked.medium(CHAN OF INT source,
                              CHAN OF SIGNAL end.of.source,
                              CHAN OF INT sink            )
  -- Copy characters from source to sink until a
  -- signal is received from end.of.source
  CHAN OF BLOCK blocked.medium :
  PAR
    encode.into.blocks(source, end.of.source, blocked.medium)
    decode.from.blocks(blocked.medium, sink)
:
```

were left in the last block of the message. When all of the bits of the last block have gone, *unpack.bits.from.blocks* accepts the *end.of.block.source* signal, and terminates causing an *end.of.bit.stream* signal to be sent to terminate the *discard* process.

Process 14.12 and Process 14.14 can be operated concurrently to emulate a buffer (Process 14.15) with each communication on the *blocked.medium* being a transfer of a block of the predetermined fixed size.

The *copy.over.blocked.medium* procedure is not quite as good an implementation of a buffer as is the bit-serial copy. Consider what communications must happen before the first character is output on *sink*. This is a restriction on the contexts in which *copy.over.blocked.medium* can be substituted for *copy*.

Adapting the code to the message

So far, Huffman's assumption that the code is predetermined and remains fixed throughout the transmission of a given message has been accepted. This is reasonable in case the probability distribution of the characters in the message is known in advance, or if the message can be read through in advance. Gallager suggests an alternative encoding that tends in the long run towards the fixed Huffman encoding, but which starts with no knowledge of the probability distribution of the characters, adapting the code as the message is being sent.

Each character is encoded with a Huffman code that would be optimal for a message consisting of all those characters that have gone before it. This encoding technique has the startling property that, since the decoder has already decoded the preceding characters, it can deduce from the received message what code should be used to decode each character. There is no longer a problem in communicating the code as well as the message!

It might seem that Gallager's adaptive coder requires that a new coding tree be constructed for each character of the transmitted and received message. Fortunately, this is not the case: the accumulated character probabilities change little, so the shape of the tree tends to settle down; successive trees are sufficiently similar that it is fairly easy to construct each from its predecessor.

The idea is to write a process *increase.weight*(*tree, char*) which modifies the coding tree so as to be consistent with a frequency distribution with one more occurrence of the character *char* than previously. Were relative probabilities used as before, whenever a character arrived the weights of all the components of the tree would have to change, to reflect the reduced likelihood of every other character. This problem is avoided by using absolute character frequencies. The probability is diminished by increasing the implicit denominator, the total number of characters received, while leaving the numerators unchanged except in the branch of the tree containing the representative of the newly arrived character.

To keep track of the accumulated frequencies, the *weight* (now implemented by []INT, rather than []REAL32) must become a permanent part of the representation of the tree

```
VAL INT number.of.arrays IS 5 :
VAL INT weight.index IS 4 :
```

and we will normally refer to this new component by another abbreviation

```
[]INT weight IS tree[weight.index] :
```

The encoding process becomes Process 14.16, and the corresponding decoding process is Process 14.17.

In order to increment the recorded frequency of a character, it is necessary to increment the weight of its representative leaf

```
VAL INT node IS representative[index(char)] :
weight[node] := weight[node] + 1
```

There are two ways in which this may have damaged the structure of the tree. First of all, unless the tree has only the one node, the weight of the parent of *node* is no longer the sum of the weights of its children: it will be necessary to increment the weights of the parent of the node, and all of its ancestors up to the root

```
INT node :
SEQ
  node := representative[index(char)]
  WHILE node <> root
    SEQ
      weight[node] := weight[node] + 1
      node := parent[node]
  weight[root] := weight[root] + 1
```

Secondly, each time the weight of a node, be that the original leaf or one of its ancestors, is increased there is a danger that the ordering of the weights may be upset. If this is the case then it is time to reorganize the tree, and change the encoding.

Assuming that the tree is initially properly ordered, then the ordering will first fail when $weight[node - 1] = weight[node]$ and the weight of *node* is about to be incremented. Now, the trees rooted at nodes of equal weight must be disjoint trees, that is either the nodes are siblings, or they have ancestors which are siblings. This follows from the fact that the weight of a node is always less than that of its ancestors, and greater than that of its descendants, so another node with the same weight is neither an ancestor nor a descendant.

To preserve the ordering on the nodes, it would be possible to exchange the trees rooted at *node* and *node* − 1, and then to increment the weight of the light node in its new position. Since there might be many nodes with the same weight, however, this would have to be done repeatedly, shuffling the imminently overweight node leftwards in the tree, by a process like

```
WHILE weight[node-1] = weight[node]
  SEQ
    swap.trees(tree, node, node - 1)
    node := node - 1
```

Process 14.16

```
PROC copy.encoding(CHAN OF INT source,
                   CHAN OF SIGNAL end.of.source,
                   CHAN OF BIT sink             )
  BOOL more.characters.expected :
  [number.of.arrays][size.of.tree]INT tree :
  SEQ
    initialize.tree(tree)
    more.characters.expected := TRUE
    WHILE more.characters.expected
      ALT
        INT char :
        source ? char
          SEQ
            encode.character(sink, tree, char)
            increase.weight(tree, char)
        end.of.source ? CASE signal
          more.characters.expected := FALSE
    encode.character(sink, tree, end.of.message)
:
```

Process 14.17

```
PROC copy.decoding(CHAN OF BIT source,
                   CHAN OF INT sink   )
  BOOL more.characters.expected :
  [number.of.arrays][size.of.tree]INT tree :
  SEQ
    initialize.tree(tree)
    more.characters.expected := TRUE
    WHILE more.characters.expected
      INT char :
      SEQ
        decode.character(source, tree, char)
        IF
          char <> end.of.message
            SEQ
              sink ! char
              increase.weight(tree, char)
          char = end.of.message
            more.characters.expected := FALSE
:
```

An alternative solution is to look for the leftmost node of the given weight, and exchange with that node, directly. The same argument about the weight of a node being less than that of its ancestors shows that there is always a sequence of nodes for which

$$weight[(node - i) - 1] > weight[node - i] = \ldots = weight[node]$$

This leftmost node, indexed $node - i$, is identified, and the exchange performed, by something like

```
IF i = 1 FOR (node - root) - 1
  weight[(node - i) - 1] > weight[node]
    SEQ
      swap.trees(tree, node, node - i)
      node := node - i
```

Unfortunately neither this nor the simpler WHILE loop would be legal in occam 2: in the scope of an abbreviation of the *weight* component of *tree*, mention of *tree* is allowed only in making further, non-overlapping abbreviations. Passing *tree* as an argument to *swap.trees* is therefore not allowed, as the procedure call is within the scope of whichever abbreviation makes *weight* accessible in the Boolean condition.

There are several ways to circumvent this clash of scopes. The test could use the unabbreviated forms like *tree*[*weight.index*][*node*]. Another possibility is to make the declaration of *swap.trees* local to the routine that calls it, so that it inherits the abbreviated components of *tree* as free variables. The technique adopted here is to encapsulate the reference to *weight* in a new scope, that of the body of a function *compare.weights* (Process 14.18).

Process 14.18

```
VAL INT lighter IS -1 :
VAL INT same.weight IS 0 :
VAL INT heavier IS 1 :
INT FUNCTION compare.weights(VAL [][]INT tree, VAL INT a, b)
  INT result :
  VALOF
    VAL []INT weight IS tree[weight.index] :
    IF
      weight[a] < weight[b]
        result := lighter
      weight[a] = weight[b]
        result := same.weight
      weight[a] > weight[b]
        result := heavier
    RESULT result
  :
```

Combining these fragments yields an algorithm which normally increments the weight of a node, and each of its ancestors; and if this would unbalance the tree, moves the node to where it is safe to increment its weight:

```
INT node :
SEQ
  ... abbreviate representative from tree in next line only
  node := representative[index(char)]
  WHILE node <> root
    CASE compare.weights(tree, node - 1, node)
      heavier
        ... abbreviate parent and weight from tree
        SEQ
          weight[node] := weight[node] + 1
          node := parent[node]
      same.weight
        IF i = 1 FOR (node - root) - 1
          compare.weights(tree, (node-i)-1, node) = heavier
            SEQ
              swap.trees(tree, node, node - i)
              node := node - i
  ... abbreviate weight from tree
  weight[root] := weight[root] + 1
```

The procedure *swap.trees* must exchange the positions in *tree* of two disjoint sub-trees. This must, amongst other things, achieve the effect of

```
eldest[i], eldest[j] := eldest[j], eldest[i]
```

where i and j are the node indices passed as parameters to the call of *swap.trees*. Unfortunately, it is not immediately obvious that *eldest*[i] and *eldest*[j] are distinct components of the array *eldest*, so the variables in that particular multiple assignment would not be detectably disjoint.

The programmer's intention that they will always be disjoint can be made explicit by abbreviating the two variables:

```
INT ei IS eldest[i] :
INT ej IS eldest[j] :
ei, ej := ej, ei
```

forcing a compiler to check, or to cause a check during execution, that *ei* and *ej* are distinct. The same effect can be achieved by using the procedure parameter mechanism to make the abbreviations

```
PROC swap.ints(INT a, b)
  a, b := b, a
:
swap.ints(eldest[i], eldest[j])
```

Process 14.19

```
PROC swap.trees([][]INT tree, VAL INT i, j)
  -- Exchange disjoint sub-trees rooted at i and j
  PROC swap.ints(INT a, b)
    a, b := b, a
  :
  ... abbreviate eldest, parent, etc. from tree
  PROC adjust.offspring(VAL INT i)
    -- restore downstream pointers to node i
    IF
      eldest[i] = root
        representative[index(character[i])] := i
      eldest[i] <> root
        SEQ child = eldest[i] FOR 2
          parent[child] := i
  :
  SEQ
    swap.ints(eldest[i], eldest[j])
    swap.ints(character[i], character[j])
    adjust.offspring(i)
    adjust.offspring(j)
:
```

Process 14.19 achieves the exchange of a pair of disjoint sub-trees: first the upstream pointers, *eldest* and *character*, to the nodes are exchanged, then the process *adjust.offspring* restores the downstream pointers that are no longer correct. There is, of course, no need to exchange the weights of the nodes, since they were known to be equal.

The only remaining problem is to decide the shape of the initial coding tree: what encoding should be used to send the first character? The simplest solution would be to construct the initial tree on the assumption that all characters are equally likely to turn up, say *weight[node]* = 1 for all *representative* nodes. This means that, to begin with, the code is a fixed-length one, each character being encoded by *bits.in.character* number of bits.

An alternative technique is to keep in the coding tree only representations of characters that have actually been sent and received. Whenever a character is to be sent for the first time in the message, the code of a special escape 'character' is sent, followed by some standard representation of the new character, say its ASCII code. A new leaf must then be added to the tree to represent the new character.

In order to accommodate the escape character, the space allocated for the tree must be enlarged

```
VAL INT number.of.codes IS number.of.characters + 1 :
```

and, since the tree grows, some way must be found of recording its size. As each escape is the representation of a character that has never occurred at

all (you may not yet know which character, but you do know this), it should
be given a very low weight. This means that it is reasonable to represent it
by the rightmost (least likely) leaf of the tree. Doing this means that a single
variable *escape* will serve the purpose of recording which node represents the
escape, and which is the rightmost node of the tree. The index of the escape
node is an essential part of the coding of the tree, so it is proper to use part
of the spare space in the component of *tree* not fully filled by *representative*:

```
INT escape IS
          tree[representative.index][number.of.characters] :
```

Since the value of *escape* changes, it will not do to use it as an initial
value for the elements of *representative*. Define, instead,

```
VAL INT not.a.node IS size.of.tree :
```

then creating the initial tree is just a matter of making the escape leaf, and
initializing the array of representatives to *not.a.node* with Process 14.20.

Process 14.20

```
PROC initialize.tree([][]INT tree)
  ... abbreviate eldest, escape, etc. from tree
  SEQ
    escape := root
    weight[escape] := 1        -- minimum legal weight
    eldest[escape] := root   -- it is a leaf
    SEQ char = 0 FOR number.of.characters
      representative[char] := not.a.node
  :
```

Encoding using the new tree is substantially unchanged, excepting
that some provision must be made for sending escaped characters. First of
all, the encoding is potentially larger by the *bits.in.character* number of bits
in the unencoded representation, so we must define

```
VAL INT size.of.encoding IS
                bits.in.character + (number.of.codes - 1) :
```

The bits of the unencoded character representation can then be stored before
the encoding of the escape, to be transmitted after it:

```
SEQ i = 0 FOR bits.in.character
  encoding[i] := ((char >> i) /\ 1) = 1
```

The encoding of the escape changes as the tree is modified. It is of
course found by applying to the node representing escape the same algorithm as would be applied to the representative of any genuine character.
Process 14.21 thus performs the encoding process. The very first character

Process 14.21

```
PROC encode.character(CHAN OF BIT output,
                      VAL [][]INT tree,
                      VAL INT char          )
  -- Transmit the encoding of char along output
  ... abbreviate values of eldest, parent, etc. from tree
  [size.of.encoding]BOOL encoding :
  INT length, node :
  SEQ
    VAL INT leaf IS representative[index(char)] :
    IF
      leaf <> not.a.node
        length, node := 0, leaf
      leaf = not.a.node
        SEQ
          SEQ i = 0 FOR bits.in.character
            encoding[i] := ((char >> i) /\ 1) = 1
                           -- i'th bit of unencoded char
          length, node := bits.in.character, escape
    WHILE node <> root
      SEQ
        encoding[length] := node <> eldest[parent[node]]
        length, node := length + 1, parent[node]
    SEQ i = 1 FOR length
      output ! encoding[length - i]
  :
```

to be sent will be escaped, and since the representative node for *escape* is initially *root* the encoding of the escape will be the null sequence of bits. This means that the first transmitted bit will be the first bit of the unencoded character representation.

Decoding is also similar to decoding with a fixed code, excepting that on receipt of the coding for escape, the bits which made up the unencoded, escaped character must be read and that character reassembled. The first bit of an escaped sequence is TRUE precisely when the character is negative, and the decision

```
SEQ
  input ? bit
  IF
    bit
      char := BITNOT 0
    NOT bit
      char := 0
```

therefore correctly extends that bit to the left, so that subsequent bits can simply be shifted in from the right.

Whatever the character to be decoded, escaped or not, the first action must be to accept enough bits to represent a leaf node: initially a sequence of no bits is enough to represent the only leaf, which is *escape*. Then, if the leaf represents a character, that character has been decoded; if the leaf represents the escape, the character code must be reconstructed. Process 14.22 is a modified *decode.character* which does this.

Process 14.22

```
PROC decode.character(CHAN OF BIT input,
                      VAL [][]INT tree,
                      INT char            )
  -- Receive an encoding along input and store the
  -- corresponding character in char
  ... abbreviate values of eldest, character, etc. from tree
  INT node :
  SEQ
    node := root
    WHILE eldest[node] <> root
      BOOL go.right :
      SEQ
        input ? go.right
        IF
          go.right
            node := eldest[node] + 1
          NOT go.right
            node := eldest[node]
    IF
      node < escape
        char := character[node]
      node = escape
        BOOL bit :    -- read bits of signed character code
        SEQ
          input ? bit
          IF
            bit
              char := BITNOT 0
            NOT bit
              char := 0
          SEQ i = 2 FOR bits.in.character - 1
            SEQ
              input ? bit
              char := (char << 1) \/ (INT bit)
:
```

In order to increment the frequency of a character not yet in the tree, it is necessary to be able to construct a new leaf to be the representative of the new character. The new character has never previously been received, so its initial weight should be as low as possible, which means that it belongs next to the *escape* node, at the low-probability end of the tree.

The simplest way of adding a node to the tree is to create a node of zero weight, and then increment its weight (to one) exactly as though it had previously existed. This can be achieved by dividing the escape leaf into three: two new leaves and their parent. The new leaf has no weight when created, so there is no effect on the weights of its ancestors. Notice that a brand new leaf having no weight, the earlier data invariant – that no node has the same weight as its parent – is breached by the *escape* node and its parent. This invariant was used to show that the sub-tree exchanging was correct, so that argument has to be re-constructed. The statement of the invariant must be strengthened: no node, excepting the *escape* node, has the same weight as its parent. This is sufficient (as you should check) because it is never required that the one-node tree rooted at *escape* be exchanged with any other. Process 14.23 is the requisite *create.leaf* process.

Creating a new representative with zero weight makes new characters like those already present in the tree. In either case, recording the arrival of a character is a matter of finding a representative leaf for it, and then incrementing the weight of that leaf and making the consequential adjustments to the tree by Process 14.24.

There is one more refinement that could be added to the process *increase.weight*. At present, once the weight of the *root* (which is the total number of characters sent in the message, plus one for the *escape* node) reaches MOSTPOS INT, the next character will cause an arithmetic overflow error. This could be a serious practical problem on machines where the 'natural' integer type is the same as INT16, as messages longer than about thirty-two thousand characters would break the transmission medium. Even using explicit INT64 variables would be setting potential time-bombs for our (many-times-great-) grandchildren, were the encoding and decoding processes built into some long-lived communications system. Using cyclic arithmetic (PLUS) generates negative weights, and neither '>' nor AFTER can be guaranteed to compare the results in the correct sense. Using floating-point numbers would be no solution, either, because the rounding of the result of adding one in order to increment a frequency would eventually leave the number unchanged. The tree would therefore tend to become balanced, representing equal-length codewords.

The proper solution is to detect the problem just before it occurs, and to take avoiding action. It is arguable that the frequency of the earliest characters sent should have little bearing on the encoding of later sections of the message, especially if the data stream is in fact the concatenation of a sequence of different messages separated by some distinguished control value. Two strategies for exploiting this observation suggest themselves: the entire tree could be thrown away, and reinitialized; or less drastically, the existing weights could be scaled down. The disadvantage of the former is that each distinct character used in the rest of the message has to be re-sent in its

Process 14.23

```
PROC create.leaf(INT new.leaf, [][]INT tree, VAL INT char)
  -- Extend the tree by fission of the escape into two new leaves
  ... abbreviate eldest, parent, etc. from tree
  INT new.escape :
  SEQ
    new.leaf, new.escape := escape + 1, escape + 2
    eldest[escape] := new.leaf -- old escape is new parent
    weight[new.leaf],   eldest[new.leaf],   parent[new.leaf] :=
      0,                root,               escape
    character[new.leaf], representative[index(char)] :=
      char,              new.leaf
    weight[new.escape], eldest[new.escape], parent[new.escape] :=
      1,                root,               escape
    escape := new.escape
:
```

Process 14.24

```
PROC increase.weight([][]INT tree, VAL INT char)
  INT node :
  SEQ
    ... abbreviate representative from tree for next line only
    node := representative[index(char)]
    IF
      node <> not.a.node
        SKIP
      node = not.a.node
        create.leaf(node, tree, char)
    WHILE node <> root
      CASE compare.weights(tree, node - 1, node)
        heavier
          ... abbreviate parent and weight from tree
          SEQ
            weight[node] := weight[node] + 1
            node := parent[node]
        same.weight
          IF i = [1 FOR (node - root) - 1]
            compare.weights(tree, (node-i)-1, node) = heavier
              SEQ
                swap.trees(tree, node, node - i)
                node := node - i
    ... abbreviate weight from tree
    weight[root] := weight[root] + 1
:
```

escaped form. The latter is not as straightforward as it might seem at first sight, as one has to be careful not to scale anything down to a weight of zero; simply rounding up can lead to breaking the invariants on the tree, requiring the non-leaf nodes to be rebuilt. For the sake of the present example, the former strategy is adopted.

Since the weight of the *root* node is the sum of the (non-negative) weights of its two children, it is clear that it is *weight*[*root*] that is first in danger of overflowing. Thus if that value is tested at the start of the *increase.weight* phase, corrective action can be taken before an error occurs.

Process 14.25

```
PROC increase.weight([][]INT tree, VAL INT char)
  INT node :
  SEQ
    VAL INT limiting.weight IS MOSTPOS INT :
    INT FUNCTION heaviest.weight(VAL [][]INT tree) IS
                                    tree[weight.index][root] :
    IF
      heaviest.weight(tree) < limiting.weight
        SKIP
      heaviest.weight(tree) = limiting.weight
        initialize.tree(tree)

    ... abbreviate representative from tree for next line only
    node := representative[index(char)]
    IF
      node <> not.a.node
        SKIP
      node = not.a.node
        create.leaf(node, tree, char)

    WHILE node <> root
      CASE compare.weights(tree, node - 1, node)
        heavier
          ... abbreviate parent and weight from tree
          SEQ
            weight[node] := weight[node] + 1
            node := parent[node]
        same.weight
          IF i = 1 FOR (node - root) - 1
            compare.weights(tree, (node-i)-1, node) = heavier
              SEQ
                swap.trees(tree, node, node - i)
                node := node - i
    ... abbreviate weight from tree
    weight[root] := weight[root] + 1
  :
```

Process 14.25 is the component required for an eternal adaptive coder, provided both ends of the communication share the same natural integer size. If not, some value that both can represent as an INT should be substituted for *limiting.weight*.

That completes the adaptive coder. Notice that, since the processes *copy.encoding* and *copy.decoding* have the same interfaces as the corresponding processes in the fixed-code coder, they may be substituted into the example *copy.—* processes. There is no need to change the processes that convey the bit stream from encoder to decoder.

15

The occam 2 notation

This chapter contains a summary of the programming language, based on that in INMOS's *occam 2 Reference Manual*[4]. The intention is that this chapter will help you over any ambiguities in the informal presentation in the early chapters of the book.

The productions which describe the syntax are not the same as those in the *Reference Manual*, and if regarded as a context-free grammar they generate a smaller language. With the qualifications in the accompanying prose in each, both this chapter and the *Reference Manual* describe the same language.

The notation used in this chapter

The structure of the language is described by productions in a BNF modified to cope with the two-dimensional syntax of **occam**. Items in rectangular boxes represent literal text, and words in italics stand for syntactic classes.

Vertical bars separate alternative parses of a class. A production like

$$base.type \ = \ \boxed{\text{BOOL}} \ | \ \boxed{\text{BYTE}} \ | \ int.type \ | \ float.type$$

means that an instance of the syntactic class *base.type* can be either of the symbols BOOL or BYTE, or it can be an instance of either of the classes *int.type* or *float.type*.

Horizontal juxtaposition means that the components of a parse can appear after each other in a single (logical) line. The production

$$sequential.definition \ = \ \boxed{\text{PROTOCOL}} \ name \ \boxed{\text{IS}} \ sequential.protocol \ \boxed{:}$$

means that an instance of *sequential.definition* consists of five things: the symbol PROTOCOL, a *name*, the symbol IS, a *sequential.protocol* and a colon symbol in that sequence, all on the same line. Logical lines may be broken, and redundant spaces may be added between symbols on a line, as detailed later.

As a special case, the only parse of

$empty =$

consists of nothing at all.

Vertical juxtaposition means that the components of a parse must appear above each other, on separate logical lines. The production

$value.proc =$ | $\boxed{\text{VALOF}}$ | $specification$
| $process$ | $value.proc$
| $\boxed{\text{RESULT}}\, expr.list$ |

means that a *value.proc* could be denoted by the symbol VALOF with a *process* laid out below it, and the symbol RESULT and an *expr.list* on another line below that. While the VALOF has the indentation of the whole *value.proc*, the RESULT is indented a further two columns, and the intervening *process* has an additional two spaces indentation on each line. Wherever one line is slightly indented from the line above, the offset is always exactly two additional spaces. On the other hand, a *value.proc* could be a *specification* above a *value.proc*, and in this case both parts of the parse have the same indentation.

There are two abbreviations in our notation for sequences of instances of the same kind.

$case.input =$ $channel\,\boxed{?}\boxed{\text{CASE}}$
$\{ variant \}$

A *case.input* can have any number of instances of *variant* in it, arranged one above the other at the same indentation, which is in this case two spaces to the right of the indentation of the *channel*.

$fun.heading = \{_1\boxed{,}\ base.type\}\boxed{\text{FUNCTION}}\,name\,\boxed{(}\{_0\boxed{,}\ fun.formals\}\boxed{)}$

A *fun.heading* is layed out along a line. It begins with a sequence of instances of *base.type*, at least one of them, separated by commas. Between the parentheses there is a possibly empty sequence of instances of *fun.formals* separated by commas.

Micro-syntax and program layout

The layout of an occam program is significant in a way unusual in a modern programming language. A program is written as a sequence of *logical lines*, each line preceded by an indentation the depth of which is significant to the structure of the program.

A logical line can be broken into several *physical lines* by breaking it after a comma, semicolon, assignment symbol, FOR, FROM, IS or an operator in an expression. The indentation of the logical line is the number of leading spaces on its first physical line, and each of its physical lines must begin with at least this many spaces. A logical line can also be broken after an asterisk in a string denotation; in that case the subsequent physical line must begin with an asterisk preceded by at least as many spaces as the indentation of the logical line. The pair of asterisks and the intervening line break and spaces are not a part of the sequence of characters represented by the string.

A physical line ends at an end-of-line, or at the first occurrence outside matched quotation marks of two consecutive minus signs, --, which introduce a comment that extends to the end-of-line. Within a physical line, spaces are significant only between quotes, or where they separate two words or numbers that might otherwise form a single word or number, or two symbols that might be a single symbol.

A *name* is a sequence of letters and digits and full-stop characters, the first of which is a letter. Two names are different unless they are the same sequence of characters. The following sequences of upper-case letters are not names, but are reserved for use as symbols

AFTER	FOR	OR	RETYPES
ALT	FROM	PAR	ROUND
AND	FUNCTION	PLACE	SEQ
ANY	IF	PLACED	SIZE
AT	IS	PLUS	SKIP
BITAND	INT	PORT	STOP
BITNOT	INT16	PRI	TIMER
BITOR	INT32	PROC	TIMES
BOOL	INT64	PROCESSOR	TRUE
BYTE	MINUS	PROTOCOL	TRUNC
CASE	MOSTNEG	REAL32	VAL
CHAN	MOSTPOS	REAL64	VALOF
ELSE	NOT	REM	WHILE
FALSE	OF	RESULT	

A sequence of decimal digits is a *decimal* numeral; it stands for the non-negative integer so expressed to base ten. A sequence of hexadecimal digits – decimal digits, or upper-case letters from A to F inclusive – preceded by either a hash sign, #, or a dollar sign, $, is a *hexadecimal* numeral; it stands for the integer so expressed to base sixteen.

A *real* numeral consists of two sequences of digits separated by a full stop character, representing the decimal point, followed by an exponent denoted by a letter E, either a + sign or a - sign, and a sequence of decimal digits. The *real* numeral stands for the number with that decimal expansion, multiplied by ten raised to the power of the signed integer represented in

decimal in the exponent. The whole exponent may be omitted, in which case
E+0 is assumed.

A character denotation between a pair of single quotes is a *byte* numeral. Except for the single quote, double quote and asterisk characters, any printable ASCII character, that is one with a code greater than 31_{10} and less than 127_{10}, is a character denotation; its value is the corresponding code. The following are also character denotations, whose values are the codes of these characters

*c or *C	carriage return	13_{10}
*n or *N	new line	10_{10}
*s or *S	space	32_{10}
*t or *T	horizontal tab	9_{10}
*'	single quote	39_{10}
*"	double quote	34_{10}
**	asterisk	42_{10}

Any number between zero and 255_{10} also has a corresponding character denotation consisting of an asterisk, followed by a hash sign and two hexadecimal digits.

A sequence of character denotations between a pair of double quotes is a *string* constant. Its value is an array of BYTE, the length of which is the number of character denotations, and the bytes of which are the values of the character denotations taken in sequence.

Data types

Every expression in **occam 2** has a type which constrains the values which it may take.

$base.type$ = $\boxed{\text{BOOL}}$ | $\boxed{\text{BYTE}}$ | *int.type* | *float.type*

The Boolean type, denoted BOOL, has two values denoting truth and falsity. The byte or character type, denoted BYTE, is the range of integers from zero to 255_{10}.

$int.type$ = $\boxed{\text{INT16}}$ | $\boxed{\text{INT32}}$ | $\boxed{\text{INT64}}$ | $\boxed{\text{INT}}$

The integer types denote the ranges of integers with twos-complement representations in sixteen, thirty-two or sixty-four bits, respectively. The type INT is the range of integers representable in twos-complement in a bit pattern of length determined by each implementation. This would normally be the integer type on which an implementation could most efficiently perform arithmetic.

$float.type$ = $\boxed{\text{REAL32}}$ | $\boxed{\text{REAL64}}$

The floating-point types denote those approximate reals representable according to ANSI/IEEE Standard 754-1985 in thirty-two bits (sign bit, eight bit exponent, twenty-three bit fraction) and sixty-four bits (sign bit, eleven bit exponent, fifty-two bit fraction) respectively.

$$data.type \;\; = \;\; base.type \;\; | \;\; \boxed{[}\, expr\, \boxed{]}\; data.type$$

The data types in occam 2 are these primitive types, and the types of finite homogeneous sequences of other data types. An array type has a *size* or length which is determined by the value of an expression of type INT between brackets; the values of an array type are sequences of the given size, each component of the sequence being of the type given after the brackets.

Protocols

Communications in occam 2 conform to protocols in the same way that values have types.

$$
\begin{aligned}
protocol &\quad= \quad name \mid simple.protocol \mid anarchic\\
protocol.definition &\quad= \quad sequential.definition \mid discriminated.definition
\end{aligned}
$$

A *protocol* may be denoted by a *name* bound in a protocol definition, or may be given as a simple protocol expression.

$$
\begin{aligned}
simple.protocol &\;=\; data.type \mid count.type\,\boxed{::}\,\boxed{[}\boxed{]}\; data.type\\
count.type &\;=\; int.type \mid \boxed{\text{BYTE}}
\end{aligned}
$$

To each data type there corresponds a simple protocol with the same name; a communication conforms to this protocol if and only if both the value sent and the variable into which it is received are of the corresponding type. A counted array protocol is described by a *count.type*, and the *data.type* of the components of an array; a communication conforms to this protocol if it consists of a size of the *count.type* and a segment of that size from an array of components of the *data.type*.

$$
\begin{aligned}
sequential.definition &\;=\; \boxed{\text{PROTOCOL}}\; name\,\boxed{\text{IS}}\; sequential.protocol\,\boxed{:}\\
sequential.protocol &\;=\; \{_1\boxed{;}\; simple.protocol\}
\end{aligned}
$$

In the scope of a sequential protocol definition, the *name* is bound to a sequential protocol. A sequential protocol is denoted by a semicolon-separated sequence of simple protocols. A communication conforms to the sequential protocol if it is an input or output of a sequence of items each component of which conforms to the corresponding simple protocol.

$$discriminated.definition \quad = \quad \boxed{\text{PROTOCOL}} \; name$$
$$\boxed{\text{CASE}}$$
$$\{ tagged.protocol \}$$
$$\boxed{:}$$
$$tagged.protocol \quad = \quad tag \; | \; tag \, \boxed{;} \, sequential.protocol$$
$$tag \quad = \quad name$$

In the scope of a discriminated protocol definition, its *name* denotes a discriminated protocol; the definition also binds in its scope the names of each *tag*, each of which must be distinct from the others. An output conforms to the discriminated protocol if it consists of a *tag* of the protocol, and a possibly empty sequence of values which conforms to any corresponding sequential protocol. An input conforms to the discriminated protocol if it is a case input over some or all of the *tag*s of the protocol, each branch of which is an input that conforms to a *tagged.protocol* of the protocol.

$$anarchic \quad = \quad \boxed{\text{ANY}}$$

An output of a value of any data type conforms to the *anarchic* protocol, as does an input into a variable of any type. An output to a channel with this protocol sends the sequence of bytes which retypes the value; an input from a channel with this protocol assigns a sequence of bytes to that variable as if it had been retyped to a sequence of bytes. It is invalid for a co-operating output and input to send and expect byte sequences of different lengths.

Literals

A *literal* constant denotes a specific value of its type, independently of its context.

$$literal \quad = \quad bool.literal \; | \; byte.literal \; | \; int.literal \; | \; float.literal$$

There are *literal*s of each of the base data types.

$$bool.literal \quad = \quad \boxed{\text{TRUE}} \; | \; \boxed{\text{FALSE}}$$

The constants TRUE and FALSE denote truth and falsity, respectively, and are of type BOOL.

$$byte.literal \quad = \quad byte \; | \; byte \, \boxed{(} \boxed{\text{BYTE}} \boxed{)} \; | \; integer \, \boxed{(} \boxed{\text{BYTE}} \boxed{)}$$

A *byte* numeral optionally followed by BYTE in parentheses represents its value, of type BYTE. An *integer* between zero and 255_{10} followed by BYTE in parentheses represents the BYTE of that value.

$$int.literal \quad = \quad integer \; | \; integer \, \boxed{(} int.type \boxed{)} \; | \; byte \, \boxed{(} int.type \boxed{)}$$

integer   =   *decimal* | *hexadecimal*

A *decimal* numeral followed by the name of an integer type in parentheses represents the value of that constant in that type, provided that it lies between zero and the most positive value of its type.

A *hexadecimal* numeral followed by the name of an integer type in parentheses is also an *int.literal*. It represents the signed integer of the given type with that twos-complement representation in the number of bits appropriate to that type which, when regarded as an unsigned binary number, would have the value of the *hexadecimal* numeral. It is valid only if its value lies between the most negative and most positive values of its type.

A *byte* numeral followed by the name of an integer type in parentheses represents the value of that constant in the given type.

If an *int.literal* appears without a specified type, (INT) is assumed.

float.literal   =   *real* $\lceil$ (*float.type*) $\rceil$

A *real* numeral followed by the name of a floating-point type in parentheses is a constant of that type. Its value is that of the numeral rounded to a value of the type, provided that this is in the range of values representable in the type.

Rounding takes a real number within the range of the type to the floating-point number which differs in value by less than half of the weight of its least significant bit; or if there are two numbers differing from it by exactly half the weight of the least significant bit, to the one with zero as its least significant bit.

Arrays

A *table* denotes a sequence of values all of the same type.

table   = $\lceil$ [{ 1 , } *expr* }] $\rceil$ | *string* | *name*

A *table* expression consists of a sequence of expressions all of the same type, separated by commas and enclosed in brackets. Its size is the number of expressions, and its type is that of arrays of that many components of the type of each expression. Its value is the sequence of values of the expressions, taken in order. A *string* is equivalent to the *table* expression with the same value. A *name* bound to a *table* value can be used to stand for the value.

part   =   *table* | *part* $\lceil$ [*expr*] $\rceil$ | $\lceil$ [*part* FROM *expr* FOR *expr*] $\rceil$

An INT indexing expression in brackets after a *part* of array type selects a component from the value of the *part*. The value of the expression must be no less than zero, and strictly less than the size of the array. The value of the selection is that component of the value of the array with the given index, counting from zero for the first component.

A contiguous segment of an array value is specified by giving two INT expressions: the first is an index into the array value, which component is the first of the segment; the second is the size of the segment. A segment is valid only if each component of it is a valid component of the array from which it is drawn.

Specification and scope

A *specification* binds some names within its scope.

> *specification* = *declaration* | *abbreviation* | *definition*
>
> *definition*   = *protocol.definition* | *proc.definition* | *fun.definition*

In the text of the syntactic entity that follows the *specification* a *name* bound in the *specification* refers to that to which it is bound by that *specification*. The scope of a *specification* is the text of the syntactic entity following the *specification*, excluding any text in the scope of a *specification* of the same *name* contained in that syntactic entity.

Declaration

Every declared object or array of objects has a *type*.

> *type* = *data.type* | *channel.type* | *port.type* | *timer.type*

A *specifier* denotes a range of types.

> *specifier*   = *type* | $[\![$ *expr.option* $]\!]$ *specifier*
>
> *expr.option*   = *expr* | *empty*

If the *specifier* has the form of a *type*, it consists of just that *type*. A *specifier* preceded by an INT expression in brackets contains the types of all arrays with size equal to the value of the expression, and with components in the *specifier*. A *specifier* preceded by an empty pair of brackets consists of the types of all arrays with components that have types in the component *specifier*, irrespective of the sizes of the arrays.

A *declaration* introduces new variables, channels, ports or timers, and gives names to them.

> *declaration* = *type* { 1 $[\![,]\!]$ *name* } $[\![:]\!]$

In each case, a multiple *declaration*

$$type\ name_1,\ name_2,\ \dots,\ name_N :$$
$$scope$$

is equivalent to

$$type'\ name_1 :$$
$$type'\ name_2 :$$
$$\dots$$
$$type'\ name_N :$$
$$scope$$

where *type'* denotes the same type as *type*, but contains no occurrences of the declared names.

A *declaration* of a *name* with a *data.type* introduces a new variable of that type, and binds the *name* to that *variable*:

$$variable\ =\ name\ |\ variable\,\boxed{[}\,expr\,\boxed{]}\ |\ \boxed{[}\,variable\,\boxed{\text{FROM}}\,expr\,\boxed{\text{FOR}}\,expr\,\boxed{]}$$

In the scope of the declaration, the *name* can be used to refer to that *variable* for assignment, or to the value most recently assigned to that *variable*.

A component of a *variable* which has an array type is denoted by following the *variable* by an INT expression in brackets. The value of the expression must be non-negative and strictly less than the size of the array; the denoted *variable* is the component of the array with that index, the first component having index zero.

A contiguous segment of a *variable* which has an array type is specified by a pair of INT expressions: the value of the first is the index in the *variable* of the first component of the segment; the value of the second is the size of the segment. A segment selection is valid only if each component of it is a valid component of the *variable* array from which it is drawn.

A *declaration* of a *name* with a *channel.type* introduces a new channel or array of channels, and binds the *name* to that new object:

$$channel.type\ =\ \boxed{\text{CHAN}}\,\boxed{\text{OF}}\,protocol\ |\ \boxed{[}\,expr\,\boxed{]}\,channel.type$$

To each *protocol* there corresponds a *channel.type*, all communications on channels having that *channel.type* being required to conform to the *protocol*. The type of an array of channels is denoted by giving the size of the array in brackets before the type of the component.

$$channel\ =\ name\ |\ channel\,\boxed{[}\,expr\,\boxed{]}\ |\ \boxed{[}\,channel\,\boxed{\text{FROM}}\,expr\,\boxed{\text{FOR}}\,expr\,\boxed{]}$$

In the scope of a channel declaration, the bound *name* can be used to refer to the collection of channels. Components and segments of arrays of channels can be selected exactly as with variables. A *channel* which has the *channel.type* of a single channel of some protocol can be used for communications which conform to that protocol.

A *declaration* of a *name* with a *port.type* introduces a new port or array of ports, and binds the *name* to that new object:

port.type = $\boxed{\text{PORT}}\boxed{\text{OF}}$ *data.type* | $\boxed{\text{[}}$ *expr* $\boxed{\text{]}}$ *port.type*

To each *data.type* there corresponds a *port.type*, it being allowed on ports having that *port.type* to read and write values of that *data.type*. The type of an array of ports is denoted by giving the size of the array in brackets before the type of the component.

port = *name* | *port* $\boxed{\text{[}}$ *expr* $\boxed{\text{]}}$ | $\boxed{\text{[}}$ *port* $\boxed{\text{FROM}}$ *expr* $\boxed{\text{FOR}}$ *expr* $\boxed{\text{]}}$

In the scope of a port declaration, the bound *name* can be used to refer to the collection of ports. Components and segments of arrays of ports can be selected exactly as with variables. A *port* which has the *port.type* of a single port of some data type can be used for reading and writing values of that type.

A *declaration* of a *name* with a *timer.type* introduces a new timer or array of timers, and binds the *name* to that new object:

timer.type = $\boxed{\text{TIMER}}$ | $\boxed{\text{[}}$ *expr* $\boxed{\text{]}}$ *timer.type*

The type of a single timer is denoted TIMER and the type of an array of timers is denoted by giving the size of the array in brackets before the type of the component.

timer = *name* | *timer* $\boxed{\text{[}}$ *expr* $\boxed{\text{]}}$ | $\boxed{\text{[}}$ *timer* $\boxed{\text{FROM}}$ *expr* $\boxed{\text{FOR}}$ *expr* $\boxed{\text{]}}$

In the scope of a timer declaration, the bound *name* can be used to refer to the collection of timers. Components and segments of arrays of timers can be selected exactly as with variables. A *timer* which has the *timer.type* of a single timer can be used for reading the time on the corresponding clock, or for delaying execution.

Abbreviation

An *abbreviation* makes a new binding of a name to an existing object or to the value of an expression:

abbreviation = *value.abbreviation* | *object.abbreviation* | *retyping*

In the scope of a *value.abbreviation* the newly bound *name* can be used to stand for the value of the abbreviated expression:

value.abbreviation = $\boxed{\text{VAL}}$ *specifier.option name* $\boxed{\text{IS}}$ *expr* $\boxed{:}$

specifier.option   = *specifier* | *empty*

If a *specifier* is quoted in the abbreviation, the abbreviated expression must have a type in that *specifier*.

The *value.abbreviation* is invalid if the *expr* which it abbreviates is invalid. It is invalid in the scope of a *value.abbreviation* to change the value of any *variable* used in the *expr* being abbreviated.

A *variable*, *channel*, *port*, *timer*, or an array, or array of arrays of these, or a component or segment of such an array, can be given a new name by an abbreviation:

object.abbreviation = *specifier.option name* $\boxed{\text{IS}}$ *object* $\boxed{:}$

object   = *variable* | *channel* | *port* | *timer*

In the scope of the *abbreviation* the newly bound *name* can be used to stand for the abbreviated object. If a *specifier* is quoted, the abbreviated object must have a *type* in that *specifier*.

The *object.abbreviation* is invalid if the *object* which it abbreviates is invalid. It is invalid in the scope of an *object.abbreviation* to refer to the abbreviated object except by means of the *name* bound in the abbreviation. It is also invalid in the scope of an *object.abbreviation* to change the value of any *variable* used in selecting the *object* being abbreviated.

It is invalid in the scope of an abbreviation of a component and segment of an array to refer to any part of the array, except that it may be referred to in other abbreviations of components and segments, provided that the abbreviated components and segments are mutually disjoint.

retyping = *value.retyping* | *object.retyping*

A *retyping* conversion makes an implementation-dependent binding of a *name* with one type to an expression or value of another. In the scope of the *retyping*, the type of the *name* bound is in the given *specifier*. It is necessary that the number of bits in the representation of values of both types be the same.

value.retyping = $\boxed{\text{VAL}}$ *specifier name* $\boxed{\text{RETYPES}}$ *expr* $\boxed{:}$

A *value.retyping* behaves like a *value.abbreviation* of an *expr*, except that the value to which the *name* is bound is that value of the specified type which has the same representation as the value of the *expr* abbreviated.

object.retyping = *specifier name* $\boxed{\text{RETYPES}}$ *variable* $\boxed{:}$

An *object.retyping* behaves like an *object.abbreviation* of a *variable*, except that the value of the *name* is that value of the specified type which has the same representation as the value of the *variable* abbreviated, and values assigned to the *name* are stored as that value of the type of the abbreviated *variable* which has the same representation.

Expressions

An expression has a type which is fixed and is determined by the types of the constants and variables that occur in it. It has also a value determined by the values of the constants that occur in it and the values, when it is evaluated, of the variables that occur in it.

If a process requires the evaluation of an expression which leads to the evaluation of a sub-expression which is invalid, the process behaves like STOP.

$$expr \;\; = \;\; rand \mid mon.op\,rand \mid rand\,rator\,rand \mid conversion \mid extremum$$

$$rand \;\; = \;\; literal \mid part \mid variable \mid \boxed{(}\,expr\,\boxed{)} \mid \begin{array}{c}\boxed{(}\,value.proc\\\boxed{)}\end{array} \mid fun.call$$

$$rator \;\; = \;\; number.op \mid modulo.op \mid bit.op \mid logic.op \mid shift.op \mid relate.op$$

The type and value of an expression which is a *literal* or *part* are those of the *literal* or *part*. The type of an expression which is a *variable* is that of the *variable*, and its value is the value most recently assigned to the *variable*.

Expressions containing two or more applications of an operator must be grouped by parentheses to specify the order of evaluation.

A *value.proc* or *fun.call* which occurs in an *expr* must return a single value; the type and value of such an expression are those of the returned value.

$$mon.op \;\; = \;\; \boxed{-} \mid \boxed{\text{MINUS}} \mid \boxed{\char`\~} \mid \boxed{\text{BITNOT}} \mid \boxed{\text{NOT}} \mid \boxed{\text{SIZE}}$$

If x has any *int.type* or *float.type*, and *zero* is the zero of the same type, then $-x$ is the same as $zero - x$, and if x has any *int.type*, MINUS x is the same as *zero* MINUS x.

If x has any *int.type*, and *ones* is the minus one of the same type, represented by a bit pattern every bit of which is one, then $\char`\~x$ and BITNOT x are both the same as *ones* >< x.

If x has type BOOL, so does NOTx; and its value is true or false according as the value of x is false or true, respectively.

If x has an array type, $[n]T$, the type of SIZE x is INT, and its value is the number, n, of components in x.

$$number.op \;\; = \;\; \boxed{+} \mid \boxed{-} \mid \boxed{*} \mid \boxed{/} \mid \boxed{\backslash} \mid \boxed{\text{REM}}$$

If x and y have the same *int.type* and $\oplus$ is a *number.op*, then the type of $x \oplus y$ is the same *int.type*. The value of $x + y$ is the sum of the values of x and y, that of $x - y$ is the difference of their values, that of $x * y$ is the product of their values. Provided that y is not zero, the value of $x \,/\, y$ is the quotient of x by y truncated to an integer, and the value of $x \,\backslash\, y$ is the remainder from that division. If the division is not exact, the sign of the remainder is the same as that of x, so that provided it is valid $((x \ / \ y) * y) + (x \setminus y)$ has the same value as x.

In each case the expression is invalid if its value has no representation of the type; division or remainder by zero is invalid.

If x and y have the same *float.type* and $\oplus$ is a *number.op*, then the type of $x \oplus y$ is the same *float.type*. In each case the value is rounded to the nearest value of its type, as specified by ANSI/IEEE Standard 754-1985. The value of $x + y$ is the sum of the values of x and y, that of $x - y$ is the difference of their values, that of $x * y$ is the product of their values, and provided that y is not zero that of $x \ / \ y$ is the quotient of x by y. The value of $x \setminus y$ is the remainder on taking from x a number of multiples of y which is $x \ / \ y$ rounded to an integer.

In each case the expression is invalid if its value is outside the range representable by proper values of the type; division or remainder by zero is invalid. That is, an expression is invalid if the Standard would require its value to be an 'infinity' or a 'not a number' value.

The remainder operation can also be denoted REM which is a synonym for \.

modulo.op = PLUS | MINUS | TIMES

If x and y have the same *int.type* and $\oplus$ is a *modulo.op*, then the type of $x \oplus y$ is the same *int.type*. In each case, the value is calculated modulo the number of representable values of that type. The value of x PLUS y differs from the sum of the values of x and y by a multiple of the range of its type, that of x MINUS y from the difference of their values, and that of x TIMES y from the product of their values.

Thus, for example, if x and y are of INT16 the value of x PLUS y is that INT16 which differs from $x + y$ by a multiple of 2^{16}.

logic.op = AND | OR

If x and y are both of type BOOL, and $\oplus$ is a *logic.op*, then $x \oplus y$ has type BOOL. If x is false, then so is x AND y and it need not be valid to evaluate y, otherwise its value is that of y. If x is true, then so is x OR y and it need not be valid to evaluate y, otherwise its value is that of y.

As a concession to the associativity of AND and OR, expressions in these operators need not be fully parenthesized; $(x$ AND $y)$ AND z may be written x AND y AND z, and $(x$ OR $y)$ OR z may be written x OR y OR z.

bit.op = /\ | BITAND | \/ | BITOR | ><

If x and y have the same *int.type* and $\oplus$ is a *bit.op*, then the type of $x \oplus y$ is the same *int.type*. In each case, the value has a representation each bit of which is determined by the corresponding bit in the representations of the values of x and y. A bit in $x /\backslash y$ is one when both of the corresponding bits in x and y are one, a bit in $x \backslash/ y$ is zero when both of the corresponding bits in x and y are zero, and a bit in $x >< y$ is one when the corresponding bits in x and y differ. BITAND is a synonym for $/\backslash$, and BITOR is a synonym for $\backslash/$.

$$shift.op \;=\; \boxed{<<} \;\Big|\; \boxed{>>}$$

If x has an *int.type*, y is of type INT, and $\oplus$ is a *shift.op*, then the type of $x \oplus y$ is the same as that of x. In each case, the value has a representation obtained by shifting the representation of the value of x by a number of bit positions determined by the value of y. Bits which are shifted out of the representation are discarded, vacated bit positions are filled by zero bits. The value of $x << y$ is x shifted away from the least significant bit (leftwards) by y bits; that of $x >> y$ is x shifted away from the most significant bit (rightwards) by y bits.

It is invalid for the value of y to be negative, or to exceed the number of bits in the representation of the type being shifted.

$$relate.op \;=\; equality \;\mid\; inequality \;\mid\; after$$
$$equality \;=\; \boxed{=} \;\Big|\; \boxed{<>}$$

If x and y have the same *base.type* and $\oplus$ is an *equality*, then $x \oplus y$ has type BOOL. The value of $x = y$ is true if x and y are equal, and false otherwise; that of $x <> y$ is false if x and y are equal, and true otherwise.

$$inequality \;=\; \boxed{<} \;\Big|\; \boxed{<=} \;\Big|\; \boxed{>} \;\Big|\; \boxed{>=}$$

If x and y have the same *int.type* or *float.type*, or are both of type BYTE, and $\oplus$ is an *inequality*, then $x \oplus y$ has type BOOL. The value of $x < y$ is true if x is less than y, and false otherwise; that of $x <= y$ is false if x is greater than y, and true otherwise; that of $x > y$ is true if x is greater than y, and false otherwise; that of $x >= y$ is false if x is less than y, and true otherwise.

$$after \;=\; \boxed{AFTER}$$

If x and y have the same *int.type*, then x AFTER y has type BOOL. If *zero* is the zero of the same type as x and y, the value of x AFTER y is the same as that of $(x$ MINUS $y) >$ *zero*.

$$conversion \;=\; base.type \; rounding \; rand$$
$$rounding \;=\; empty \;\Big|\; \boxed{ROUND} \;\Big|\; \boxed{TRUNC}$$

Data type conversion renders a value of one *base.type* as a numerically similar value of another *base.type*. In each case, the type of the *conversion* is the *base.type* specified. The value is approximately that of the *rand* which must itself be of some *base.type*.

Conversions are exact within and between *int.type*, BYTE and BOOL. The conversion $T\ x$ is of type T and its value is the same integer as that of x. It is invalid if the value of x is outside the range of values of T. For the purpose of conversion, FALSE is treated as zero, and TRUE is treated as one. If x has a *float.type*, the conversion REAL64 x is the REAL64 with the same value as x.

For other conversions to or from a *float.type*, either rounding or truncation must be specified. The conversion T ROUND x is of type T and has the value of x rounded to a value representable in that type. The conversion TTRUNCx is of type T and has the value of x truncated by discarding bits less significant than the least significant bit in the representation of the result. Both are invalid if the value of the result of rounding or truncation would be outside the range of values of T.

$$extremum\ =\ \boxed{\text{MOSTPOS}}\ int.type\ \mid\ \boxed{\text{MOSTNEG}}\ int.type$$

If T is any *int.type*, the value of MOSTPOS T is the largest of that type, and that of MOSTNEG T is the smallest (most negative) of that type. In both cases the type of the expression is T.

$$
value.proc\ =\ \begin{array}{l|l} \boxed{\text{VALOF}} & specification \\ process & value.proc \\ \boxed{\text{RESULT}}\ expr.list & \end{array}
$$

A *value.proc* returns the values of a list of expressions, evaluated after the execution of the *process* in its body. If a *specification* precedes a *value.proc*, the scope of the *specification* is the *value.proc* including its returned *expr.list*, but not the text of the *specification* itself.

The *process* in a *value.proc* may not assign to variables with a scope extending beyond the *value.proc* and any immediately preceding *specification*; nor may it contain any communication, nor alternation, nor parallel process. If it stops or fails to terminate, then so does any *process* which evaluates the *value.proc*.

Processes

The unit of program structure is the *process*

$$process\ =\ atom\ \mid\ construct\ \mid\ discrimination\ \mid\ loop\ \mid\ instance\ \mid\ block$$

Every *process* in a program is either a simple *atom*, or is constructed of a number of simpler processes, or is an invocation of a named process.

$$
block\ =\ \begin{array}{l|l} specification & allocation \\ process & process \end{array}
$$

If a *specification* precedes a *process*, the scope of the *specification* is the *process*, but not the text of the *specification* itself. An *allocation* may precede a *process* to locate declared objects in the store of the processor on which the *process* is to be executed.

$atom$ = $\boxed{SKIP}$ | $\boxed{STOP}$ | *assignment* | *input* | *output*

The process SKIP is immediately ready to perform no action, and always terminates. The process STOP performs no actions, and never terminates. Implementations of **occam** may provide assistance in detecting the execution of STOP.

Assignment

Assignment processes calculate the values of expressions, and store them in variables.

$$assignment = variable.list \boxed{:=} expr.list$$

$$variable.list = \{_1 \boxed{,} \; variable\}$$

$$expr.list = \{_1 \boxed{,} \; expr\} \; \bigg| \; \begin{matrix} \boxed{(} \\ \boxed{)} \end{matrix} value.proc \; \bigg| \; fun.call$$

An *assignment* stores in a list of variables the values, before the assignment, of a list of expressions; the number of variables and expressions must agree, and the type of each variable must be the same as that of the corresponding expression. An anonymous function or a call on a named function can appear in place of the list of expressions, and must return a list of values of the same number and types as the list of variables.

   If there are two or more variables assigned together, they must be detectably disjoint; the meaning of

$$v_1, \ldots, v_n := e_1, \ldots, e_n$$

is the same as

```
SEQ
  PAR
    t₁ := e₁
    ...
    tₙ := eₙ
  PAR
    v₁ := t₁
    ...
    vₙ := tₙ
```

where $t_1, \ldots, t_n$ are new variables of the same types as the corresponding expressions.

Communication

Output processes evaluate expressions and communicate their values to other processes.

$$
\begin{aligned}
output &= channel.output \mid port.output \\
channel.output &= channel\boxed{!}\,source.list \mid channel\boxed{!}\,tagged.source.list
\end{aligned}
$$

An output to a channel selects the *channel*, waits for the corresponding input to be ready, and implements a sequence of communications.

$$
\begin{aligned}
tagged.source.list &= tag \mid tag\,\boxed{;}\,source.list \\
source.list &= \{_1\boxed{;}\ source\} \\
source &= expr \mid expr\,\boxed{::}\,expr
\end{aligned}
$$

In the course of a *channel.output*, each *source* is evaluated. If the list of sources starts with a *tag*, that *tag* is sent; the value of each *source* in the *source.list* is then sent in sequence.

The value of a *source* which is an expression is the value of the expression. The value of a *source* which is a counted array consists of the size, which is the value of the first expression, and of a segment of that number of components from the start of the value of the second expression.

The sequence of an optional *tag* and *source.list* must conform to the protocol of the channel.

$$
port.output = port\boxed{!}\,expr
$$

An output to a port selects the *port*, evaluates its expression, and sends the values of the expression to that *port*. The type of the *port* must be PORT of the type of the expression.

$$
input = channel.input \mid port.input \mid timer.input \mid delay
$$

Input processes generally assign to variables some values drawn from outside the process.

$$
channel.input = channel\boxed{?}\,target.list \mid channel\boxed{?}\,\boxed{CASE}\,tagged.list
$$

An input from a channel selects the *channel*, waits for the corresponding output to be ready, and then implements a sequence of communications.

$$
\begin{aligned}
tagged.list &= tag \mid tag\,\boxed{;}\,target.list \\
target.list &= \{_1\boxed{;}\ target\} \\
target &= variable \mid variable\,\boxed{::}\,variable
\end{aligned}
$$

If the list of targets starts with a *tag*, the input process stops unless the received value matches the expected *tag*. When the next *target* is a *variable*, the *variable* is selected and the received value is assigned to it. When the next *target* is a counted array, the two variables are selected, the communicated size is stored in the first *variable*, and the communicated array is stored in a segment of that number of components at the start of the second variable. The sequence of an optional *tag* and *target.list* must conform to the protocol of the channel.

> *port.input* = *port* $\boxed{?}$ *variable*

An input from a port selects the *port*, selects a *variable*, and assigns to that *variable* a value read from that *port*. The type of the *port* must be PORT of the type of the *variable*.

> *timer.input* = *timer* $\boxed{?}$ *variable*

An input from a timer selects the *timer*, selects a *variable*, and assigns to that *variable* the reading of the clock corresponding to that *timer*.

> *delay* = *timer* $\boxed{?}$ $\boxed{\text{AFTER}}$ *expr*

A *delay* process terminates with no effect once the reading on the selected *timer* has satisfied *reading* AFTER *expr*.

Constructed processes

Processes can be constructed from components all of which are executed in sequence or in parallel, or one of which is selected for execution.

> *construct* = *sequence* | *conditional* | *parallel* | *alternation*

In each case, the representation of a constructed processes consists of a constructing keyword followed by a number of components.

For each of these constructions, a regular array of processes can be composed by replication.

> *replicator* = *name* $\boxed{=}$ *expr* $\boxed{\text{FOR}}$ *expr*

A *replicator* attached to a constructor replicates the single component of that construct, introducing in each copy a new binding for its *name*. The value of the second expression, which must be a non-negative INT, gives the number of replications. In each case

> *cons i = b* FOR *c*
>   *component*

is the same as an empty *cons* construction if the value of *c* is zero. If the
value of *c* is one, it is the same as a *cons* construction with one component
the same as *component* except that *i* is bound, as if by a value abbreviation,
to the value of the INT expression *b*. For larger positive *c*, it is equivalent to

```
cons
  cons i = b FOR 1
    component
  cons i = (b) + 1 FOR (c) − 1
    component
```

Implementations may require that the number of replications of some constructions, in particular *parallel* constructions, be constants determinable by
a compiler.

Sequential processes

Processes constructed by SEQ execute by executing all their components in
sequence.

$$sequence \;=\; \boxed{\text{SEQ}} \qquad \Big| \quad \boxed{\text{SEQ}}\; replicator$$
$$\{process\} \qquad\quad process$$

A *sequence* starts with the execution of its first component process, each
subsequent process starts if and when its predecessor has terminated, and
the whole sequence terminates when and only when the last component has
terminated.

A *sequence* is invalid if there is a channel which may be used only
for input by one of its components, and only for output by another of its
components.

Conditional processes

Processes constructed by IF execute by executing one of their components,
the selection of the component depending on the values of variables.

$$conditional \;=\; \boxed{\text{IF}} \qquad\quad \Big| \quad \boxed{\text{IF}}\; replicator$$
$$\{choice\} \qquad\quad choice$$

$$choice \;=\; guarded.choice \;\Big|\; conditional \;\Big|\; \begin{matrix} specification \\ choice \end{matrix}$$

$$guarded.choice \;=\; expr$$
$$process$$

When a *conditional* executes it evaluates in textual order the expressions
guarding its *guarded.choices* and those of its components. These expressions

must be of type BOOL. A simple *guarded.choice* is ready if its condition is TRUE, and a *conditional* is ready if it has a ready component. A ready *conditional* executes by executing the first of its ready components, and a ready *guarded.choice* executes by executing its *process* part. An unready *conditional* executes exactly like STOP, and fails to terminate.

If a *specification* precedes a *choice*, the scope of the *specification* is the *choice*, but not the text of the *specification* itself.

Homogeneous choice

There are two constructions which express particular forms of conditional discrimination, on the value of a single expression and on the tag of a communication.

$$
\begin{aligned}
\textit{discrimination} \;&=\; \textit{selection} \;\mid\; \textit{case.input}\\
\textit{selection} \;&=\; \boxed{\text{CASE}}\; \textit{expr}\\
&\qquad \{\,\textit{option}\,\}\\
\textit{option} \;&=\; \{\,\text{1}\boxed{,}\; \textit{expr}\,\}\; \mid\; \boxed{\text{ELSE}}\; \mid\; \textit{specification}\\
&\qquad \textit{process} \;\mid\; \textit{process} \;\mid\; \textit{option}
\end{aligned}
$$

The expression at the head of a *selection* is the selector, and must have an integer or byte type. The expressions listed in each *option* must be constants of the same type as the selector, and must be distinct from each other. At most one *option* in each *selection* may be indicated, by the keyword ELSE, to be selected in case no other *option* can be selected.

A *selection* executes by evaluating its selector and executing the *process* part of the *option* listing the constant with the same value. If the value of the selector does not correspond to any listed expression, the *process* part of the default *option* is executed. If the value of the selector does not correspond to any listed expression, and there is no default *option*, the *selection* stops.

If a *specification* precedes an *option*, the scope of the *specification* is the *option*, but not the text of the *specification* itself.

A *case.input* makes a discrimination on the *tag* received by input from a *channel*, which must have a discriminated protocol.

$$
\begin{aligned}
\textit{case.input} \;&=\; \textit{channel}\;\boxed{?}\boxed{\text{CASE}}\\
&\qquad \{\,\textit{variant}\,\}\\
\textit{variant} \;&=\; \textit{tagged.list} \;\mid\; \textit{specification}\\
&\qquad \textit{process} \;\mid\; \textit{variant}
\end{aligned}
$$

A *case.input* selects its *channel* and performs an input from that *channel*. The input performed is that described by the *tagged.list* which begins with the *tag* received at the beginning of the input. Each *tagged.list* must conform to the protocol of the *channel*, and the *tag* of each must be distinct from the others. If there is no *tagged.list* which begins with the *tag* received, the *case.input* stops.

If a *specification* precedes a *variant*, the scope of the *specification* is the *variant*, but not the text of the *specification* itself.

Parallel processes

Processes constructed by PAR execute by the concurrent execution of all their components.

$$parallel \ = \ \boxed{\text{PAR}} \ \bigg| \ \boxed{\text{PAR}} \ replicator \ \bigg| \ placed.parallel \ \bigg| \ pri.parallel$$
$$\{processor\} \qquad \quad processor$$

When a *parallel* construct executes, each of its component processes is executed. The whole construct terminates when and only when all of the components have terminated.

A *parallel* construct is invalid if any of its components may change the value of a variable which may be used in any other of its components. It is invalid if there is a channel which may be used by two of the component processes, both using the channel for input, or both using it for output. It is invalid if there is a port which is used in two of the component processes.

It is invalid for two or more components of a *parallel* to select, using subscripting expressions containing variables, components or segments of a single array of variables or channels or ports, and to use those components or segments in a way which would be invalid were the segments and components not disjoint.

A *parallel* construct may be decorated with configuration directives to indicate that its components be executed on different processors.

$$placed.parallel \ = \ \boxed{\text{PLACED}}\boxed{\text{PAR}} \ \bigg| \ \boxed{\text{PLACED}}\boxed{\text{PAR}} \ replicator$$
$$\{placement\} \qquad placement$$

$$placement \qquad = \ singleton \ | \ placed.parallel$$

$$singleton \qquad = \ \boxed{\text{PROCESSOR}} \ expr$$
$$process$$

Each *singleton* is executed by a processor selected, in a way determined by the implementation, by the value of its *expr* which is of type INT. Apart from this constraint, a placed *parallel* executes by the concurrent execution of its component processes, in the same way as the corresponding undecorated construct. Particular implementations may require or allow other annotations on a *singleton*, indicating for example the properties of the processor.

A placed *parallel* is invalid if it uses any variables, ports or timers declared in an enclosing scope.

In a process executed on a single processor, declared variables, channels, ports, timers, and arrays of these objects can be fixed at known locations in the store.

allocation = $\boxed{\text{PLACE}}$ *name* $\boxed{\text{AT}}$ *expr* $\boxed{:}$

The *expr* in an *allocation* must be of type INT. Its value is used as an index into a memory map which is an array of type $[\,]$ INT that occupies, in an implementation-dependent way, the whole store of the processor on which the process including the *allocation* will be executed.

The *name* must be bound to a variable, channel, port, timer, or array of these, and the effect of the *allocation* is to ensure that the named object is at the same absolute store location as the selected component of the memory map. An *allocation* is invalid if it places an object at a location which does not implement that kind of object, or if it causes several variables, channels, ports or timers to occupy the same location.

A *parallel* construct which is to be executed on a single processor may be decorated with directives to indicate the relative priority of its components.

pri.parallel = $\boxed{\text{PRI}}\boxed{\text{PAR}}$ $\quad\Big|\quad$ $\boxed{\text{PRI}}\boxed{\text{PAR}}$ *replicator*
$\qquad\qquad\qquad$ { *process* } $\qquad$ *process*

An asymmetric *parallel* executes by the concurrent execution of its component processes, in the same way as the corresponding symmetric construct, except that it is guaranteed that no component executes unless all syntactically preceding components are unable to proceed, either because they are waiting for communication or because they have terminated. An implementation may impose a limit on the number of components in an asymmetric *parallel*.

Alternative processes

Processes constructed by ALT execute by executing one of their components, the selection of the component depending on the readiness of other processes to communicate.

alternation = $\boxed{\text{ALT}}$ $\quad\Big|\quad$ $\boxed{\text{ALT}}$ *replicator* $\;\Big|\;$ *pri.alternation*
$\qquad\qquad\qquad$ { *alternative* } $\qquad$ *alternative*

An *alternation* can be ready or not; it is ready if at least one of its *alternatives* is ready. A ready *alternation* executes by executing exactly one of its ready *alternatives*. An *alternation* which is not ready suspends its execution until it becomes ready, and then executes exactly one of its *alternatives* which became ready.

$$
\begin{aligned}
alternative \quad &= \; simple.alternative \mid alternation \mid \begin{array}{l} specification \\ alternative \end{array} \\
simple.alternative \; &= \; guarded.alternative \mid case.alternative
\end{aligned}
$$

If a *specification* precedes an *alternative*, the scope of the *specification* is the *alternative*, but not the text of the *specification* itself.

$$
\begin{aligned}
guarded.alternative \; &= \; \begin{array}{l} guard \\ \quad process \end{array} \\
guard \qquad\qquad\quad &= \; \boxed{\text{SKIP}} \mid expr\,\boxed{\&}\,\boxed{\text{SKIP}} \mid input \mid expr\,\boxed{\&}\,input
\end{aligned}
$$

A simple *guarded.alternative* is ready if its *guard* is ready, and executes by executing the process appearing in its *guard* and its guarded *process* in sequence.

When SKIP appears in a *guard*, it is ready immediately the *alternative* of which it is a part is executed. A *guard* which is a *delay* is ready when the *delay* can terminate. A *guard* which is an *input* from a channel is ready when the corresponding output process is executing, even if the *input* expects a *tag* which is not being offered. A *guard* which is an *input* of any other kind is ready immediately the *alternative* of which it is a part is executed.

If the process in a *guard* is preceded by an expression, the type of that expression must be BOOL, and the *guard* is ready only if the Boolean is true and the process part is ready. A symmetric *alternation* is not valid if it contains a SKIP guard not accompanied by a Boolean expression.

$$
case.alternative \; = \; \begin{array}{l} channel\,\boxed{?}\,\boxed{\text{CASE}} \\ \quad \{\, variant \,\} \end{array} \; \Bigg| \; \begin{array}{l} expr\,\boxed{\&}\,channel\,\boxed{?}\,\boxed{\text{CASE}} \\ \quad \{\, variant \,\} \end{array}
$$

An *alternative* which consists of a *case.input* is ready when the corresponding output is executing, even if the *tag* being offered does not correspond to any *variant*. If the *case.input* is preceded by an expression, the type of that expression must be BOOL, and the *guard* is ready only if the Boolean is true and the *case.input* is ready. A ready *case.alternative* executes by executing the corresponding *case.input*.

An *alternation* preceded by a PRI is asymmetric.

$$
pri.alternation \; = \; \begin{array}{l} \boxed{\text{PRI}}\,\boxed{\text{ALT}} \\ \quad \{\, alternative \,\} \end{array} \; \Bigg| \; \begin{array}{l} \boxed{\text{PRI}}\,\boxed{\text{ALT}}\; replicator \\ \quad alternative \end{array}
$$

An asymmetric *alternation* behaves like the corresponding symmetric construct, except that no *alternative* can be selected for execution which is later in the text than the first *alternative* of the *alternation* to become ready.

Unbounded loops

An unbounded loop consists of a Boolean expression and a process.

$loop$ = $\boxed{\text{WHILE}}$ *expr*
          process

It executes as if it were

```
IF
  expr
    SEQ
      process
      WHILE expr
        process
  NOT (expr)
    SKIP
```

Procedure abstraction

A procedure definition binds a *name* to a process made parametric on a list of names.

proc.definition = *proc.heading*
                       process
                    $\boxed{:}$

proc.heading = $\boxed{\text{PROC}}$ *name* $\boxed{(}$ { 0 $\boxed{,}$ *proc.formals* } $\boxed{)}$

Names free in the *process* and which do not appear in the list of formal parameters are bound by the definitions in the scope of which the *proc.definition* occurs.

The procedure definition is invalid if its body uses for both input and output any channel which appears either as a free name of its body or as formal parameter.

An *instance* of such a procedure executes by executing the *process* in the context of additional bindings to the names of the formal parameters.

proc.formals = *specifier* { 1 $\boxed{,}$ *name* } $\mid$ $\boxed{\text{VAL}}$ *specifier* { 1 $\boxed{,}$ *name* }

A list of formal parameters with a single *specifier*

$spec\ name_1,\ name_2,\ \ldots,\ name_N$

is equivalent to

$spec'\ name_1,\ spec'\ name_2,\ \ldots,\ spec'\ name_N$

where *spec'* denotes the same *specifier* as *spec*, but contains no occurrences of the names; similarly

> VAL *spec* $name_1$, $name_2$, ..., $name_N$

is equivalent to

> VAL *spec'* $name_1$, VAL *spec'* $name_2$, ..., VAL *spec'* $name_N$

An *instance* of a *name* bound to a procedure must be accompanied by as many actual parameters as there are formal parameters to the procedure.

> *instance*   = *name* $\boxed{(}$ {o $\boxed{,}$ *proc.actual* } $\boxed{)}$
> *proc.actual* = *object* | *expr*

Its meaning is that of the body of the procedure preceded by a sequence of abbreviations, each binding the name of a formal parameter to the corresponding actual parameter. For the *instance* to be valid these abbreviations must be valid, and the process in the body of the procedure must be valid in the context of these abbreviations.

Function abstraction

A function definition binds a *name* to a list of expressions made parametric on a list of names.

> *fun.definition* = *fun.heading* $\boxed{\text{IS}}$ *expr.list* $\boxed{:}$ | *fun.heading*
>   *value.proc*
> $\boxed{:}$
>
> *fun.heading* = {1 $\boxed{,}$ *base.type* } $\boxed{\text{FUNCTION}}$ *name* $\boxed{(}$ {o $\boxed{,}$ *fun.formals* } $\boxed{)}$

Names free in the *value.proc* or *expr.list* and which do not appear in the list of formal parameters are bound by the definitions in the scope of which the *fun.definition* occurs. The form

> *fun.heading*
>   *value.proc*
> :

is entirely equivalent to

> *fun.heading* IS (*value.proc*
>   ) :

A *fun.call* returns a list of values, the type of each value being the corresponding *base.type* in the *fun.heading*; the values being those of the *expr.list* or those returned by the *value.proc*, evaluated in the context of additional bindings to the names of the formal parameters.

$$fun.formals \ = \ \boxed{\text{VAL}} \ specifier \{_1 \boxed{,} \ name\}$$

A list of formal parameters with a single *specifier*

VAL *spec name*$_1$, *name*$_2$, ..., *name*$_N$

is equivalent to

VAL *spec'* *name*$_1$, VAL *spec'* *name*$_2$, ..., VAL *spec'* *name*$_N$

where *spec'* denotes the same *specifier* as *spec*, but contains no occurrences of the names.

$$fun.call \quad = \quad name\boxed{(}\{_0\boxed{,} \ fun.actual\}\boxed{)}$$
$$fun.actual \ = \ expr$$

A *fun.call* of a *name* bound to a function must be accompanied by as many actual parameters as there are formal parameters to the function.

Its meaning is that of the body of the function, preceded by a sequence of value abbreviations, each binding the name of a formal parameter to the value of the corresponding actual parameter. For the *fun.call* to be valid these abbreviations must be valid, and the body of the function must be valid in the context of these abbreviations.

Index of syntactic classes

Roman face page numbers, like 229, refer to the BNF production which defines the class; references in an italic face, like *229*, are to informal definitions in the prose.

Codes of the programs

In the following pages are the programs referred to in the earlier chapters of the book. They are transcribed as faithfully as circumstances permitted from originals composed and executed using an **occam** programming system. In the transcription, the structure of the text has been removed, leaving only the sequence of lines which you see here.

The programming system contains an editor for structured, folded texts. A fold is a sequence of lines that can be concealed behind a single line of the document, in the way that an inverted pleat conceals a length of material. The fixed format of **occam** programs makes it both easy, and desirable, to use hierarchical folding of a program to reveal the structure of the program.

It is harder to read 'flat', un-folded **occam** on paper than it is to read a well structured text using an editor that allows exploration of that structure. The need to present the code in this flat form has influenced its style somewhat: there are more small procedures than there might otherwise have been, and their definitions are less deeply nested than they might otherwise have been. In particular, almost none of the procedures in these programs have any free variables, as opposed to free names bound to constants.

Packing and unpacking routines

```
--  This chapter contains routines for packing and unpacking bits
--  and bytes in bytes and blocks.


--
--  access to bytes in blocks
--

VAL INT bytes.in.a.block IS 512 :

PROTOCOL BLOCK IS [bytes.in.a.block]BYTE :

--
--  accesses to bits in bytes
--

VAL INT bits.in.a.byte IS 8 :

PROTOCOL BIT IS BOOL :

PROC set.bit(BYTE byte, VAL INT bit.number, VAL BOOL bit)
  IF
    NOT bit
      byte := BYTE ((INT byte) /\ (~(1 << bit.number)))
    bit
      byte := BYTE ((INT byte) \/ (1 << bit.number))
  :

BOOL FUNCTION get.bit(VAL BYTE byte, VAL INT bit.number) IS
                        (((INT byte) >> bit.number) /\ 1) <> 0 :
```

```
--
--  pack bytes into blocks
--

PROC pack.bytes.into.blocks(CHAN OF BYTE byte.source,
                            CHAN OF SIGNAL end.of.source,
                            CHAN OF BLOCK block.sink     )
  BOOL more.bytes.expected :
  SEQ
    more.bytes.expected := TRUE
    WHILE more.bytes.expected
      [bytes.in.a.block]BYTE buffer :
      ALT
        byte.source ? buffer[0]
          SEQ
            SEQ byte.number = 1 FOR bytes.in.a.block - 1
              BYTE byte IS buffer[byte.number] :
              ALT
                more.bytes.expected & byte.source ? byte
                  SKIP
                more.bytes.expected & end.of.source ? CASE signal
                  more.bytes.expected := FALSE
                NOT more.bytes.expected & SKIP
                  SKIP
            block.sink ! buffer
        end.of.source ? CASE signal
          more.bytes.expected := FALSE
:


--
--  unpack bytes from blocks
--

PROC unpack.bytes.from.blocks(CHAN OF BLOCK block.source,
                              CHAN OF SIGNAL end.of.source,
                              CHAN OF BYTE byte.sink       )
  BOOL more.blocks.expected :
  SEQ
    more.blocks.expected := TRUE
    WHILE more.blocks.expected
      ALT
        [bytes.in.a.block]BYTE buffer :
        block.source ? buffer
          SEQ byte.number = 0 FOR bytes.in.a.block
            byte.sink ! buffer[byte.number]
        end.of.source ? CASE signal
          more.blocks.expected := FALSE
:
```

```
--
--   bit packing routines
--

PROC pack.bits.into.bytes(CHAN OF BIT bit.source,
                          CHAN OF SIGNAL end.of.source,
                          CHAN OF BYTE byte.sink        )
  BOOL more.bits.expected :
  SEQ
    more.bits.expected := TRUE
    WHILE more.bits.expected
      BYTE byte :
      ALT
        BOOL bit :
        bit.source ? bit
          SEQ
            set.bit(byte, 0, bit)
            SEQ bit.number = 1 FOR bits.in.a.byte - 1
              ALT
                more.bits.expected & bit.source ? bit
                  set.bit(byte, bit.number, bit)
                more.bits.expected & end.of.source ? CASE signal
                  more.bits.expected := FALSE
                NOT more.bits.expected & SKIP
                  SKIP
            byte.sink ! byte
        end.of.source ? CASE signal
          more.bits.expected := FALSE
:

PROC pack.bits.into.blocks(CHAN OF BIT bit.source,
                           CHAN OF SIGNAL end.of.source,
                           CHAN OF BLOCK block.sink      )
  CHAN OF BYTE bytes :
  CHAN OF SIGNAL end.of.bytes :
  PAR
    SEQ
      pack.bits.into.bytes(bit.source, end.of.source, bytes)
      end.of.bytes ! signal
    pack.bytes.into.blocks(bytes, end.of.bytes, block.sink)
:
```

```
--
--  bit unpacking routines
--

PROC unpack.bits.from.bytes(CHAN OF BYTE byte.source,
                            CHAN OF SIGNAL end.of.source,
                            CHAN OF BIT bit.sink          )
  BOOL more.bytes.expected :
  SEQ
    more.bytes.expected := TRUE
    WHILE more.bytes.expected
      ALT
        BYTE byte :
        byte.source ? byte
          SEQ bit.number = 0 FOR bits.in.a.byte
            bit.sink ! get.bit(byte, bit.number)
        end.of.source ? CASE signal
          more.bytes.expected := FALSE
:


PROC unpack.bits.from.blocks(CHAN OF BLOCK block.source,
                             CHAN OF SIGNAL end.of.source,
                             CHAN OF BIT bit.sink          )
  CHAN OF BYTE bytes :
  CHAN OF SIGNAL end.of.bytes :
  PAR
    SEQ
      unpack.bytes.from.blocks(block.source, end.of.source, bytes)
      end.of.bytes ! signal
    unpack.bits.from.bytes(bytes, end.of.bytes, bit.sink)
:
```

Distributed
implementation of buffers

```
--  This chapter implements procedures safe.multiplex and
--  safe.demultiplex for which the process
--
--     CHAN OF TAGGED.MESSAGE link :
--     CHAN OF INT back :
--     PAR
--       safe.multiplex(from.producer, link, back)
--       safe.demultiplex(link, back, to.consumer)
--
--  behaves like
--
--     PAR i = 0 FOR width
--       buffer(from.producer[i], to.consumer[i])
--


--
--  sizing constants and protocols
--

VAL INT width IS ... :              -- number of virtual channels

VAL INT longest.message IS ... :    -- length of the longest string

PROTOCOL MESSAGE IS INT::[]BYTE :

PROTOCOL SIGNAL
  CASE
    signal
:

PROTOCOL TAGGED.MESSAGE IS INT; INT::[]BYTE :
```

```
--
--   templates for the 'user' procedures
--


PROC producer(VAL INT i, CHAN OF MESSAGE output)
  --  writes some messages to output, using
  --
  --     output ! n :: v
  --
  ... omitted code
:


PROC consumer(VAL INT i, CHAN OF MESSAGE input)
  --  reads some messages from input, using
  --
  --     input ? n :: s
  --
  ... omitted code
:


--
--   component multiplexers and demultiplexers
--

PROC multiplex([]CHAN OF MESSAGE local,
               CHAN OF TAGGED.MESSAGE link )
  WHILE TRUE
    SEQ favoured = 0 FOR width
      INT count :
      [longest.message]BYTE string :
      PRI ALT
        local[favoured] ? count::string
          link ! favoured; count::string
        ALT source = 0 FOR width
          local[source] ? count::string
            link ! source; count::string
:


PROC demultiplex(CHAN OF TAGGED.MESSAGE link,
                 []CHAN OF MESSAGE local    )
  WHILE TRUE
    INT destination, count :
    [longest.message]BYTE string :
    SEQ
      link ? destination; count::string
      local[destination] ! count::string
:
```

```
PROC request.buffer(CHAN OF SIGNAL request,
                    CHAN OF MESSAGE source, sink )
  WHILE TRUE
    INT count :
    [longest.message]BYTE string :
    SEQ
      request ! signal
      source ? count::string
      sink ! count::string
:


--
--   safe.multiplex and safe.demultiplex
--

PROC safe.demultiplex(CHAN OF TAGGED.MESSAGE link,
                      CHAN OF INT back,
                      []CHAN OF MESSAGE local    )
  [width]CHAN OF SIGNAL ack :
  [width]CHAN OF MESSAGE fwd :
  PAR
    demultiplex(link, fwd)
    PAR i = 0 FOR width
      request.buffer(ack[i], fwd[i], local[i])
    WHILE TRUE
      SEQ favoured = 0 FOR width
        PRI ALT
          ack[favoured] ? CASE signal
            back ! favoured
          ALT i = 0 FOR width
            ack[i] ? CASE signal
              back ! i
:

PROC safe.multiplex([]CHAN OF MESSAGE local,
                    CHAN OF TAGGED.MESSAGE link,
                    CHAN OF INT back            )
  [width]CHAN OF SIGNAL ack :
  [width]CHAN OF MESSAGE fwd :
  PAR
    PAR i = 0 FOR width
      request.buffer(ack[i], local[i], fwd[i])
    multiplex(fwd, link)
    WHILE TRUE
      INT i :
      SEQ
        back ? i
        ack[i] ? CASE signal
:
```

```
--
--  program using the mechanism
--

CHAN OF TAGGED.MESSAGE link :
CHAN OF INT back :
PAR
  --
  --  producer processes
  --
  [width]CHAN OF MESSAGE local :
  PAR
    PAR i = 0 FOR width
      producer(i, local[i])
    safe.multiplex(local, link, back)
  --
  --  consumer processes
  --
  [width]CHAN OF MESSAGE local :
  PAR
    safe.demultiplex(link, back, local)
    PAR i = 0 FOR width
      consumer(i, local[i])
```

Process farming

```
--   This chapter uses about 'number.of.workers' processes to compute
--   the effect of
--
--      SEQ i = 0 FOR N
--        result[i] := f(task[i]))
--
--   in a way that could be executed about 'number.of.workers' times
--   more quickly on that many processors.


--
--   sizing constants
--

VAL INT N IS ... :              -- the number of independent tasks

VAL INT number.of.workers IS ... :
                                -- the number of tasks executed at once

REAL64 FUNCTION f(VAL REAL64 x) IS ... :
                                -- the task to be performed N times

VAL [N]REAL64 task IS ... :     -- the N items of data to be f(.)'d

[N]REAL64 result :              -- and the output variable
```

```
--
--   protocols
--

PROTOCOL TASK.STREAM
  CASE
    new.task; INT; REAL64
    no.more.tasks
:

PROTOCOL RESULT.STREAM
  CASE
    new.result; INT; REAL64
    no.more.results
:

PROTOCOL ADDR.TASK.STREAM
  CASE
    new.task.packet; INT; INT; REAL64
    no.more.task.packets
:

PROTOCOL ADDR.RESULT.STREAM
  CASE
    new.result.packet; INT; INT; REAL64
    no.more.result.packets
:


--
--   worker: processes a sequence of tasks
--

PROC worker(CHAN OF TASK.STREAM task.in,
            CHAN OF RESULT.STREAM result.out )
  BOOL more.tasks :
  SEQ
    more.tasks := TRUE
    WHILE more.tasks
      task.in ? CASE
        INT index :
        REAL64 task :
        new.task; index; task
          REAL64 result :
          SEQ
            result := f(task)
            result.out ! new.result; index; result
        no.more.tasks
          more.tasks := FALSE
    result.out ! no.more.results
:
```

```
--
--   foremen
--
--      task.foreman divides a stream of addressed tasks into a stream
--         of tasks for its worker, and a stream of addressed tasks for
--         the rest of the farm
--      result.foreman combines a stream of results from its worker
--         with a stream of addressed results from the rest of the farm
--

PROC task.foreman(CHAN OF ADDR.TASK.STREAM from.farmer,
                  CHAN OF TASK.STREAM to.worker,
                  CHAN OF ADDR.TASK.STREAM to.farm        )
  BOOL more.tasks :
  SEQ
    more.tasks := TRUE
    WHILE more.tasks
      from.farmer ? CASE
        INT addr, index :
        REAL64 task :
        new.task.packet; addr; index; task
          IF
            addr = 0
              to.worker ! new.task; index; task
            addr > 0
              to.farm ! new.task.packet; addr - 1; index; task
        no.more.task.packets
          more.tasks := FALSE
    to.worker ! no.more.tasks
    to.farm ! no.more.task.packets
  :
```

```
PROC result.foreman(CHAN OF ADDR.RESULT.STREAM from.farm,
                    CHAN OF RESULT.STREAM from.worker,
                    CHAN OF ADDR.RESULT.STREAM to.farmer)
  BOOL more.from.worker, more.from.farm :
  SEQ
    more.from.worker, more.from.farm := TRUE, TRUE
    WHILE more.from.worker OR more.from.farm
      ALT
        more.from.worker & from.worker ? CASE
          INT index :
          REAL64 task :
          new.result; index; task
            to.farmer ! new.result.packet; 0; index; task
          no.more.results
            more.from.worker := FALSE
        more.from.farm & from.farm ? CASE
          INT addr, index :
          REAL64 result :
          new.result.packet; addr; index; result
            to.farmer ! new.result.packet; addr + 1; index; result
          no.more.result.packets
            more.from.farm := FALSE
    to.farmer ! no.more.result.packets
:


--
--  work.detail runs a worker and a smaller farm
--

PROC work.detail(CHAN OF ADDR.TASK.STREAM from.farmer, to.farm,
                 CHAN OF ADDR.RESULT.STREAM from.farm, to.farmer )
  CHAN OF TASK.STREAM to.worker :
  CHAN OF RESULT.STREAM from.worker :
  PAR
    task.foreman(from.farmer, to.worker, to.farm)
    worker(to.worker, from.worker)
    result.foreman(from.farm, from.worker, to.farmer)
:
--
--  farmer's boy implements a farm consisting of no workers
--

PROC farmers.boy(CHAN OF ADDR.TASK.STREAM from.farm,
                 CHAN OF ADDR.RESULT.STREAM to.farm )
  PAR
    from.farm ? CASE no.more.task.packets
    to.farm ! no.more.result.packets
:
```

```
--
--  farmer distributes addressed tasks to a fixed-sized farm
--

PROC farmer(VAL []REAL64 task,
                       CHAN OF ADDR.TASK.STREAM out,
                       CHAN OF ADDR.RESULT.STREAM in,
                                    []REAL64 result )
  [number.of.workers]BOOL idle :
  INT begun, completed :
  SEQ
    SEQ i = 0 FOR number.of.workers
      idle[i] := TRUE
    begun, completed := 0, 0
    WHILE completed < (SIZE task)
      ALT   .
        INT addr, index :
        in ? CASE new.result.packet; addr; index; result[index]
          completed, idle[addr] := completed + 1, TRUE
        (begun < (completed + number.of.workers)) AND
                                    (begun < (SIZE task)) & SKIP
          IF addr = 0 FOR number.of.workers
            idle[addr]
              SEQ
                out ! new.task.packet; addr; begun; task[begun]
                begun, idle[addr] := begun + 1, FALSE
    out ! no.more.task.packets
    in ? CASE no.more.result.packets
:


--
--  the structure of the farm
--

[number.of.workers + 1]CHAN OF ADDR.TASK.STREAM outgoing :
[number.of.workers + 1]CHAN OF ADDR.RESULT.STREAM incoming :
PAR
  farmer(task, outgoing[0], incoming[0], result)
  PAR i = 0 FOR number.of.workers
    work.detail(outgoing[i], outgoing[i+1],
                incoming[i+1], incoming[i] )
  farmers.boy(outgoing[number.of.workers],
              incoming[number.of.workers] )
```

Handling interrupts

```
--  This chapter contains routines for implementing a stand-alone
--  terminal handler.
--

PROTOCOL SIGNAL
  CASE
    signal
:


--
--  hardware constants
--


VAL INT keyboard.interface IS ... : -- address of keyboard channel
VAL INT vdu.interface      IS ... : -- address of screen channel


--
--  screen output handler
--


PROC screen.handler(CHAN OF BYTE outgoing, CHAN OF SIGNAL error)

  CHAN OF BYTE screen.out :
  PLACE screen.out AT vdu.interface :

  VAL BYTE bell.character IS '*#07' :
  WHILE TRUE
    PRI ALT
      error ? CASE signal
        screen.out ! bell.character
      BYTE char :
      outgoing ? char
        screen.out ! char
:
```

```
--
--  keyboard input handler
--

VAL INT type.ahead IS 100 :        -- number of characters that can be
                                   -- typed ahead of being wanted

PROC keyboard.handler(CHAN OF SIGNAL request,
                      CHAN OF BYTE reply,
                      CHAN OF SIGNAL error   )

  -- Characters typed at the keyboard can be read from reply. A
  -- signal is required on request before each item is read. If
  -- more than type.ahead are typed ahead, an error is signalled.

  CHAN OF BYTE keystroke.in :
  PLACE keystroke.in AT keyboard.interface :

  INT reader, writer, count :
  SEQ
    reader, writer, count := 0, 0, type.ahead

    [type.ahead]BYTE datum :
    WHILE TRUE
      ALT

        BYTE lost :
        count = 0 & keystroke.in ? lost
          error ! signal

        count > 0 & keystroke.in ? datum[writer]
          count, writer := count - 1, (writer + 1) \ type.ahead

        count < type.ahead & request ? CASE signal
          SEQ
            reply ! datum[reader]
            count, reader := count + 1, (reader + 1) \ type.ahead
:
```

```
--
--  handler for echoing of input to output
--

VAL BYTE release IS 0(BYTE) :

PROC echo.handler(CHAN OF SIGNAL request,
                  CHAN OF BYTE reply, echo, inward )
  VAL BYTE enter IS '*c' :
  WHILE TRUE
    BYTE char :
    SEQ
      request ! signal
      reply ? char
      inward ! char     -- Transmit character to user
      IF
        ('*s' <= char) AND (char <= '~')
          echo ! char          -- Echo visible input to screen
        char = enter
          SEQ
            echo ! '*c'     -- Echo carriage return ...
            echo ! '*n'     -- ... and newline
            echo ! release  -- Release screen at end of line
        TRUE
          SKIP                 -- No action on other characters
:


--
--  multiplexer for screen output
--

PROC output.multiplexer([]CHAN OF BYTE from, CHAN OF BYTE outgoing )
  WHILE TRUE
    ALT selected.process = 0 FOR SIZE from
      BYTE char :
      from[selected.process] ? char
        WHILE char <> release
          SEQ
            outgoing ! char
            from[selected.process] ? char
:


--
--  template for user process
--

PROC user(CHAN OF BYTE terminal.keyboard, terminal.screen)
  ... omitted code
:
```

```
--
--   structure of the program
--

CHAN OF BYTE reply, outgoing, from.keyboard :

CHAN OF SIGNAL request, error :

VAL INT from.echo.handler IS 0 :
VAL INT from.user        IS 1 :
VAL INT number.of.outputs IS 2 :

[number.of.outputs]CHAN OF BYTE to.screen :

PRI PAR
  --
  --   high priority processes
  --
  PAR
    keyboard.handler(request, reply, error)
    echo.handler(request, reply,
                   to.screen[from.echo.handler],
                   from.keyboard               )
    screen.handler(outgoing, error)
  --
  --   low priority processes
  --
  PAR
    output.multiplexer(to.screen, outgoing)
    user(from.keyboard, to.screen[from.user])
```

Formatted input and output

```
--  This chapter defines routines to be used in other programs for
--  converting between internal and textual representations of data,
--  principally
--
--      write.string, write.decimal.int, write.hexadecimal.int, etc
--      read.signed, read.line
--      write.formatted
--      make.decimal.string.int
--


--
--  write.character, write.string, write.bool
--

PROC write.character(CHAN OF BYTE output, VAL BYTE character)
  output ! character
:

PROC write.string(CHAN OF BYTE output, VAL []BYTE string)
  SEQ i = 0 FOR SIZE string
    output ! string[i]
:

VAL []BYTE true.string  IS "true" :
VAL []BYTE false.string IS "false" :

PROC write.bool(CHAN OF BYTE output, VAL BOOL condition)
  IF
    condition
      write.string(output, true.string)
    NOT condition
      write.string(output, false.string)
:
```

```
--
--   write.hexadecimal
--

PROC write.hexadecimal.int64(CHAN OF BYTE output, VAL INT64 bits)
  VAL []BYTE hex.digit IS "0123456789abcdef" :
  SEQ i = 1 FOR 64 / 4
    VAL nibble IS INT ((bits >> (64 - (4 * i))) /\ #F(INT64)) :
    output ! hex.digit[nibble]
:

PROC write.hexadecimal.byte(CHAN OF BYTE output, VAL BYTE bits)
  write.hexadecimal.int64(output, (INT64 bits))
:

PROC write.hexadecimal.int(CHAN OF BYTE output, VAL INT bits)
  VAL INT64 mask IS (INT64 (MOSTNEG INT)) << 1 :
  write.hexadecimal.int64(output, (INT64 bits) /\ (BITNOT mask))
:

PROC write.hexadecimal.int16(CHAN OF BYTE output, VAL INT16 bits)
  VAL INT64 mask IS (INT64 (MOSTNEG INT16)) << 1 :
  write.hexadecimal.int64(output, (INT64 bits) /\ (BITNOT mask))
:

PROC write.hexadecimal.int32(CHAN OF BYTE output, VAL INT32 bits)
  VAL INT64 mask IS (INT64 (MOSTNEG INT32)) << 1 :
  write.hexadecimal.int64(output, (INT64 bits) /\ (BITNOT mask))
:
```

```
--
--  write.decimal
--

BYTE FUNCTION decimal(VAL INT d) IS BYTE (d + (INT '0')) :

PROC write.decimal.int64(CHAN OF BYTE output, VAL INT64 number)
  VAL INT64 ten.to.the.eighteen IS 1000000000000000000(INT64) :
  INT64 tens :
  SEQ
    IF
      number < 0(INT64)
        SEQ
          output ! '-'
          tens := ten.to.the.eighteen
      number >= 0(INT64)
        SEQ
          output ! '+'
          tens := -ten.to.the.eighteen
    WHILE tens <> 0(INT64)
      SEQ
        output ! decimal(INT (-((number / tens) \ 10(INT64))))
        tens := tens / 10(INT64)
:

PROC write.decimal.byte(CHAN OF BYTE output, VAL BYTE number)
  write.decimal.int64(output, (INT64 number))
:

PROC write.decimal.int(CHAN OF BYTE output, VAL INT number)
  write.decimal.int64(output, (INT64 number))
:

PROC write.decimal.int16(CHAN OF BYTE output, VAL INT16 number)
  write.decimal.int64(output, (INT64 number))
:

PROC write.decimal.int32(CHAN OF BYTE output, VAL INT32 number)
  write.decimal.int64(output, (INT64 number))
:
```

```
--
--  read.signed
--

VAL BOOL otherwise IS TRUE :

PROC read.signed(CHAN OF BYTE input, INT n, BOOL ok)
  --  read an (optionally signed) decimal numeral from the input
  --  returning the corresponding value in n, and TRUE in ok
  --  precisely if the conversion succeeded
  BYTE char, sign :
  SEQ

    input ? char
    WHILE char = '*s'               -- skip leading spaces
      input ? char

    IF
      (char = '+') OR (char = '-')  -- read a possible sign
        SEQ
          sign := char
          input ? char
      (char <> '+') AND (char <> '-')
        sign := '+'

    WHILE char = '*s'               -- skip any spaces after the sign
      input ? char

    n := 0
    ok := ('0' <= char) AND (char <= '9')  -- check for digits

    WHILE ('0' <= char) AND (char <= '9')  -- and read them
      SEQ
        VAL INT digit IS (INT char) - (INT '0') :
        IF
          (sign = '+') AND (n <= (((MOSTPOS INT) - digit) / 10))
            n := (10 * n) + digit
          (sign = '-') AND ((((MOSTNEG INT) + digit) / 10) <= n)
            n := (10 * n) - digit
          otherwise
            ok := FALSE              -- an error has occurred
        input ? char
:
```

```
--
--  read.line
--

PROC read.line(CHAN OF BYTE keyboard, echo, []BYTE s, INT n)
  VAL BYTE backspace IS '*#08' :   -- control-H
  VAL BYTE bell      IS '*#07' :   -- control-G
  VAL BYTE cancel    IS '*#15' :   -- control-U
  VAL BYTE delete    IS '*#7F' :
  VAL BYTE enter     IS '*c' :
  VAL INT max.contents IS (SIZE s) - 1 : -- leave room for enter
  SEQ
    n := 0    -- string intially empty
    BYTE char :                      -- most recent char typed
    WHILE (n = 0) OR (char <> enter)   -- not used before set
      SEQ
        keyboard ? char
        CASE char
          backspace
            IF
              n > 0  -- string not empty
                SEQ
                  echo ! backspace
                  echo ! '*s'
                  echo ! backspace
                  n := n - 1
              n = 0  -- nothing to delete
                echo ! bell
          cancel
            WHILE n >= 0            -- cancel
              SEQ                   --    backspaces over the
                n := n - 1          --    whole of the line
                echo ! backspace
                echo ! '*s'
                echo ! backspace
          enter
            SEQ                              -- carriage return
              s[n] := enter       --   is added to the string
              n := n + 1          --   and terminates the loop
          ELSE
            IF
              (n < max.contents) AND
                ('*s' <= char) AND (char < delete)
                SEQ  -- if there is room and char is printable
                  echo ! char       -- it is echoed
                  s[n] := char      -- and added to the string
                  n := n + 1
              otherwise    -- anything else is an error
                echo ! bell
:
```

```
--
--   routines used throughout write.formatted
--


--
--   min, max, lower.case, upper.case
--

INT FUNCTION min(VAL INT a, b)
  INT min :
  VALOF
    IF
      a <= b
        min := a
      b <= a
        min := b
    RESULT min
:

INT FUNCTION max(VAL INT a, b)
  INT max :
  VALOF
    IF
      a >= b
        max := a
      b >= a
        max := b
    RESULT max
:

BYTE FUNCTION lower.case(VAL BYTE char)
  BYTE result :
  VALOF
    IF
      ('A' <= char) AND (char <= 'Z')
        result := BYTE ((INT char) >< ((INT 'A') >< (INT 'a')))
      (char < 'A') OR ('Z' < char)
        result := char
    RESULT result
:

BYTE FUNCTION upper.case(VAL BYTE char)
  BYTE result :
  VALOF
    IF
      ('a' <= char) AND (char <= 'z')
        result := BYTE ((INT char) >< ((INT 'A') >< (INT 'a')))
      (char < 'a') OR ('z' < char)
        result := char
    RESULT result
:
```

```
--
--  the DATA.ITEM protocol
--

PROTOCOL DATA.ITEM
  CASE
     data.bool;   BOOL
     data.byte;   BYTE
     data.int;    INT
     data.int16;  INT16
     data.int32;  INT32
     data.int64;  INT64
     data.real32; REAL32
     data.real64; REAL64
     data.string; INT:: []BYTE
     data.abort
:


--
--  digits in numeric text, precision constants
--

VAL INT decimal.raw       IS 1+19 : -- sign and digits from decimal
VAL INT hexadecimal.raw   IS 16 :   -- and hexadecimal raw output

VAL INT real32.precision    IS  9 :
VAL INT real64.precision    IS 17 :
VAL INT nibbles.in.a.byte   IS  2 :
VAL INT nibbles.in.an.int16 IS  4 :
VAL INT nibbles.in.an.int32 IS  8 :
VAL INT nibbles.in.an.int64 IS 16 :


--
--  indexing constants for flag and field arrays
--

VAL INT left.justify IS 0 :
VAL INT    sign.plus IS 1 :
VAL INT   sign.blank IS 2 :
VAL INT number.of.flags IS 3 :

VAL INT   get.flag IS -1 :
VAL INT      width IS  0 :
VAL INT  precision IS  1 :
VAL INT field.numbers IS 2 :
```

```
--
--   discard.input, set.unless.specified, conditionally.repeat,
--   get.first.significant, split.real32, split.real64
--

PROC discard.input(CHAN OF BYTE input, VAL INT unwanted)
  SEQ i = 0 FOR unwanted
    BYTE discard :
    input ? discard
:

PROC set.unless.specified(INT parameter, VAL INT default)
  IF
    parameter >  0  -- already specified
      SKIP
    parameter <= 0  -- left to default
      parameter := default
:

PROC conditionally.repeat(VAL BOOL condition,
                          VAL INT count, VAL BYTE char,
                          CHAN OF BYTE output           )
  IF
    condition
      SEQ i = 1 FOR count
        output ! char
    NOT condition
      SKIP
:

PROC get.first.significant(CHAN OF BYTE input,
                           INT number.of.digits, BYTE digit )
  SEQ
    input ? digit
    WHILE (number.of.digits > 1) AND (digit = '0')
      SEQ
        input ? digit
        number.of.digits := number.of.digits - 1
:

INT, INT64 FUNCTION split.real32(VAL REAL32 r)
  ... code omitted
:

INT, INT64 FUNCTION split.real64(VAL REAL64 r)
  ... code omitted
:
```

```
--
--  raw.output
--

PROC raw.output(CHAN OF DATA.ITEM data, VAL BYTE format,
                CHAN OF INT info, CHAN OF BYTE uncooked )
  CASE format
    '%'  --  percent sign: no data item; just write.character
      write.character(uncooked, '%')

    'b'  --  Boolean: accept data.bool for write.bool after 'info'
      BOOL condition :
      SEQ
        data ? CASE data.bool; condition
        IF
          condition
            info ! SIZE true.string
          NOT condition
            info ! SIZE false.string
        write.bool(uncooked, condition)

    'c'  --  character: accept data.byte for write.character
      BYTE character :
      SEQ
        data ? CASE data.byte; character
        write.character(uncooked, character)

    'd'  --  decimal (signed) integer
      data ? CASE
        BYTE number :
        data.byte; number
          write.decimal.byte(uncooked, number)
        INT number :
        data.int; number
          write.decimal.int(uncooked, number)
        INT16 number :
        data.int16; number
          write.decimal.int16(uncooked, number)
        INT32 number :
        data.int32; number
          write.decimal.int32(uncooked, number)
        INT64 number :
        data.int64; number
          write.decimal.int64(uncooked, number)
```

```
'e'  --  exponential form of real
INT exponent :
INT64 mantissa :
SEQ
  data ? CASE
    REAL32 float :
    data.real32; float
      SEQ
        exponent, mantissa := split.real32(float)
        info ! real32.precision
    REAL64 float :
    data.real64; float
      SEQ
        exponent, mantissa := split.real64(float)
        info ! real64.precision
  write.decimal.int64(uncooked, mantissa)
  write.decimal.int(uncooked, exponent)

'f'  --  positional form of real
INT exponent :
INT64 mantissa :
SEQ
  data ? CASE
    REAL32 float :
    data.real32; float
      SEQ
        exponent, mantissa := split.real32(float)
        info ! real32.precision
    REAL64 float :
    data.real64; float
      SEQ
        exponent, mantissa := split.real64(float)
        info ! real64.precision
  PAR
    write.decimal.int64(uncooked, mantissa)
    info ! exponent
```

```
'x' -- hexadecimal (unsigned) integer
data ? CASE
  BYTE number :
  data.byte; number
    SEQ
      info ! nibbles.in.a.byte
      write.hexadecimal.byte(uncooked, number)
  INT16 number :
  data.int16; number
    SEQ
      info ! nibbles.in.an.int16
      write.hexadecimal.int16(uncooked, number)
  INT32 number :
  data.int32; number
    SEQ
      info ! nibbles.in.an.int32
      write.hexadecimal.int32(uncooked, number)
  INT64 number :
  data.int64; number
    SEQ
      info ! nibbles.in.an.int64
      write.hexadecimal.int64(uncooked, number)
  INT number :
  data.int; number
    SEQ
      VAL []BYTE count.bytes RETYPES number :
      info ! (SIZE count.bytes) * nibbles.in.a.byte
      write.hexadecimal.int(uncooked, number)
:
```

```
--
--  copy.translating
--

PROC copy.translating(VAL BOOL change, CHAN OF BYTE source,
                      VAL INT count, VAL BYTE first,
                      CHAN OF BYTE sink                )
  BYTE char :
  IF
    change        -- letters must be made capital
      SEQ
        sink ! upper.case(first)
        SEQ i = 2 FOR count - 1
          SEQ
            source ? char
            sink ! upper.case(char)
    NOT change    -- send unchanged
      SEQ
        sink ! first
        SEQ i = 2 FOR count - 1
          SEQ
            source ? char
            sink ! char
:


--
--  set.padding
--

PROC set.padding(VAL []INT field, VAL BOOL signed,
                 VAL INT significant.chars,
                 INT pad.zeros, pad.spaces, wanted, unwanted )
  VAL INT total.width IS field[width] :
  VAL INT displayed IS field[precision] :
  SEQ
    VAL INT discrepancy IS displayed - significant.chars :
    IF
      discrepancy >= 0  -- not enough uncooked text
        pad.zeros, wanted, unwanted :=
                        discrepancy, significant.chars, 0
      discrepancy <= 0  -- too much
        pad.zeros, wanted, unwanted := 0, displayed, -discrepancy
    pad.spaces := total.width - displayed
    IF
      signed
        pad.spaces := max(0, pad.spaces - 1)
      NOT signed
        pad.spaces := max(0, pad.spaces)
:
```

```
--
--  cook.output
--

PROC cook.output(CHAN OF BYTE uncooked, CHAN OF INT info,
                 VAL BYTE format, VAL []BOOL flag, []INT field,
                 CHAN OF BYTE cooked                          )
  VAL BYTE format.type IS lower.case(format) :
  INT raw.size, text.size :
  BOOL signed :
  BYTE sign.char, first :
  SEQ
    --
    --  set up expected numbers of characters etc
    --
    CASE format.type
      '%', 'c'
        raw.size, field[precision] := 1, 1

      'b'
        INT max.chars IS field[precision] :
        INT default.precision :
        SEQ
          info ? default.precision
          set.unless.specified(max.chars, default.precision)
          raw.size, max.chars :=
                  default.precision, min(max.chars, default.precision)

      'd'
        raw.size := decimal.raw

      'e', 'f'
        INT max.chars IS field[precision] :
        INT default.precision :
        SEQ
          info ? default.precision
          set.unless.specified(max.chars, default.precision)
          raw.size, max.chars :=
                  decimal.raw, min(max.chars, default.precision)

      'x'
        INT min.chars IS field[precision] :
        INT default.precision :
        SEQ
          info ? default.precision
          set.unless.specified(min.chars, default.precision)
          raw.size := hexadecimal.raw
```

```
--
--   process signs and leading zeros
--
CASE format.type
  '%', 'b', 'c'
    SEQ
      text.size, signed := raw.size, FALSE
      uncooked ? first

  'd', 'e', 'f'
    VAL BOOL plus  IS flag[sign.plus] :
    VAL BOOL blank IS flag[sign.blank] :
    SEQ
      uncooked ? sign.char
      signed := (sign.char = '-') OR plus OR blank
      IF
        signed AND blank AND (sign.char = '+')
          sign.char := '*s'  -- replace '+' by space
        otherwise
          SKIP
      text.size := raw.size - 1  -- sign dealt with already
      get.first.significant(uncooked, text.size, first)
      IF
        format = 'd'
          field[precision] := max(text.size, field[precision])
        format <> 'd'
          SKIP

  'x'
    SEQ
      text.size, signed := raw.size, FALSE
      get.first.significant(uncooked, text.size, first)
      field[precision] := max(text.size, field[precision])
```

```
--
--   output the massaged representation
--
VAL BOOL left   IS flag[left.justify] :
VAL BOOL right IS NOT left :
VAL BOOL upper IS format <> format.type :
INT zero.pad, space.pad, copy, truncate :
CASE format.type
  '%', 'b', 'c', 'd', 'x'
    SEQ
      set.padding(field, signed, text.size,
                            zero.pad, space.pad, copy, truncate )
      conditionally.repeat(right, space.pad, '*s', cooked)
      conditionally.repeat(signed, 1, sign.char, cooked)
      conditionally.repeat(TRUE, zero.pad, '0', cooked)
      copy.translating(upper, uncooked, copy, first, cooked)
      discard.input(uncooked, truncate)
      conditionally.repeat(left, space.pad, '*s', cooked)

  'e'
    VAL INT exp IS 3 :   -- digits of exponent
    SEQ
      -- adjust for punctuation:   point   E  sign
      field[width] := field[width] - (1 + (1 + (1 + exp)))
      set.padding(field, signed, text.size,
                            zero.pad, space.pad, copy, truncate )
      conditionally.repeat(right, space.pad, '*s', cooked)
      SEQ  -- mantissa
        conditionally.repeat(signed, 1, sign.char, cooked)
        cooked ! '.'   -- decimal point
        copy.translating(upper, uncooked, copy, first, cooked)
        conditionally.repeat(TRUE, zero.pad, '0', cooked)
        discard.input(uncooked, truncate)
      SEQ  -- exponent
        -- E and exponent sign
        copy.translating(upper, uncooked, 2, 'e', cooked)
        -- and then exponent digits
        text.size := raw.size - 1  -- sign already read
        get.first.significant(uncooked, text.size, first)
        field[precision] := exp
        INT ignored :
        set.padding(field, TRUE, text.size,
                              zero.pad, ignored, copy, truncate )
        conditionally.repeat(TRUE, zero.pad, '0', cooked)
        copy.translating(upper, uncooked, copy, first, cooked)
        discard.input(uncooked, truncate)
      conditionally.repeat(left, space.pad, '*s', cooked)
```

```
'f'
  INT exponent, number.of.digits, extra.zeros :
  SEQ
    field[width] := field[width] - 1  -- allow for point
    info ? exponent
    INT sig.figs IS field[precision] :
    IF
      exponent > 0  -- number of digits before point
        number.of.digits := max(exponent, sig.figs)
      exponent <= 0  -- MINUS number of zeros after point
        number.of.digits := sig.figs - exponent
    INT ignored :
    set.padding(field, signed, text.size,
                              zero.pad, ignored, copy, truncate )
    text.size, field[precision] :=
                              field[precision], number.of.digits
    INT ignored1, ignored2 :
    set.padding(field, signed, text.size,
                        extra.zeros, space.pad, ignored1, ignored2 )
    conditionally.repeat(right, space.pad, '*s', cooked)
    IF
      exponent >= copy                -- all digits before point
        SEQ
          zero.pad := zero.pad + extra.zeros
          copy.translating(upper, uncooked,
                                    copy, first, cooked )
          conditionally.repeat(TRUE, zero.pad, '0', cooked)
          cooked ! '.'

      (0 < exponent) AND (exponent < copy)
                                      -- split across point
        SEQ
          copy.translating(upper, uncooked,
                              exponent, first, cooked )
          copy.translating(upper, uncooked,
                        (copy - exponent) + 1, '.', cooked )

      exponent <= 0                   -- all after point
        SEQ
          cooked ! '.'
          conditionally.repeat(TRUE, extra.zeros, '0', cooked)
          copy.translating(upper, uncooked,
                                      copy, first, cooked )
          conditionally.repeat(TRUE, zero.pad, '0', cooked)

    discard.input(uncooked, truncate)
    conditionally.repeat(left, space.pad, '*s', cooked)

  :
```

```
--
--   formatted.output
--


PROC formatted.output(VAL BYTE format,
                      VAL []BOOL flag, []INT field,
                      CHAN OF DATA.ITEM data,
                      CHAN OF BYTE output          )
  VAL BYTE format.type IS lower.case(format) :
  CASE format.type
    '%', 'b', 'c', 'd', 'e', 'f', 'x'
      CHAN OF BYTE uncooked :
      CHAN OF INT info :
      PAR
        raw.output(data, format.type, info, uncooked)
        cook.output(uncooked, info, format, flag, field, output)
    ELSE  -- unrecognized format character
      SEQ
        write.string(output, "<format error>")  -- e.g.
        STOP
:


--
--   process.item
--


PROC process.item(CHAN OF DATA.ITEM data,
                  VAL []BYTE control, INT i,
                  CHAN OF BYTE output        )
  [number.of.flags]BOOL flag :
  [field.numbers]INT field :
  INT which.field :
  BOOL this.format :
  BYTE format.char :
  VAL INT size IS SIZE control :
  SEQ
    flag, field := [FALSE, FALSE, FALSE], [-1, -1]
    which.field, this.format := get.flag, TRUE
    format.char := '*#00' -- not a valid format type
    WHILE this.format AND (i < size)
      SEQ
        format.char, i := control[i], i + 1
        CASE format.char

          ELSE
            this.format := FALSE  -- parsed format successfully
```

```
    '-', '+', '*s'
      IF
        which.field = get.flag
          CASE format.char
            '-'
              flag[left.justify] := TRUE
            '+'
              flag[sign.plus] := TRUE
            '*s'
              flag[sign.blank] := TRUE
        which.field > get.flag
          this.format := FALSE  -- error case

    '.'
      IF
        which.field < precision
          which.field, field[precision] := precision, 0
        which.field >= precision
          this.format := FALSE  -- error case

    '**'
      IF
        (which.field < width) AND (field[width] < 0)
          SEQ
            which.field := width
            data ? CASE data.int; field[width]
            this.format := field[width] >= 0  -- error?
        (which.field = precision) AND (field[precision] < 0)
          SEQ
            data ? CASE data.int; field[precision]
            this.format := field[precision] >= 0  -- error?
        otherwise
          this.format := FALSE  -- error case

    '0', '1', '2', '3', '4', '5', '6', '7', '8', '9'
      VAL INT digit IS (INT format.char) - (INT '0') :
      CASE which.field
        get.flag
          which.field, field[width] := width, digit
        width, precision
          INT parameter IS field[which.field] :
          IF
            parameter <= (((MOSTPOS INT) - digit) / 10)
              parameter := (parameter * 10) + digit
            parameter > (((MOSTPOS INT) - digit) / 10)
              this.format := FALSE  -- error case

formatted.output(format.char, flag, field, data, output)

:
```

```
--
--   write.formatted
--

PROC write.formatted(CHAN OF BYTE output,
                     VAL []BYTE control,
                     CHAN OF DATA.ITEM data )
  INT i :
  SEQ
    i := 0
    VAL INT size IS SIZE control :
    WHILE i < size
      IF
        control[i] <> '%'
          SEQ
            output ! control[i]
            i := i + 1
        control[i] = '%'
          SEQ
            i := i + 1
            process.item(data, control, i, output)
  :
```

```
--
--  make.decimal.string.int
--

PROC make.decimal.string.int([]BYTE buffer, VAL INT number)
  CHAN OF BYTE internal :
  PAR
    write.decimal.int(internal, number)
    BYTE sign, digit :
    INT size :
    VAL INT length IS SIZE buffer :
    SEQ
      internal ? sign
      size := decimal.raw - 1  -- sign already read
      get.first.significant(internal, size, digit)
      IF
        (size < length) OR ((size = length) AND (sign = '+'))
          --  put blanks, sign, and digits in correct place
          VAL INT spaces IS length - size :
          SEQ
            SEQ i = 0 FOR spaces
              buffer[i] := '*s'
            CASE sign
              '-'
                buffer[spaces - 1] := sign  -- there is room
              '+'
                SKIP
            buffer[spaces] := digit
            SEQ i = spaces + 1 FOR size - 1 -- remaining digits
              internal ? buffer[i]

        (size > length) OR ((size = length) AND (sign = '-'))
          --  too large to fit, so fill with '*' characters
          SEQ
            SEQ i = 0 FOR length
              buffer[i] := '**'
            discard.input(internal, size - 1)  -- discard digits
  :
```

Parallel matrix multiplier

```
--   This program applies an affine transformation
--
--     v = a . u + k
--     -   -   -   -
--   to an infinite sequence of vectors, u, overlapping
--   the multiplications of the components.


--
--   the multiplier cell
--

PROC multiplier(VAL REAL32 aij,
                CHAN OF REAL32 north, south, west, east )
  REAL32 uj,  aij.times.uj,  vi :
  SEQ
    north ? uj
    WHILE TRUE
      SEQ
        PAR
          south ! uj
          aij.times.uj := aij * uj
          west ? vi
        PAR
          east ! vi + aij.times.uj
          north ? uj
:
```

```
--
--   the other component processes of the array
--

PROC offset(VAL REAL32 ki, CHAN  OF REAL32 east)
  WHILE TRUE
    east ! ki
:

PROC sink(CHAN OF REAL32 north)
  WHILE TRUE
    REAL32 discard :
    north ? discard
:


--
--   configuration constants and interface procedures
--

VAL INT n IS 3 :        -- size of the matrix

VAL [n][n]REAL32 a IS   -- example value for the matrix
        [[ 0.980085(REAL32), -0.14112(REAL32),  -0.139708(REAL32) ],
         [-0.139708(REAL32), -0.989992(REAL32),  0.0199149(REAL32)],
         [-0.14112(REAL32) ,  0.0(REAL32),       -0.989992(REAL32) ]] :

VAL [n]REAL32 k IS      -- example value of the offset
         [ 0.1(REAL32),       2.0(REAL32),      30.0(REAL32)] :

PROC produce.u([n]CHAN OF REAL32 out)
  --
  --   produce an infinite sequence of vectors
  --
  ... omitted code
:

PROC consume.v([n]CHAN OF REAL32 in)
  --
  --   consume an infinite sequence of result vectors
  --
  ... omitted code
:
```

```
--
--   structure of the program
--

[n+1][n]CHAN OF REAL32 north.south, west.east :
PAR
  --
  --   producer of co-ordinates u[j]
  --
  produce.u(north.south[0])
  --
  -- the matrix multiplier array
  --
  PAR
    PAR i = 0 FOR n
      offset(k[i], west.east[0][i])
    PAR i = 0 FOR n
      PAR j = 0 FOR n
        multiplier(a[i][j],
                   north.south[i][j], north.south[i+1][j],
                   west.east  [j][i], west.east  [j+1][i] )
    PAR j = 0 FOR n
      sink(north.south[n][j])
  --
  --   consumer of co-ordinates v[i]
  --
  consume.v(west.east[n])
```

Monitoring communication

```
--   This chapter contains the code of a simple sorting program
--   implemented by a tree-shaped array of processes, and the code
--   needed to monitor on a screen the execution of the sorter.
--

--
--   configuration constants
--

-- size and shape of the tree

VAL INT depth.of.tree       IS 3 :
VAL INT number.of.leaves    IS 1 << depth.of.tree :
VAL INT number.of.forks     IS number.of.leaves - 1 :
VAL INT number.of.processes IS number.of.forks + number.of.leaves :
VAL INT number.of.channels  IS number.of.processes :

-- indexing of the tree

VAL INT root       IS 0 :
VAL INT first.fork IS root :
VAL INT first.leaf IS first.fork + number.of.forks :

-- and for the monitoring code

VAL INT collect IS 0 :
VAL INT deliver IS 1 :

VAL INT number.of.probes IS number.of.channels + number.of.leaves :

VAL INT first.channel.probe IS 0 :
VAL INT first.leaf.probe    IS number.of.channels :
```

```
--
--   protocols
--

PROTOCOL INT.STREAM
  CASE
    another.int; INT
    no.more.ints
:

PROTOCOL DISPLAY.STREAM
  CASE
    display.number; INT
    display.empty
    display.stop
:

PROTOCOL MULTIPLEX.STREAM
  CASE
    multiplex.number; INT; INT              -- probe; data
    multiplex.empty; INT                    -- probe
    multiplex.stop                          -- all probes stopped
:

VAL INT field.width IS 3 :

PROTOCOL TERMINAL.STREAM
  CASE
    terminal.item; INT; INT; [field.width]BYTE  -- x; y; characters
    terminal.stop
:
```

```
--
-- leaf processes
--

PROC leaf(CHAN OF INT.STREAM from.parent, to.parent,
         CHAN OF DISPLAY.STREAM probe          )
  SEQ
    from.parent ? CASE

      INT number :
      another.int; number
        SEQ
          probe ! display.number; number

          from.parent ? CASE no.more.ints

            to.parent ! another.int; number
            probe ! display.empty

      no.more.ints
        SKIP

    to.parent ! no.more.ints
    probe ! display.stop
:


--
-- fork processes
--

VAL INT left IS 0 :
VAL INT right IS 1 :

PROC fork.distribute(CHAN OF INT.STREAM from.parent,
                     [2]CHAN OF INT.STREAM to.children )
  INT child :
  BOOL more :
  SEQ
    child, more := left, TRUE
    WHILE more
      from.parent ? CASE
        INT number :
        another.int; number
          SEQ
            to.children[child] ! another.int; number
            child := child >< (left >< right)
        no.more.ints
          more := FALSE
    PAR child = left FOR 2
      to.children[child] ! no.more.ints
:
```

```
PROC fork.gather(CHAN OF INT.STREAM to.parent,
                 [2]CHAN OF INT.STREAM from.children )
  [2]BOOL more :
  [2]INT minimum :
  SEQ
    PAR child = left FOR 2
      from.children[child] ? CASE
        another.int; minimum[child]
          more[child] := TRUE
        no.more.ints
          more[child] := FALSE
    WHILE more[left] OR more[right]
      IF child = left FOR 2
        VAL INT other IS child >< (left >< right) :
        more[child] AND
                ((NOT more[other]) OR
                 (minimum[child] <= minimum[other]))
          SEQ
            to.parent ! another.int; minimum[child]
            from.children[child] ? CASE
              another.int; minimum[child]
                SKIP
              no.more.ints
                more[child] := FALSE
      to.parent ! no.more.ints
:

PROC fork(CHAN OF INT.STREAM from.parent, to.parent,
          [2]CHAN OF INT.STREAM from.children, to.children )
  SEQ
    fork.distribute(from.parent, to.children)
    fork.gather(to.parent, from.children)
:
```

```
--
--  monitor process
--

PROC monitor(CHAN OF INT.STREAM up.collect, down.collect,
                                up.deliver, down.deliver,
             CHAN OF DISPLAY.STREAM probe               )

  PROC copy.monitoring(CHAN OF INT.STREAM collector, deliverer,
                       CHAN OF DISPLAY.STREAM probe           )
    BOOL more :
    SEQ
      more := TRUE
      WHILE more
        collector ? CASE
          INT number :
          another.int; number
            SEQ
              probe ! display.number; number
              deliverer ! another.int; number
              probe ! display.empty
          no.more.ints
            more := FALSE
      deliverer ! no.more.ints
  :

  SEQ
    copy.monitoring(up.collect, up.deliver, probe)
    copy.monitoring(down.collect, down.deliver, probe)
    probe ! display.stop
:
```

```
--
--  multiplex process
--

PROC multiplex([]CHAN OF DISPLAY.STREAM probe,
               CHAN OF MULTIPLEX.STREAM all.probes )
  INT active.probes :
  [number.of.probes]BOOL more.from :
  SEQ
    active.probes := number.of.probes
    SEQ i = 0 FOR number.of.probes
      more.from[i] := TRUE
    WHILE active.probes > 0
      ALT i = 0 FOR number.of.probes
        more.from[i] & probe[i] ? CASE
          INT number :
          display.number; number
            all.probes ! multiplex.number; i; number
          display.empty
            all.probes ! multiplex.empty; i
          display.stop
            active.probes, more.from[i] := active.probes - 1, FALSE
    all.probes ! multiplex.stop
:


--
--  terminal-independent display processes
--

INT, INT FUNCTION make.cartesian(VAL INT index)
  INT x, y :
  VALOF
    IF
      IF line = 1 FOR depth.of.tree + 1
        index < ((1 << line) - 1)
          VAL INT column IS index - ((1 << (line - 1)) - 1) :
          VAL INT spread IS number.of.leaves >> (line - 1) :
          x, y := ((2 * column) + 1) * spread, line
      index >= number.of.channels
        VAL INT column IS index - number.of.channels :
        x, y := (2 * column) + 1, depth.of.tree + 2
    RESULT x, y
:
```

```
PROC independent(CHAN OF MULTIPLEX.STREAM source,
                 CHAN OF TERMINAL.STREAM sink   )
  [field.width]BYTE blanks :
  BOOL running :
  SEQ
    SEQ i = 0 FOR field.width
      blanks[i] := '*s'
    running := TRUE

    WHILE running
      source ? CASE

        INT index, number :
        multiplex.number; index; number
          INT x, y :
          [field.width]BYTE buffer :
          SEQ
            x, y := make.cartesian(index)
            make.decimal.string.int(buffer, number)
            sink ! terminal.item; x; y; buffer

        INT index :
        multiplex.empty; index
          INT x, y :
          SEQ
            x, y := make.cartesian(index)
            sink ! terminal.item; x; y; blanks

        multiplex.stop
          running := FALSE

      sink ! terminal.stop
  :


  --
  --  terminal-dependent display processes
  --

  VAL INT virtual.height IS depth.of.tree + 1 :
  VAL INT virtual.width  IS (2 * number.of.leaves) - 1 :

  VAL INT screen.height IS 24 :
  VAL INT screen.width  IS 80 :

  VAL INT height.scale IS
                (screen.height - 1) / virtual.height :
  VAL INT width.scale  IS
                (screen.width - field.width) / virtual.width :
```

```
PROC clear.screen(CHAN OF BYTE terminal)
  -- clear screen sequence for an ANSI terminal
  write.string(terminal, "*#1B[2J")
:


PROC move.cursor(CHAN OF BYTE terminal, VAL INT x, y)
  -- lefthanded co-ordinates, origin 0,0 at top left
  CHAN OF DATA.ITEM c :
  PAR
    write.formatted(terminal, "*#1B[%d;%dH", c)
    SEQ
      c ! data.int; y + 1
      c ! data.int; x + 1
:


PROC dependent(CHAN OF TERMINAL.STREAM source,
              CHAN OF BYTE terminal            )
  -- terminal-dependent code for driving ANSI terminal
  BOOL more :
  SEQ
    clear.screen(terminal)
    more := TRUE
    WHILE more
      source ? CASE
        INT x, y :
        [field.width]BYTE buffer :
        terminal.item; x; y; buffer
          SEQ
            move.cursor(terminal, (x - 1)  * width.scale,
                (virtual.height - (y - 1)) * height.scale )
            write.string(terminal, buffer)
        terminal.stop
          more := FALSE
    move.cursor(terminal, 0, screen.height - 1)
:


--
-- display process
--

PROC display(CHAN OF MULTIPLEX.STREAM source, CHAN OF BYTE sink)
  CHAN OF TERMINAL.STREAM internal :
  PAR
    independent(source, internal)
    dependent(internal, sink)
:
```

```
--
-- driver
--

VAL INT mask IS BITNOT ((BITNOT 0) << 9) :

PROC shift(INT state)
  SEQ i = 1 FOR 9
    state := ((state << 1) /\ mask) \/
                            (((state >> 4) >< (state >> 8)) /\ 1)
:

PROC driver(CHAN OF INT.STREAM up.to.tree, down.from.tree)
  VAL INT second IS ... :  -- number of clock ticks per second
  TIMER clock :
  SEQ
    INT event, number :
    SEQ
      clock ? event
      number :=  (event /\ mask) \/ 1
      SEQ i = 0 FOR number.of.leaves
        SEQ
          event := event PLUS second
          shift(number)
          up.to.tree ! another.int; number
          clock ? AFTER event
      up.to.tree ! no.more.ints
    INT event :
    SEQ
      clock ? event
      SEQ i = 0 FOR number.of.leaves
        SEQ
          event := event PLUS second
          INT discard :
          down.from.tree ? CASE another.int; discard
          clock ? AFTER event
      down.from.tree ? CASE no.more.ints
:
```

```
--
-- structure of the program
--


[2][number.of.channels]CHAN OF INT.STREAM up, down :
[number.of.probes]CHAN OF DISPLAY.STREAM probe :
CHAN OF MULTIPLEX.STREAM all.probes :

PAR
  --
  -- sequential driver process
  --
  driver(up[collect][root], down[deliver][root])
  --
  -- parallel sorter
  --
  PAR
    --
    -- fork nodes in the tree
    --
    PAR i = first.fork FOR number.of.forks
      VAL INT first.born IS (2 * i) + 1 :
      fork(up[deliver][i], down[collect][i],
           [down[deliver] FROM first.born FOR 2],
           [up[collect] FROM first.born FOR 2]   )
    --
    -- leaf nodes in the tree
    --
    []CHAN OF DISPLAY.STREAM leaf.probe IS
            [probe FROM first.leaf.probe FOR number.of.leaves] :
    PAR i = first.leaf FOR number.of.leaves
      leaf(up[deliver][i], down[collect][i],
                                leaf.probe[i - first.leaf] )
    --
    -- monitoring buffers
    --
    []CHAN OF DISPLAY.STREAM channel.probe IS
            [probe FROM first.channel.probe FOR number.of.channels] :
    PAR i = root FOR number.of.channels
      monitor(up[collect][i], down[collect][i],
              up[deliver][i], down[deliver][i], channel.probe[i] )
  --
  -- display control processes
  --
  multiplex(probe, all.probes)
  display(all.probes, terminal.screen)
```

Conway's game of Life

```
--   The program in this chapter plays Life on a terminal screen.
--


--
--   configuration constants
--

VAL INT array.width  IS ... :     -- number of cells across the board
VAL INT array.height IS ... :     -- number of cells down the board

VAL INT radius      IS 1 :        -- of the 'sphere of influence'
VAL INT diameter    IS (2 * radius) + 1 :
VAL INT neighbours IS (diameter * diameter) - 1 :

VAL INT number.of.cells IS array.height * array.width :
VAL INT number.of.links IS neighbours * number.of.cells :

--
--   protocols
--

PROTOCOL STATE IS BOOL :

VAL BOOL alive IS TRUE :
VAL BOOL dead  IS NOT alive :

PROTOCOL COMMAND
  CASE
    set.state; BOOL
    evolve
    terminate
:

PROTOCOL RESPONSE IS BOOL; BOOL :
```

```
--
--  cell processes
--

PROC broadcast.present.state([] [] []CHAN OF STATE link,
                             VAL INT x, y, VAL BOOL state )
  PAR d = 0 FOR neighbours
    link[x][y][d] ! state
:

PROC calculate.next.state([] [] []CHAN OF STATE link,
                          VAL []INT nx, ny,
                          VAL BOOL state, BOOL next.state )
  INT count :         -- number of living neighbours
  SEQ
    [neighbours]BOOL state.of.neighbour :
    SEQ
      PAR d = 0 FOR neighbours
        link[nx[d]][ny[d]][d] ? state.of.neighbour[d]
      count := 0
      SEQ d = 0 FOR neighbours
        IF
          state.of.neighbour[d] = alive
            count := count + 1
          state.of.neighbour[d] = dead
            SKIP
    IF
      count < 2     -- death from isolation
        next.state := dead
      count = 2     -- this cell is stable
        next.state := state
      count = 3     -- stable if alive, a birth if dead
        next.state := alive
      count > 3     -- death from overcrowding
        next.state := dead
:
```

```
PROC cell([][][]CHAN OF STATE link,
          VAL INT x, y, VAL []INT nx, ny,
          CHAN OF COMMAND control,
          CHAN OF RESPONSE sense          )
  BOOL state, not.finished :
  SEQ
    state := dead        -- the whole board starts off dead
    not.finished := TRUE
    WHILE not.finished
      control ? CASE

        set.state; state
          SKIP           -- state has been set to the new value

        evolve
          BOOL next.state :
          SEQ
            PAR
              broadcast.present.state(link, x, y, state)
              SEQ
                calculate.next.state(link, nx, ny,
                                     state, next.state )
                sense ! (state <> next.state); next.state
            state := next.state

        terminate
          not.finished := FALSE
:


--
--   terminal-dependent output routines
--

PROC clear.screen(CHAN OF BYTE terminal)
  -- clear screen sequence for an ANSI terminal
  write.string(terminal, "*#1B[2J")
:

PROC move.cursor(CHAN OF BYTE terminal, VAL INT x, y)
  -- left-handed co-ordinates, origin 0,0 at top left
  CHAN OF DATA.ITEM c :
  PAR
    write.formatted(terminal, "*#1B[%d;%dH", c)
    SEQ
      c ! data.int; y + 1
      c ! data.int; x + 1
:
```

```
--
--  display routines
--

PROC initialize.display(CHAN OF BYTE screen)
  -- display an entirely dead board
  clear.screen(screen)
:

PROC clean.up.display(CHAN OF BYTE screen)
  move.cursor(screen, 0, array.height)
:

PROC display.state(CHAN OF BYTE screen, VAL INT x, y, VAL BOOL state)
  SEQ
    move.cursor(screen, x, y)
    IF
      state = alive
        screen ! '**'
      state = dead
        screen ! '*s'
:


--
--  controller states
--

VAL INT idle        IS 0 :  -- controller activity values
VAL INT editing     IS 1 :
VAL INT single.step IS 2 :
VAL INT free.running IS 3 :
VAL INT terminated  IS 4 :


INT FUNCTION new.activity(VAL BYTE char)
  INT activity :
  VALOF
    CASE char      -- typed on the keyboard ...
      'q', 'Q'               -- ... Q to finish program
        activity := terminated
      's', 'S'               -- ... S to halt evolution
        activity := idle
      'e', 'E'               -- ... E to start editing
        activity := editing
      'r', 'R'               -- ... R to start evolution
        activity := free.running
      ELSE  -- ... or anything else for one generation
        activity := single.step
    RESULT activity
:
```

```
PROC display.activity(CHAN OF BYTE screen, VAL INT activity)
  SEQ
    move.cursor(screen, array.width+1, array.height/2)
    CASE activity
      idle
        write.string(screen, "Idle")
      editing
        write.string(screen, "Edit")
      single.step
        write.string(screen, "Step")
      free.running
        write.string(screen, "Busy")
      terminated
        write.string(screen, "Done")
:


--
--  generation
--

PROC generation(CHAN OF BYTE screen,
                [][]CHAN OF COMMAND control,
                [][]CHAN OF RESPONSE sense,
                BOOL active                 )
  SEQ
    PAR x = 0 FOR array.width
      PAR y = 0 FOR array.height
        control[x][y] ! evolve
    active := FALSE
    SEQ x = 0 FOR array.width
      SEQ y = 0 FOR array.height
        BOOL changed, next.state :
        SEQ
          sense[x][y] ? changed; next.state
          IF
            changed
              SEQ
                display.state(screen, x, y, next.state)
                active := TRUE
            NOT changed
              SKIP
:
```

```
--
--  editor
--

INT FUNCTION min(VAL INT a, b)
  INT min :
  VALOF
    IF
      a <= b
        min := a
      b <= a
        min := b
    RESULT min
:

INT FUNCTION max(VAL INT a, b)
  INT max :
  VALOF
    IF
      a >= b
        max := a
      b >= a
        max := b
    RESULT max
:
```

```
PROC editor(CHAN OF BYTE keyboard, screen,
            [][]CHAN OF COMMAND control   )
  INT x, y :
  BOOL editing :
  SEQ
    -- initialize co-ordinates to centre of board
    x, y := array.width / 2, array.height / 2
    editing := TRUE
    WHILE editing
      BYTE char :
      SEQ
        move.cursor(screen, x, y)
        keyboard ? char
        CASE char
          'A'         -- move up, if possible
            y := max(y - 1, 0)
          'B'         -- move down, if possible
            y := min(y + 1, array.height - 1)
          'C'         -- move right, if possible
            x := min(x + 1, array.width - 1)
          'D'         -- move left, if possible
            x := max(x - 1, 0)
          '*s', '**'
            VAL BOOL state IS (char = '**') = alive :
            PAR
              control[x][y] ! set.state; state
              display.state(screen, x, y, state)
          'q', 'Q'
            editing := FALSE
          ELSE
            SKIP    -- ignore anything else
  :
```

```
--
--  controller
--

PROC controller(CHAN OF BYTE keyboard, screen,
                [][]CHAN OF COMMAND control,
                [][]CHAN OF RESPONSE sense   )
  INT activity :
  SEQ
    activity := idle
    initialize.display(screen)
    WHILE activity <> terminated
      SEQ
        display.activity(screen, activity)
        BYTE char :
        PRI ALT
          (activity <> editing) & keyboard ? char
            activity := new.activity(char)
          (activity <> idle) & SKIP
            CASE activity
              editing
                SEQ
                  editor(keyboard, screen, control)
                  activity := idle
              free.running, single.step
                BOOL changing :
                SEQ
                  generation(screen, control, sense, changing)
                  IF
                    (activity = single.step) OR (NOT changing)
                      activity := idle ·
                    (activity = free.running) AND changing
                      SKIP
    display.activity(screen, activity)
    PAR x = 0 FOR array.width
      PAR y = 0 FOR array.height
        control[x][y] ! terminate
    clean.up.display(screen)
  :
```

```
--
--   structure of the program
--

[array.width][array.height][neighbours]CHAN OF STATE link :
[array.width][array.height]CHAN OF COMMAND control :
[array.width][array.height]CHAN OF RESPONSE sense :
PAR
  controller(terminal.keyboard, terminal.screen, control, sense)
  PAR x = 0 FOR array.width
    PAR y = 0 FOR array.height
      VAL INT left  IS ((x - 1) + array.width) \ array.width  :
      VAL INT right IS  (x + 1)                \ array.width  :
      VAL INT up    IS  (y + 1)                \ array.height :
      VAL INT down  IS ((y - 1) + array.height) \ array.height :
      VAL [neighbours]INT nx IS
            [ right, x,    left, left, left, x,  right, right ] :
      VAL [neighbours]INT ny IS
            [ down,  down, down, y,    up,  up, up,   y     ] :
      cell(link, x, y, nx, ny, control[x][y], sense[x][y])
```

Simple Huffman coder

```
--   This chapter contains routines to transmit and receive character
--   streams encoded by a fixed Huffman code.
--


--
--   character set description
--

VAL INT bits.in.character    IS 8 :
VAL INT number.of.characters IS 1 << bits.in.character :
VAL INT number.of.codes      IS number.of.characters :

VAL INT character.mask IS BITNOT ((BITNOT 0) << bits.in.character) :

INT FUNCTION index(VAL INT char) IS char /\ character.mask :

VAL [number.of.characters]REAL32 probability IS ... :
         --   table of expected probabilities of characters;
         --   probability[index(char)] is the probability of char


--
--   structure of the tree
--

VAL INT root IS 0 :
VAL INT size.of.tree IS (2 * number.of.codes) - 1 :

VAL INT number.of.arrays IS 4 :

VAL INT eldest.index         IS 0 :
VAL INT parent.index         IS 1 :
VAL INT character.index      IS 2 :
VAL INT representative.index IS 3 :
```

```
--
--   insert.new.node
--

PROC insert.new.node([][]INT tree,
                     INT left.limit,
                     VAL INT right.limit,
                     INT new.node,
                     []REAL32 weight,
                     VAL REAL32 weight.of.new.node )
  INT weight.limit :
  SEQ
    IF
      IF node = left.limit FOR right.limit - left.limit
        weight[node] <= weight.of.new.node
          weight.limit := node
      TRUE
        weight.limit := right.limit
    []INT eldest IS tree[eldest.index] :
    []INT character IS tree[character.index] :
    SEQ node = left.limit FOR weight.limit - left.limit
      character[node-1], eldest[node-1], weight[node-1] :=
        character[node],  eldest[node],   weight[node]
    left.limit, new.node := left.limit - 1, weight.limit - 1
    weight[new.node] := weight.of.new.node
:


--
-- construct leaf nodes of tree
--

PROC construct.leaves([][]INT tree,
                      INT left.limit, right.limit,
                      []REAL32 weight,
                      VAL []REAL32 probability   )
  VAL INT minimum.character IS -(number.of.characters / 2) :
  SEQ char = minimum.character FOR number.of.characters
    INT new.node :
    SEQ
      insert.new.node(tree, left.limit, right.limit,
                      new.node, weight,
                      probability[index(char)]      )
      []INT eldest IS tree[eldest.index] :
      []INT character IS tree[character.index] :
      eldest[new.node], character[new.node] := root, char
:
```

```
--
--   construct non-leaf nodes of the tree
--

PROC construct.other.nodes([][]INT tree,
                           INT left.limit, right.limit,
                           []REAL32 weight           )
  WHILE (right.limit - left.limit) <> 1
    INT new.node :
    REAL32 new.weight :
    SEQ
      right.limit := right.limit - 2
      new.weight := weight[right.limit] + weight[right.limit + 1]
      insert.new.node(tree, left.limit, right.limit,
                      new.node, weight, new.weight )
      []INT eldest IS tree[eldest.index] :
      eldest[new.node] := right.limit
:


--
--   construct parent from eldest, representative from character
--

PROC invert.representation([][]INT tree)
  []INT eldest IS tree[eldest.index] :
  []INT parent IS tree[parent.index] :
  []INT character IS tree[character.index] :
  []INT representative IS
      [tree[representative.index] FROM 0 FOR number.of.characters] :
  SEQ node = root FOR size.of.tree
    IF
      eldest[node] = root
        representative[index(character[node])] := node
      eldest[node] <> root
        SEQ child = eldest[node] FOR 2
          parent[child] := node
:
```

```
--
--   construct.tree
--

PROC construct.tree([][]INT tree, VAL []REAL32 probability)

  INT left.limit, right.limit :
  [size.of.tree]REAL32 weight :

  SEQ
    left.limit   := size.of.tree
    right.limit  := size.of.tree

    -- left.limit = size.of.tree
    -- (right.limit - left.limit) = 0

    construct.leaves(tree, left.limit, right.limit,
                           weight, probability    )

    -- left.limit = number.of.codes
    -- (right.limit - left.limit) = number.of.codes

    construct.other.nodes(tree, left.limit, right.limit, weight)

    -- left.limit = root
    -- (right.limit - left.limit) = 1

    invert.representation(tree)
  :
```

```
--
--   encode.character, decode.character
--

PROC encode.character(CHAN OF BIT output,
                      VAL [][]INT tree,
                      VAL INT char        )

  VAL []INT eldest IS tree[eldest.index] :
  VAL []INT parent IS tree[parent.index] :
  VAL []INT character IS tree[character.index] :
  VAL []INT representative IS
      [tree[representative.index] FROM 0 FOR number.of.characters] :

  VAL INT size.of.encoding IS number.of.codes - 1 :
  [size.of.encoding]BOOL encoding :
  INT length, node :
  SEQ
    length := 0
    node   := representative[index(char)]
    WHILE node <> root
      SEQ
        encoding[length] := node <> eldest[parent[node]]
        length := length + 1
        node   := parent[node]
    SEQ i = 1 FOR length
      output ! encoding[length - i]
:

PROC decode.character(CHAN OF BIT input,
                      VAL [][]INT tree,
                      INT char           )

  VAL []INT eldest IS tree[eldest.index] :
  VAL []INT character IS tree[character.index] :

  INT node :
  SEQ
    node := root
    WHILE eldest[node] <> root
      BOOL go.right :
      SEQ
        input ? go.right
        IF
          go.right
            node := eldest[node] + 1
          NOT go.right
            node := eldest[node]
    char := character[node]

:
```

```
--
--   copy.encoding, copy.decoding
--

VAL INT end.of.message IS -1 :

PROC copy.encoding(CHAN OF INT source,
                   CHAN OF SIGNAL end.of.source,
                   CHAN OF BIT sink                  )
  --
  -- read characters from source, sending their encodings along sink,
  -- until a signal is received along end.of.source
  --
  BOOL more.characters.expected :
  [number.of.arrays][size.of.tree]INT tree :
  SEQ
    construct.tree(tree, probability)
    more.characters.expected := TRUE
    WHILE more.characters.expected
      ALT
        INT char :
        source ? char
          encode.character(sink, tree, char)
        end.of.source ? CASE signal
          more.characters.expected := FALSE
      encode.character(sink, tree, end.of.message)
:

PROC copy.decoding(CHAN OF BIT source, CHAN OF INT sink)
  --
  -- read a bit stream from source, decoding it into characters and
  -- send these along sink until end.of.message is decoded
  --
  BOOL more.characters.expected :
  [number.of.arrays][size.of.tree]INT tree :
  SEQ
    construct.tree(tree, probability)
    more.characters.expected := TRUE
    WHILE more.characters.expected
      INT char :
      SEQ
        decode.character(source, tree, char)
        IF
          char <> end.of.message
            sink ! char
          char = end.of.message
            more.characters.expected := FALSE
:
```

```
--
--  encode.into.blocks, decode.from.blocks
--


--
--  this code uses the packing routines from an earlier chapter
--
--      PROC pack.bits.into.blocks(...)
--      PROC unpack.bits.from.blocks(...)
--


PROC encode.into.blocks(CHAN OF INT source,
                        CHAN OF SIGNAL end.of.source,
                        CHAN OF BLOCK sink           )
  CHAN OF BIT bit.stream :
  CHAN OF SIGNAL end.of.bit.stream :
  PAR
    SEQ
      copy.encoding(source, end.of.source, bit.stream)
      end.of.bit.stream ! signal
    pack.bits.into.blocks(bit.stream, end.of.bit.stream, sink)
:


PROC discard(CHAN OF BIT source, CHAN OF SIGNAL end.of.source)
  BOOL more.expected :
  SEQ
    more.expected := TRUE
    WHILE more.expected
      ALT
        BOOL bit :
        source ? bit
          SKIP
        end.of.source ? CASE signal
          more.expected := FALSE
:


PROC decode.from.blocks(CHAN OF BLOCK block.source, CHAN OF INT sink)
  CHAN OF SIGNAL end.of.block.source, end.of.bit.stream :
  CHAN OF BIT bit.stream :
  PAR
    SEQ
      unpack.bits.from.blocks(block.source,
                              end.of.block.source, bit.stream )
      end.of.bit.stream ! signal              -- 'feed-forward'
    SEQ
      copy.decoding(bit.stream, sink)
      PAR
        end.of.block.source ! signal          -- 'feed-back'
        discard(bit.stream, end.of.bit.stream)
:
```

```
--
--   copy.over.serial.medium, copy.over.blocked.medium
--

PROC copy.over.serial.medium(CHAN OF INT source,
                             CHAN OF SIGNAL end.of.source,
                             CHAN OF INT sink              )
  --
  --   copy characters from source to sink until a signal is received
  --   from end.of.source
  --
  CHAN OF BIT serial.medium :
  PAR
    copy.encoding(source, end.of.source, serial.medium)
    copy.decoding(serial.medium, sink)
:

PROC copy.over.blocked.medium(CHAN OF INT source,
                              CHAN OF SIGNAL end.of.source,
                              CHAN OF INT sink              )
  --
  --   copy characters from source to sink until a signal is received
  --   from end.of.source
  --
  CHAN OF BLOCK blocked.medium :
  PAR
    encode.into.blocks(source, end.of.source, blocked.medium)
    decode.from.blocks(blocked.medium, sink)
:
```

Adaptive Huffman coder

```
--  This chapter contains routines to transmit and receive character
--  streams encoded by an adaptive Huffman code. The code used for
--  each character is one given by Huffman's algorithm for those
--  characters which have preceded it.
--

--
--  character set description
--

VAL INT bits.in.character    IS 8 :
VAL INT number.of.characters IS 1 << bits.in.character :
VAL INT number.of.codes      IS number.of.characters + 1 :

VAL INT character.mask IS BITNOT ((BITNOT 0) << bits.in.character) :

INT FUNCTION index(VAL INT char) IS char /\ character.mask :

--
--  structure of the tree
--

VAL INT root IS 0 :
VAL INT size.of.tree IS (2 * number.of.codes) - 1 :

VAL INT not.a.node IS size.of.tree :

VAL INT number.of.arrays IS 5 :

VAL INT eldest.index         IS 0 :
VAL INT parent.index         IS 1 :
VAL INT character.index      IS 2 :
VAL INT representative.index IS 3 :
VAL INT weight.index         IS 4 :
```

```
--
--   create.leaf
--

PROC create.leaf(INT new.leaf, [][]INT tree, VAL INT char)
  --
  --  extend the tree by fission of the escape into two new leaves
  --
  []INT eldest IS tree[eldest.index] :
  []INT parent IS tree[parent.index] :
  []INT character IS tree[character.index] :
  []INT representative IS
      [tree[representative.index] FROM 0 FOR number.of.characters] :
  []INT weight IS tree[weight.index] :
  INT escape IS tree[representative.index][number.of.characters] :

  INT new.escape :
  SEQ
    new.leaf, new.escape := escape + 1, escape + 2
    eldest[escape] := new.leaf -- old escape is new parent
    weight[new.leaf],    eldest[new.leaf],    parent[new.leaf] :=
        0,                   root,                escape
    character[new.leaf], representative[index(char)] :=
        char,                new.leaf
    weight[new.escape], eldest[new.escape], parent[new.escape] :=
        1,                  root,               escape
    escape := new.escape
:


--
--   compare.weights
--

VAL INT lighter      IS -1 :
VAL INT same.weight  IS  0 :
VAL INT heavier      IS  1 :

INT FUNCTION compare.weights(VAL [][]INT tree, VAL INT a, b)
  INT result :
  VALOF
    VAL []INT weight IS tree[weight.index] :
    IF
      weight[a] < weight[b]
        result := lighter
      weight[a] = weight[b]
        result := same.weight
      weight[a] > weight[b]
        result := heavier
    RESULT result
:
```

```
--
--   initialize.tree, swap.trees
--

PROC initialize.tree([][]INT tree)

  []INT eldest IS tree[eldest.index] :
  []INT representative IS
      [tree[representative.index] FROM 0 FOR number.of.characters] :
  []INT weight IS tree[weight.index] :
  INT escape IS tree[representative.index][number.of.characters] :
  SEQ
    escape := root
    weight[escape] := 1        -- minimum legal weight
    eldest[escape] := root  -- it is a leaf
    SEQ char = 0 FOR number.of.characters
      representative[char] := not.a.node
:

PROC swap.trees([][]INT tree, VAL INT i, j)
  --
  --   exchange disjoint sub-trees rooted at i and j
  --
  PROC swap.ints(INT a, b)
    a, b := b, a
  :

  []INT eldest IS tree[eldest.index] :
  []INT parent IS tree[parent.index] :
  []INT character IS tree[character.index] :
  []INT representative IS
      [tree[representative.index] FROM 0 FOR number.of.characters] :

  PROC adjust.offspring(VAL INT i)
    --
    --   restore downstream pointers to node i
    --
    IF
      eldest[i] = root
        representative[index(character[i])] := i
      eldest[i] <> root
        SEQ child = eldest[i] FOR 2
          parent[child] := i
  :

  SEQ
    swap.ints(eldest[i],    eldest[j])
    swap.ints(character[i], character[j])
    adjust.offspring(i)
    adjust.offspring(j)
:
```

```
--
--   increase.weight
--

PROC increase.weight([][]INT tree, VAL INT char)
  INT node :
  SEQ
    --
    --   check that the tree is not at its maximum weight
    --
    VAL INT limiting.weight IS MOSTPOS INT :
    INT FUNCTION heaviest.weight(VAL [][]INT tree) IS
                                      tree[weight.index][root] :
    IF
      heaviest.weight(tree) < limiting.weight
        SKIP
      heaviest.weight(tree) = limiting.weight
        initialize.tree(tree)
    --
    --   find a leaf to represent 'char'
    --
    []INT representative IS
      [tree[representative.index] FROM 0 FOR number.of.characters] :
    node := representative[index(char)]
    IF
      node <> not.a.node
        SKIP
      node = not.a.node
        create.leaf(node, tree, char)
    --
    --   increment the weight of 'node' and all of its ancestors
    --
    WHILE node <> root
      CASE compare.weights(tree, node - 1, node)
        heavier
          --   abbreviate parent and weight from tree
          []INT parent IS tree[parent.index] :
          []INT weight IS tree[weight.index] :

          SEQ
            weight[node] := weight[node] + 1
            node := parent[node]
        same.weight
          IF i = 1 FOR (node - root) - 1
            compare.weights(tree, (node-i)-1, node) = heavier
              SEQ
                swap.trees(tree, node, node - i)
                node := node - i
    []INT weight IS tree[weight.index] :
    weight[root] := weight[root] + 1
  :
```

```
--
--  encode.character
--

PROC encode.character(CHAN OF BIT output,
                      VAL [][]INT tree, VAL INT char )

  VAL []INT eldest IS tree[eldest.index] :
  VAL []INT parent IS tree[parent.index] :
  VAL []INT representative IS
      [tree[representative.index] FROM 0 FOR number.of.characters] :
  VAL INT escape IS
                  tree[representative.index][number.of.characters] :

  VAL INT size.of.encoding IS
                            bits.in.character + (number.of.codes - 1) :
  [size.of.encoding]BOOL encoding :
  INT length, node :
  SEQ
    VAL INT leaf IS representative[index(char)] :
    IF
      leaf <> not.a.node
        length, node := 0, leaf
      leaf = not.a.node
        SEQ
          SEQ i = 0 FOR bits.in.character
            encoding[i] := ((char >> i) /\ 1) = 1
                            -- i'th bit of unencoded char
          length, node := bits.in.character, escape
    WHILE node <> root
      SEQ
        encoding[length] := node <> eldest[parent[node]]
        length, node := length + 1, parent[node]
    SEQ i = 1 FOR length
      output ! encoding[length - i]
:
```

```
--
--   decode.character
--

PROC decode.character(CHAN OF BIT input, VAL [][]INT tree, INT char)

  VAL []INT eldest IS tree[eldest.index] :
  VAL []INT character IS tree[character.index] :
  VAL INT escape IS
                  tree[representative.index][number.of.characters] :

  INT node :
  SEQ
    node := root
    WHILE eldest[node] <> root
      BOOL go.right :
      SEQ
        input ? go.right
        IF
          go.right
            node := eldest[node] + 1
          NOT go.right
            node := eldest[node]
    IF
      node < escape
        char := character[node]
      node = escape
        BOOL bit :    -- read bits of signed character code
        SEQ
          input ? bit
          IF
            bit
              char := BITNOT 0
            NOT bit
              char := 0
          SEQ i = 2 FOR bits.in.character - 1
            SEQ
              input ? bit
              char := (char << 1) \/ (INT bit)
:
```

```
--
--   copy.encoding
--

VAL INT end.of.message IS -1 :

PROC copy.encoding(CHAN OF INT source,
                   CHAN OF SIGNAL end.of.source,
                   CHAN OF BIT sink                )
  --
  -- read characters from source, sending their encodings along sink,
  -- until a signal is received along end.of.source
  --
  BOOL more.characters.expected :
  [number.of.arrays][size.of.tree]INT tree :
  SEQ
    initialize.tree(tree)
    more.characters.expected := TRUE
    WHILE more.characters.expected
      ALT
        INT char :
        source ? char
          SEQ
            encode.character(sink, tree, char)
            increase.weight(tree, char)
        end.of.source ? CASE signal
          more.characters.expected := FALSE
    encode.character(sink, tree, end.of.message)
:
```

```
--
--   copy.decoding
--

PROC copy.decoding(CHAN OF BIT source, CHAN OF INT sink)
  --
  --   read a bit stream from source, decoding it into characters and
  --   send these along sink until end.of.message is decoded
  --
  BOOL more.characters.expected :
  [number.of.arrays][size.of.tree]INT tree :
  SEQ
    initialize.tree(tree)
    more.characters.expected := TRUE
    WHILE more.characters.expected
      INT char :
      SEQ
        decode.character(source, tree, char)
        IF
          char <> end.of.message
            SEQ
              sink ! char
              increase.weight(tree, char)
          char = end.of.message
            more.characters.expected := FALSE
:
```

```
--
--   The interfaces of the copy.encoding and copy.decoding procedures
--   in this chapter are the same as those in the preceding chapter,
--   so we could here define
--
--       PROC encode.into.blocks(...)
--       PROC decode.from.blocks(...)
--       PROC copy.over.serial.medium(...)
--       PROC copy.over.blocked.medium(...)
--
--   by repeating the texts of their definitions from that chapter.
--
```

Bibliography

This short list of books and papers is not intended to be exhaustive, but to point in the direction of further reading about occam, parallel programming, and some of the subjects touched upon in the course of this book.

About occam 2

The authoritative reference on the occam 2 language is

1. INMOS Limited (1988) occam 2 *Reference Manual*, Prentice Hall International, Hemel Hempstead,

and it is the document against which we measured our material for this book for its accuracy. In addition to the language definition, the *Reference Manual* contains small illustrative examples of each feature of the language, and details of the functions and procedures to be provided by standard libraries in an occam programming system.

2. Dick Pountain, David May (1987) *A Tutorial Introduction to* occam *Programming*, Blackwell Scientific Publications, Oxford.

A very gentle introduction to parallel programming is oddly bound in this book with an extremely terse (only twenty-two page) language definition by the designer of occam 2.

There are a couple of small historical discrepancies between the language described in this book and the *Reference Manual*, apparently to be removed in a forthcoming edition. The same sorts of slight variations from the reference language are also present in

3. Alan Burns (1988) *Programming in* occam 2, Addison-Wesley Publishing Company, Wokingham,

308

which is a broader survey. As well as the kind of introduction to occam 2 in the first few chapters of the present book, Burns touches on the implementation of occam on transputers, and relates it to other languages.

About occam

The revolutionary program structures possible in the present occam language were first introduced in a simpler language, sometimes called 'proto-occam', or occam 1. Indeed the principal differences between that and occam 2 are to do with data typing, and other matters which are just as important in sequential programs.

The original reference on occam is

4. INMOS Limited (1984) occam *Programming Manual*, Prentice Hall International, Hemel Hempstead,

which bears a family resemblance to the language summary in [2].

A more discursive approach will be found in

5. Geraint Jones (1987) *Programming in* occam, Prentice Hall International, Hemel Hempstead,

which was the prototype for the present book. It contains treatments in proto-occam of most of the same examples as the present book, together with a summary of the language.

Another collection of examples of occam programs will be found in

6. Jon Kerridge (1987) occam *programming: a practical approach*, Blackwell Scientific Publications, Oxford.

About reasoning about occam

Parallel programming is potentially much more complicated than sequential programming, yet occam is more tractable than many a sequential language, and occam programs can be more elegant than programs in other languages. Much of this is attributable to a sound mathematical foundation.

The outline of the occam language is very close to the surface in

7. C.A.R. Hoare (1978) Communicating sequential processes, *Commun ACM*, **21**(8) 666–677,

which is now one of the classic papers about writing and reasoning about parallel programs.

The theory of CSP has developed a great deal in the intervening decade, and a programmer who seeks a deeper insight into the theory of concurrency and synchronization should certainly look at

8. C.A.R. Hoare (1985) *Communicating Sequential Processes*, Prentice Hall International, Hemel Hempstead,

which sets out the theory of concurrency as a course suitable for mathematically competent programmers, as all programmers should surely be.

A mathematician taking an interest in programming might be happier to start with a different, more abstract and algebraic approach of the calculus of communicating systems (CCS)

9. Robin Milner (1989) Operational and algebraic semantics of concurrent processes, in *Handbook of Theoretical Computer Science* (ed Jan van Leeuwen), North Holland, Amsterdam (to appear),

which yet seems on first sight to be much closer to the reality of occam than is that of CSP.

For our purpose here, the principal virtue of these underlying theories is that they give us a way of understanding and reasoning about the programs which we want to write. As

10. A.W. Roscoe, C.A.R. Hoare (1986) *The Laws of* occam *Programming*, Programming Research Group technical monograph PRG-53, Oxford,

notes, one of the beauties of occam is the large number of memorable algebraic laws which relate programs written in it. This paper sets out a semantics of occam which is based on these laws, and has been the basis for work on mechanical manipulation of occam programs.

One of the characteristic signs of the insecure parallel programmer is a morbid fear of deadlock, and a shining success of the theory is that it has started to tame this dragon. A short but important paper about analysing networks of processes

11. A.W. Roscoe, Naiem Dathi (1987) The pursuit of deadlock freedom, *Information and Computation*, **75**(3) 289–327,

presents some techniques for showing that networks do not become deadlocked, in essentially the same sorts of ways that one would show that a sequential program terminated.

About the transputer

Although we have been concerned with parallel programming, rather than with the programming of parallel computers, we should acknowledge that a driving force behind the development of occam has been the transputer and the availability of parallel computers built of transputers.

The engineer's reference manual

12. INMOS Limited (1988) *Transputer Reference Manual,* Prentice Hall
International, Hemel Hempstead,

explains the architecture, which supports the duality of many processes executed by one processor and many processors executing one program. It also describes the INMOS link mechanism which implements synchronization between processes executing on distinct transputers.

About floating-point arithmetic

One of the substantial differences between occam 2 and earlier dialects of occam is the integration of approximate real arithmetic into the language. It was a design commitment that the arithmetic operations should conform to the accepted standard for floating-point arithmetic, which is

13. *IEEE Standard for Binary Floating-Point Arithmetic,* ANSI/IEEE
Std 754-1985, New York, August 1985.

This is a lengthy document which attempts, by a combination of formality and natural language, to specify precisely the performance to be expected from an implementation of floating-point arithmetic.

Our understanding of the Standard is based on a formal presentation of its requirements,

14. Geoff Barrett (1987) *Formal Methods Applied to a Floating Point
Number System,* Programming Research Group technical
monograph PRG-58, Oxford,

which sets out formally the arithmetic operations, and shows the first steps in a rigorous development of implementations from these specifications. This work was taken further within INMOS, to transform the occam programs into the microcode which controls the implementation of floating-point arithmetic in the IMST800 transputer.

Some of the design decisions represented in Chapter 10 of the present book are documented in

15. Jerome T. Coonen (1984) Contributions to a proposed standard for
binary floating-point arithmetic, *Ph.D. Thesis,* University of
California, Berkeley,

which has a chapter on conversion between binary and decimal representations of floating-point numbers.

About Life

The game of Life became widely known through a number of articles in Martin Gardner's column in the Scientific American. A good general introduction is to be found in, in particular,

16. M. Gardner (1970) Mathematical games, *Scientific American*, October 1970, 120–123,

and

17. M. Gardner (1971) Mathematical games, *Scientific American*, May 1971, 112–117,

but the definitive collection of pretty colonies is to be found in pages 817–850 of the second volume of the two volume

18. E.R. Berlekamp, J.H. Conway, R.K. Guy (1982) *Winning Ways for your Mathematical Plays*, Academic Press, London.

This is a mathematically taxing, but entirely beautiful work on the theory of games. Amongst other things, the section on Life demonstrates that every sufficiently well-stated mathematical problem can be reduced to a question about Life. It outlines the construction of a universal machine as a Life colony which performs computations with streams of gliders.

About Huffman coding

Huffman coding lies deep at the foundations of information theory. The original paper which described the idea

19. David A. Huffman (1952) A method for the construction of minimum-redundancy codes, *Proc I.R.E.*, **40**(9), 1098-1101,

is interesting both because of its status as a classic, and because it shows how much easier it has become to describe algorithms after thirty years of progress in computing.

We take our algorithm for adaptive coding, and some insights into Huffman's original algorithm, from

20. Robert G. Gallager (1978) Variations on a theme by Huffman, *IEEE Trans Information Theory*, IT-**24**(6), 668-674,

which was only prevented by publishing delays from being a twenty-fifth anniversary celebration of Huffman's work.

Index

313